BEYOND the SHADOW OF War

Diane Moody

Published by
OBT-Bookz

Cover design by Hannah Moody

Big Ben image | © Peter Zelei | iStockphoto.com
Statue of Liberty image | © kevinjeon00 | iStockphoto.com
Baseball and Glove | © eurobanks | iStockphoto.com
Old Steamship in Ocean | © kevinruss | iStockphoto.com
Christmas Candle| © my84 | iStockphoto.com
War Bride image | uswarbrides.com

In loving memory of
Joan Van Spyker

On a personal note ...

In early 2014, I received an email from a reader in England who'd just finished *Of Windmills & War*. Lydia Kindred Kirk told me that her grandfather, Percy Kindred, was the young farmer whose land was requisitioned by the government to build an airfield in the early days of WWII. That airfield became home to the 390th Bomb Group—the same base where my father was stationed in 1944-1945, and the same base where my fictionalized "Danny" was stationed. What were the chances?

But it gets even better. Lydia and her family *still live* on that farm land. Out her windows, she can see the control tower which now houses a museum dedicated to the 390th. Included in her note was an invitation to come for a visit and be guests in her home.

I got goose bumps the first time I read her email. I couldn't wait to call Dad, and as you can imagine, he was thrilled. We immediately accepted Lydia's invitation and started making plans to visit at the end of August that year. Lydia put together a full schedule of activities for us, and we could hardly wait to get there.

Writing *Of Windmills & War* was truly a labor of love for me on so many levels. But never did I dream it would one day lead us back to the base where Dad served 70 years ago, to visit the family whose land played such an important role in that war. It is indeed a small, small world.

Ours was truly the trip of a lifetime and such a joy to meet Lydia, her husband Steve, and their three children – Fliss, Tommy, and Betsy. They had decorated their home both inside and out with American flags and an enormous welcome banner in the kitchen, making us feel right at home as soon as we arrived. We spent a good deal of time at the Parham Airfield Museum located in the historic control tower. It's a fascinating museum, and the passion of the docents who volunteer their time is contagious from the moment you enter.

There we met Lydia's parents, Peter and Kath Kindred,

who manage the running of the museum. Peter is a walking, talking historian who loves sharing his knowledge about the 390th and those who served there.

By the time we left England, I could envision Danny and Anya walking hand in hand down tree-covered lanes in Framlingham. I imagined them visiting London in the aftermath of war. I wondered about the challenges they would face as they put the war years behind them, and what their future might look like. They had more stories to tell, from both sides of the Atlantic. As the months of research ensued, I badgered Lydia and her father with pages of questions and found them both to be a tremendous source of help and inspiration. I couldn't have written this sequel without them.

I'm so thankful that Lydia read my book and took the time to write to me, forever bonding our families together.

If you're interested, to see photographs and learn more about our trip to England, visit my blog posts at dianemoody.blogspot.com.

Diane Moody
December 2015

The Kirk Family
Back row: Lydia, Fliss, and Steve.
Front row: Jocelyn, Tommy, and Betsy

In this world you will have trouble.
But take heart! I have overcome the world.

John 16:33 (NIV)

Part I

1

8 June 1945

Framlingham, Suffolk, England

A shiver skittered down Anya's spine; a shadow of foreboding trailing in its wake. She cried out, but no sound emanated from her lips. She tried again. Nothing. She was lying down but had no idea where she was or how she got there.

A repulsive odor began a slow assault in her nostrils. Familiar, but she couldn't place it. She tried to cover her nose, startled to find her hands bound behind and beneath her. A surge of panic raced through her.

As her eyes grew more accustomed to the dark, she turned her head, daring to glance behind her, only to find her hands not bound by rope, but clasped tight in the bony grip of skeletal fingers. Beneath her, a pile of rotting corpses with glowing eyes all fixed on her. She cried out again and again, her efforts useless in the cavernous grave.

Oh God ... save me! Please save me!

"Anya?"

Yes God, I'm here! I hear You!

"Anya, wake up, love."

The groans of the dead grew louder as they pushed her up, up, up, until she could finally break free—

"Anya!"

She slapped at the hand patting her cheek. "Let me go! Let me go!"

"ANYA! Wake up. It's just a dream."

Her eyes flew open, her heart pounding against her chest as she gasped for air.

"Anya, it's me—Sophie. See? Look at my face. You're safe. You're here in Framlingham, in our home, and you're safe. See?"

She blinked as Sophie's face came into view, warm in the soft glow of the lamp light.

"But I—"

"Shhh, you had another nightmare. That's all. Here, let me help you sit up so you can see where you are. Today is your wedding day, Anya. Remember? No time for nightmares."

"But they were everywhere—corpses. So many corpses! And their eyes were like fire, and the smell was—"

"Shhh, look around you." Sophie stuffed a pillow behind Anya. "You're safe and sound. You're here in Framlingham, in England. Danny brought you here, remember? You've just had another bad dream. That's all."

As the remnants of the images faded away, Anya forced herself to focus on everything around her. The bedroom above Quincy's Pub. The framed photographs on the mantel of the small fireplace. The lavender sachet leaning against the lamp on the bedside table. Her hand trembled as she reached for it, then pressed it against her nose, allowing the familiar soothing scent to replace the last trace of death's stench.

And Sophie. Dear Sophie. The kind English girl who'd recently married Charlie Janssen, Danny's pilot and friend. Sophie and Charlie lived here too, in this home above her father's pub. Sophie, who'd welcomed her like a long-lost sister, and in the span of a few days, became her friend. Seated now on the bed beside her, the calming warmth of Sophie's hand over hers comforted her.

"I'm just ... I'm so sorry."

Sophie shook her head. "There's nothing for you to be sorry about."

"But I'm a guest in your home, not a stupid crybaby—" A silent sob caught in her throat.

"Anya, no one thinks you're a crybaby, least of all me. What you've been through ... it's too much. It will take time to recover; to be healed of all the painful memories. It's still too fresh. But I know someday the scars in your heart will start to heal—"

"But that's just it. I'm so afraid they *will* heal and I'll forget them. My family, my friends, the other Resistance workers. I'm scared I'll forget all of them."

Sophie pressed a handkerchief in Anya's hand. "No, you won't. You will never forget them. But time has a way of taking away the stinging pain that accompanies those memories. That's all. Your family and friends will live in your heart forever. I promise."

Anya wiped her eyes then folded and refolded the hankie. "I think it was a mistake to leave my home. I think it's a

3

mistake to marry Danny when—"

"No, it's not a mistake. He *loves* you, Anya. Before he went back for you in Holland, he was like a caged animal, so anxious to find you and take care of you. I may never know everything that happened to you during the war, but of this I'm sure—you and Danny belong together." She smiled as she squeezed Anya's hand. "Which is a good thing, since today is your wedding day."

Anya's heart skipped a beat. Just hearing the words sent another shiver down her spine. She took a shaky breath and tried so hard to compose herself.

My wedding day?

It was no use. She dropped her head in her hands and groaned. "Sophie, I can't. I can't do this."

"You can, and you will. And we shall have the most fun, you and I, getting you all dressed and ready. You'll see. I'll go make us a pot of tea. You stay here, and I'll be right back."

"You don't have to. Really."

"Nonsense. Might as well make the most of it while the house is still quiet. Charlie won't be up for another hour, and Da—well, Da could sleep through the Blitz. So we'll have it all to ourselves."

It still felt strange having someone like Sophie watching over her. After all, they'd only just met when Danny introduced them after her trip across the Channel. The same day she'd left her home in Holland on a ferry. The same day Danny picked her up at the dock.

She still couldn't quite comprehend all that had transpired.

Moments before he showed up at her abandoned home in Utrecht, she'd been curled up on the dirty floor of her bedroom. She'd lost everyone. Everyone she'd ever loved was dead. The war had ended, but she was too exhausted to celebrate. Too defeated. So she'd begged God to just take her then and there.

So foolish, to expect anything from the same God who'd remained so silent during the long years of war. How many times had she cried out to Him? How many times had she shaken her fist in His face, furious at His neglect? And how many times had she asked Him for a sign?

Anya closed her eyes, remembering the moment.

Still lying there on the floor of her room, with her view skewed at such an awkward angle, she'd noticed something. There, over in the corner ... something. What was it? Silent hiccups had quaked her body as she tried to sit up. She crawled across the floor, trying to see the tiny object barely visible in the late-afternoon shadows. She reached out and grasped it, bringing it into the light. And as she opened her palm, what she saw took her breath away.

There in her hand, with half a wing missing and a splintered snout, lay the winged piglet her brother Hans had carved for her so many years ago.

"When pigs fly," she'd whispered, cherishing the memory and missing him so much.

Footsteps had sounded behind her, someone coming down the hall. She dropped the pig in her pocket and dashed away her tears, not wanting Helga to find her blubbering like some helpless child. Clumsily she'd stood and turned to find her mother's friend standing in the doorway, the woman's gnarled hands over her mouth and the strangest expression on her face.

"Helga, what is it?"

"Anya, there's someone here to see you, dear," she'd said before moving aside.

And there, in full dress uniform with his cap in his hands, Danny McClain had stepped into the room.

"Now, that's more like it," Sophie said, returning with a tray and tea service. She set it on the bedside table.

Anya blinked at the interruption. "What do you mean?"

"You're smiling. That's progress if you ask me." She poured a cup of tea and handed it to Anya, then pulled up a chair beside the bed. "Now tell me. What were you thinking?"

"I was remembering when Danny showed up at my house last month. I still can't believe he found me."

Sophie took a sip and set her cup back on its saucer. "Ah well, of course you'd be smiling about that. It's such a sweet love story. One you'll tell your children for years to come."

Anya couldn't help smiling. "Not anytime soon, I hope."

"Perhaps not for a while yet. I trust you're keeping that little carved pig somewhere safe?"

"Yes. I keep thinking ..." Anya stared into her tea, struggling to find the words.

"What is it?"

"It's just that I keep thinking how pleased Hans would have been to know that Danny came back for me. That I wasn't alone after all."

Sophie smiled. "I'm sure he knows. At least, I like to think those in heaven know about the good things that happen in our lives."

"It's so ridiculous, of course, that Danny and I ever became friends."

"Hardly. It's so obvious the two of you were meant to be.

Your brother died, and yet in the midst of your grief, you wrote to tell his pen pal far away in America. Then he answered your letter, then you replied to his letter ... shall I go on?"

Anya smiled. "If you'd known me then, you'd know how unlikely it was for me to write to anyone, let alone my brother's pen pal." She shook her head, remembering all the letters they'd exchanged. "I'm not sure why I kept writing back to him."

"Destiny? It was certainly ordained," Sophie teased. "I keep telling you, Anya. You and Danny were meant to be."

She took a deep breath then slowly released it. "If I could only convince my heart that what you say is true. I'm not good at such things, trying to figure out emotions. Perhaps I never will be. And then what? Suppose I marry Danny and go to America and realize it was all a mistake? Suppose he tires of me once we're there?"

"Anya, stop." Sophie set her cup aside and leaned forward. "Every bride is nervous. It's the most natural thing in the world. We all try to second-guess ourselves, wondering if we're doing the right thing. So don't let all these questions worry you. You only have to think back and see how the two of you found each other in the first place—in the midst of a *war*, no less. That's no coincidence. That's no chance meeting. I have to believe with all my heart that God brought the two of you together for a purpose. How else could you explain it?"

"I want to believe that," she whispered. "I do."

"Then believe it. And today of all days, grant yourself the freedom and the joy of believing it with all your heart. Can you do that?"

Anya held her breath for a second. Then, "Yes. Yes, I think I can."

"Wonderful. Now, finish your tea. We've got to get you ready for your wedding!"

2

"Do you, Daniel Howard McClain, take Anya Liesje Versteeg to be your lawfully wedded wife, to have and to hold from this day forward, for better, for worse, for richer, for poorer, in sickness and in health, to love and to cherish til death you shall part?"

"I do."

"And do you, Anya Liesje Versteeg, take Danny Howard McClain to be your lawfully wedded husband, to have and to hold from this day forward, for better, for worse, for richer, for poorer, in sickness and in health, to love and to cherish til death you shall part?"

Tears pooled in her gray-blue eyes, a tiny crease knitting her brow. He held his breath, a stab of fear fluttering through his heart as he waited for her response. *Say it, Anya. Just say it.* She nodded ever so slightly, her eyes locked on his as a single tear broke free. Danny cupped his palm against her cheek and brushed it away.

She placed her hand over his and whispered, "I do."

His sigh of relief garnered a quiet chuckle from their friends. With Anya's hand still clasped over his, she finally smiled, and he thought it the loveliest sight he'd ever seen.

Standing there in Framlingham's United Reform Church with its centuries-old scents of musty stone and lemon-polished pews, Danny tried to stay focused on the ceremony and stop the mental gymnastics bouncing around his head; still wondering how in the world they'd made it here. Too many pieces of the puzzle had fallen in place, leading them to this moment, this altar. He couldn't have stopped the smile on his face if he'd tried.

They exchanged simple bands of gold, each repeating their vows after the vicar.

"With this ring, I thee wed, with all that I am and all that I have, I honor you. In the name of the Father, the Son, and the Holy Spirit."

Danny wove his fingers through hers, not about to let go as the vicar finished the ceremony.

"In as much as you have each pledged to the other your lifelong commitment, love, and devotion, I now pronounce you husband and wife, in the name of the Father, the Son, and the Holy Spirit. Lieutenant, you may now kiss your bride."

He pulled her into his arms and kissed her soundly, oblivious to the others gathered around them.

"Well, then," the vicar said, startled as laughter echoed through the chapel. "I suppose this is where I present to you Mr. and Mrs. Daniel McClain."

Danny leaned his forehead against hers. "I must admit, I like the sound of that. Don't you, Mrs. McClain?"

A more relaxed smile warmed her face. "Yes, I suppose I do, Mr. McClain."

Beside him, Charlie cheered as the others joined in. "Here, here!"

Danny kissed his bride once more before taking her hand and turning to face the small gathering of their friends.

Once outside, Charlie gave Danny a mighty bear hug and slapped him on his back. "Congratulations, old boy!" He stepped back and held out his arms to Anya. "And my condolences to the new Mrs. McClain. I'm afraid you've got your hands full with this one, but no doubt you'll have him toeing the line in a day or two."

"Pay no mind to him," Sophie teased, elbowing him out of the way to give Anya a hug. "When it comes to these American menfolk, it takes a tad bit longer to break them in. Trust me on that," she added with a playful wink.

Sophie's father Patrick rushed around them. "Congratulations, to both of you! Now, take your time making your way to the pub. I'm off to finish preparing our little celebration."

Sophie gave Anya's wrist a squeeze. "Oh Anya, I'm so happy for you. I know you and Danny will be just as happy as we are."

Anya's smile quivered ever so slightly as she nodded. Danny appreciated Sophie's kind words and wondered how on earth they ever would have pulled off their hasty wedding without her help. He still couldn't help feeling it was all just a dream.

The immigration process had been a nightmare. Like most

of Europe still fighting its way out of the fog of war, Holland was years away from returning to business as usual. The process of required paperwork necessary for someone to leave the country moved at a snail's pace, frustrating Danny and filling Anya with second thoughts. Even with all the forms filed, they'd been told the wait for her visa could take weeks, maybe months.

When his leave ended, saying goodbye had been brutal. He wondered if he would ever see her again. Would she change her mind? Would she convince herself to stay and help rebuild her beloved homeland? Would she find a thousand other excuses not to marry him or come with him to America?

These were the thoughts that crept through his heart day and night while he waited back in Framlingham. Then, a few weeks later, he was surprised to receive a telegram from Anya saying she'd bought a ticket on a ferry boat and would arrive in England the next day. Even now, he still couldn't believe her visa finally came through, and she'd actually made the trip. Yet here they were, five days later ... married.

Sophie was an absolute godsend, stepping in to make Anya feel as welcome as possible. How it warmed his heart to see the two of them together, Sophie ministering to her as only another woman could. Without Sophie's help, he doubted Anya would've made it to the altar today.

But oh, how she did. What a shock to see the startling transformation from the gaunt, scrawny young woman he'd first met in a safe house in Holland, to the beautiful bride now walking beside him. The simple cream-colored dress which Sophie had worn for her own wedding now graced

Anya's slender frame, the perfect fit evidence of Sophie's expertise with a needle and thread.

Like so many other war brides before her, Sophie had fashioned her wedding dress from remnants of a silk parachute. Oh, the irony. If not for a silk parachute dropping him into Holland, he never would have found Anya. Years had passed since the blackout of war had abruptly ended their exchange of letters. And yet, here she stood, elegant in the creamy silken folds of what once was a parachute.

Such a feminine look was different for Anya, but Danny thought it suited her well. A loosely woven braid gathered her dark hair down the nape of her neck as wisps of hair rustled across her forehead in the gentle breeze. He couldn't stop looking at her and didn't bother trying. He stole another kiss, then tucked her hand in the crook of his arm and covered it with his own as they turned the corner nearing Quincy's Pub.

A battered bicycle hit the ground as a crewman stiffened and threw them a salute.

"Sirs! Oh, sirs! My friends! My friends!"

Oh no.

"Oh blessed day, I can't believe it!" With his salute still locked in place, the short Italian continued. "To think a mere jaunt into town by this lowly sergeant could coincide with the very path on which you wonderful people trod—"

"At ease, Sergeant," Charlie interrupted, offering a weary salute in return. "Nothing to get excited about."

"Oh, but sirs, it is! It truly is! Do you perchance remember me? I had the esteemed honor of accompanying you on one of your Chowhound missions. Truly the highlight of my service here in the war of which we partook."

"Sure we remember you, Sergeant. How could we forget?" Danny slowed their pace, but didn't want to risk getting sidelined by the chatty crewman. "It's Cosmos, isn't it?"

"Oh boy, here we go," Charlie muttered.

Cosmos placed both hands over his heart as he nodded. "Yes, sir. That's right. Cosmos Benedetto from the great state of New Jersey. But I have to say, the fact that you actually *remembered* my name? I'm, I'm ... why, I'm utterly speechless."

"Somehow I doubt that," Charlie quipped under his breath. Danny elbowed him.

"It's nice to see you again, Sergeant Benedetto." Danny picked up their pace. "If we don't see you again before you head back to the States, have a safe trip home, okay?"

Suddenly, Cosmos was directly in their path, arms wide open, looking like a child on Christmas morning. "Oh my goodness! It has just occurred to me! Lieutenant, did you just *marry* this exquisite beauty?"

Danny finally stopped and wrapped his arm around Anya's shoulders. "Yes, I did. In fact, we just came from the church. This is my bride, Anya Vers—I mean, Anya McClain."

She reached out her hand. "It's nice to meet you, Sergeant."

He stared at her hand briefly before taking it in both of his. "Oh my dear girl, the honor is all mine. Truly, it is. And if I may, let me be the first to congratulate you on this your day of wedded matrimony. May the—" he paused as emotion stole his voice. "May the good Lord above, who has seen fit to allow all of us here to survive the troubled landscape of war these many years, bless you with a lifetime of happiness together."

Anya smiled, her hand still in his grasp. "That's very kind.

Thank you."

Charlie patted Cosmos on the back and steered him toward his bicycle. "Sergeant, I'm afraid you'll have to excuse us. There's a reception awaiting the newlyweds, and we mustn't be late. I'm sure you understand."

"Oh yes, yes! Of course. Off with you now. Mustn't be late!" He snapped another salute.

Danny returned the gesture. "Take care, Sergeant."

"You too, Lieutenant. And you as well, Mrs. Lieutenant."

As the four of them spilled into the pub, Anya felt her nerves beginning to calm. She'd never been one of those girls who'd dreamed of a fancy wedding, or getting married at all, for that matter. Yet here she was, her fingers still clutched to the crook of Danny's arm.

It hadn't been that long ago when she'd deemed him an odd duck; the young American boy who was pen pals with her brother Hans. After Hans died, Anya had struggled to write Danny about his death. His heartfelt response had touched her deeply. Almost as an afterthought, they began to write each other more often, until one day she realized how much she looked forward to finding his letters in the post and his tales of movies and baseball and a dog named Sophie.

Not a girlfriend. A dog.

"That's quite a smile on your face, Mrs. McClain." Danny tilted his head to one side as he gazed into her eyes. "Penny for your thoughts?"

She blinked out of her revelry. "What did you say?"

"A penny for your thoughts. It's an expression. Means I'm curious what you're thinking in that pretty little head of yours."

She smiled, the scene still vivid in her mind. "I was remembering the day your friend Lieutenant Pendergrass tried to warn me about the girl back home you were in love with. He was trying to spare my broken heart, or so he said, though I knew he was just flirting with me."

"Girl? What girl?"

"Oh, you know the one. That adorable girl you named your plane after. *Sweet Sophie,* wasn't it?"

He threw his head back laughing, his guffaw bouncing off the low beams of the pub's ceiling.

She couldn't help laughing. "I had the same reaction when he said it, only I'd just taken a sip of hot coffee and immediately spewed it across the table, showering my friend Frederic ..." The face of her fallen co-worker flashed through her mind, giving her pause. She shook it off, unwilling to let the memories spoil this day, and tried to find her smile again.

Danny pulled her into his arms. "Do you have *any* idea how beautiful you are when you laugh like that? Do you have any idea how much I love the sound of your laughter?"

She knew he was trying to change the subject, and she loved him for it. "Don't be silly. It's just a laugh."

He nudged her chin upward until her eyes found his again. "Yes, but after years of so little to laugh about, I believe it may be the sweetest sound I've ever heard." He kissed her gently, holding her close.

Patrick Quincy elbowed his way past them. "All right, you two. Hold off on all that kissing for now. Come and let us give you a proper toast."

Danny touched the small of her back as they joined the others near the hearth. Before it stood a table adorned with vases of wild flowers and a lovely three-tiered cake. Anya wondered how Patrick found the ingredients as rationing kept grocers' shelves sparse.

"Charlie, would you do the honors?" Patrick handed out the slender glasses. "There's not so much as a bottle of champagne to be found in all of Suffolk, so we'll simply have to make do with a drop or two of fresh cider."

Charlie raised his glass and cleared his throat. "I know the last thing Danny and I thought about when we enlisted was finding true love in the midst of war. Mostly, we just hoped to make it home in one piece." He slipped his arm around Sophie's waist. "In spite of it all, here we stand as the war is finally over, and beside us, the two most beautiful women on God's green earth."

"Here here!" Sophie cheered, raising her glass toward Anya. Anya followed her lead, clinking her glass against Sophie's.

"Today we offer our congratulations to Anya and Danny as they begin their life together as husband and wife. Someday your grandchildren will ask to hear about your love story, and my guess is they'll find it hard to believe. How two people from different sides of the world became friends through written letters while still in high school, then years later found their paths crossing in, of all places, the middle of a war." He shook his head, smiling. "If that's not providential, I

17

don't know what is.

"And so it is with great pleasure I wish you both a lifetime of happiness, a love that stands true and uncompromised no matter what life may bring your way, and hearts filled with promise and hope once again as the clouds of war are finally clearing." Charlie raised his glass higher. "To Danny and Anya."

"To Danny and Anya!"

Danny took a sip then leaned over to kiss his wife.

"Charlie, thank you for your kind words," he began. "Didn't know you had it in you, buddy."

"I practiced for weeks."

"Sure you did."

"Hours and hours."

"Of course.

"Okay, have it your way. It was ad-libbed. All of it. Spur of the moment."

"That's more like it."

They all laughed, accustomed to the familiar banter between the two.

"I thought it was splendid, love," Sophie added. "And Danny, might I add that I also wish you and Anya every happiness. Now, are you ready to cut the cake?"

"Actually, there's something I'd like to do first." Danny set down his glass then reached into the pocket of his jacket. "I received a telegram this morning from my parents, and I'd like to share it with all of you."

"Go ahead and read it, Danny," Sophie said.

He looked at Anya and gave her a wink. "All right, here's what they wrote. *'Shocked and delighted to hear of your wedding. Stop. Wish we could be there. Stop. We cannot wait to meet Anya and welcome her to our family. Stop. God bless you both today and may He bless your marriage always. Stop. All our love, Mom and Dad.'"*

When Danny's voice cracked, he busied himself folding the telegram then tucked it back in his pocket.

"How lovely," Sophie said. "A fine message to cheer you on today."

Anya reached up to kiss his cheek. "That's lovely, Danny. So thoughtful of them."

Later, after cutting the cake, the newlyweds thanked Patrick for all his kindnesses, then joined Charlie and Sophie in Patrick's automobile for the short drive to the Wickham Market Station. They chatted happily along the way, arriving in plenty of time. As the men walked ahead, carrying their luggage, Sophie looped her arm through Anya's.

"Oh Anya, I hope you and Danny have the most unforgettable honeymoon. Just relax and forget about everything else whilst you're in London. Promise?"

"We'll try."

When they arrived at their train carriage, they said their goodbyes.

"Have a wonderful time!" Sophie said. "Be sure to say hello to the king and queen for us, won't you?"

"We will!"

Then, before climbing the steps into the train, Anya stopped and turned back to Sophie, pulling her into a final hug. "How can I ever thank you for all you've done? You've been so kind to me. You didn't even know me, and yet you loaned me this beautiful dress, and helped find clothes for me, and fixed my hair today ... and helped calm my nerves after the wretched nightmares. How can I ever repay you?"

Sophie stood back and grabbed both of Anya's hands. "There's no need. It's been my pleasure, Anya."

Anya blinked away the tears and took a deep breath. "The thing is, I don't even know how to properly thank you for being ... my friend."

"And you will never know how *pleased* I am that I got to be that friend for you. It's been my honor."

"All aboard!"

"Goodbye!"

"Have fun!"

"Thanks for everything!"

"Goodbye!"

Danny stood aside and held out his hand to his wife. "After you, Mrs. McClain."

"Why, thank you, Mr. McClain."

3

With his new wife seated beside him on the train, her head tucked beneath his chin as she slept, Danny gazed out the window watching the farm fields and houses and little hamlets pass by. The thoughts rambling through his mind followed no particular script; just a jumbled maze of rabbit trails hopping here and there. But one by one, they all ended with the same thought.

We're married?

We're married!

I can't believe we're actually married!

He gently kissed the top of her head as she slept beside him, inhaling the scent of her hair, and thanking God for the miracle of their love story.

She'd been strangely quiet once they'd settled into their seats on the train. At first, they'd chatted quietly about the wedding and the honeymoon they'd be spending in London. Despite the bumpy, peculiar path their lives had taken these past few weeks, he was already learning to read the signs of her shifting moods. Eyes that wouldn't meet his, staring off at some unseen memory. The slight stiffening of her shoulders as if bracing for confrontation. The way she nibbled at her thumbnail without ever actually biting down on it.

He took a deep breath and tried to set aside such thoughts. He knew it would take some adjustment, this marriage of theirs. Anya wasn't just a new bride; she was still recovering from the war's deep and jagged scars on her emotions. But at this moment, Danny chose to shun such thoughts because this was their wedding day.

She stirred, rousing from her sleep. "Did you say something?"

He shook his head and brushed the wisps of hair away from her eyes. "No, but I do have something I need to tell you."

Her expression tensed. "Tell me what?"

He crooked his finger, motioning her closer then whispered in her ear, "I love you, Anya Liesj Versteeg McClain."

A shy smile eased her expression. "Such a mouthful, all those names."

"Yes, but they're yours and I love them. All of them. Preferably together."

"And would you prefer I call you Daniel Howard McClain?"

"Actually, I prefer *Lieutenant* Daniel Howard McClain. But I'll make an exception. Just for you."

"How gracious of you."

"Then again, I don't care what you call me as long as you call me."

"Is that so?"

"Yes, ma'am, that's affirmative." He leaned down to kiss her lips. When she didn't respond, he sat back. She motioned with her eyes, nodding toward the elderly lady in the seat facing them. The white-haired woman smiled, apparently enjoying their public display of affection.

"Got it," Danny whispered. "Okay, then." He nodded toward the window. "Take a look. We're coming into London."

"Already?"

He'd meant it as a diversion, hoping to distract the old lady. But when he saw the crumbled, massive piles of debris and still-smoldering ashes, he froze, unable to look away.

As the train gradually slowed, a number of houses flashed by, some still intact but most gutted and empty. As if a giant had walked through the neighborhoods, squashing each home to ruin with mighty, deliberate steps. In some areas, demolition had cleared block after block, leaving only crumbled foundations and an occasional chimney where homes once stood.

In the front yards of those still standing, people of all ages picked through the rubble. He wondered if they were looking for missing heirlooms, searching for anything that could be salvaged. Or were these complete strangers, pilfering through the dusty remnants of someone else's life?

With her back still leaning against him, Danny felt Anya's shiver as she gazed at the sight. He wrapped his arm around her and pulled her closer.

"Anya?"

She turned to face him, and the haunted look in her eyes almost undid him.

"It's all right. I'm here."

She grasped his hand and held it tight. "I know. It just looks—"

23

"—too much like home?"

She nodded slowly.

"That day I found you in your house. Do you remember showing me the little pig Hans had carved for you?"

"Yes. I was just thinking about that this morning."

"Do you still have it?"

"Of course. Why?"

He was stalling, trying to keep her distracted from the rubble passing by outside the window. "Oh, no reason. Just wondering. What do you call it? In Dutch, I mean?"

Her expression lightened. *"Mijn vliegend varken."*

"Main veekend farkan?"

Anya shook her head and tried not to snicker.

"What's so funny? I said it just the way you did."

She covered her face as silent laughter shook her shoulders.

"Oh, come on now. It wasn't *that* bad, was it?"

Still smiling, she finally looked up at him. "That was *worse* than bad, Danny. Please—you have to promise me you won't ever try to speak Dutch again."

"What? Why?"

Anya pressed her fingers against his lips. "Because you *sound* like a pig, and it's an insult to the Dutch language." She shook her head, still smiling. "You must not even try. Promise me."

He feigned a pout, removing her fingers from his lips. "That bad?"

"Horrible." She snorted. *"Afschuwelijk!"*

"God bless you."

"What?"

"You sneezed. I said 'God bless you.'"

"But I didn't sneeze."

"Yes, you did. You said, 'achoo-lik' or something like that."

Her laughter filled the space between. When she tried to compose herself with a deep breath, she lost it all over again.

He folded his arms across his chest. "Okay, go ahead. Have your fun. I can take it."

She dabbed at her eyes, trying to find her composure. "It never ceases to amaze me how tears can show up at the best of times as well as the worst of times. It makes no sense."

He said nothing, just stared at her.

She elbowed him. "Go ahead. I'm sure you have some clever retort just dying to spring from your lips."

He leaned toward her, his arms still folded. "No. But I admit I love to hear you laugh."

"Don't be silly. Hans used to say I laughed like a chicken—all clucks and snorts and honks."

"I bet he loved the sound of it as much as I do."

Her smile started to fade. But just a little. "I don't know. I suppose. Maybe."

"Sure he did." Danny drew her close to his side. "Anya, I want you to promise *me* something."

"Promise what?"

"We're going to see a lot of bomb damage—"

She started to turn toward the window again, but he gently nudged her chin back toward him.

"Listen to me. I must be some kind of idiot, suggesting we take our honeymoon in London. It never occurred to me that the damage from the Blitz would remind you of home and the war, when all I wanted was a chance for us to get away and have some fun."

"Danny, it's—"

"So what I want you to promise me is this. Look beyond the war's remnants. When you see sights like those out the window, remember that it's *over*. No more bombs will fall on us. In Holland and England and all the other countries damaged in the war, it's time to rebuild and make a fresh start. That doesn't mean we forget everything that happened or those we lost during the war.

"But right now," he laced his fingers with hers again, "let's try to block out everything. Even if just while we're here. Let's look beyond it and just be thankful we have each other. Can we do that?" He noted a flicker of the sadness in her eyes as she nodded, then watched it ease away with the hint of a smile.

"Promise me?"

"Yes. I'll try very hard."

"Is that a promise?"

"I promise."

With a quick glance at the elderly woman across from them, Danny turned and gave his wife a resounding kiss. "There. That seals the deal. Veekend farkan or no veekend farkan!"

Anya groaned a laugh. "No, you promised!"

"Newlyweds?" the woman across from them asked.

"Yes, ma'am," Danny said. "Married this morning."

"And isn't that lovely?" She tilted her head as she studied them. "I wish you both the best. My husband and I have been married for over fifty-six years."

Danny blew a whistle. "That's a long time. What's your secret?"

"Very simple, I think. You have to make sure you marry the right person, of course. But I can see you've already done that." Her eyes twinkled as she continued. "Then you get up every morning and ask the good Lord to give you one thing you can do that day to show your love for her, and her for you. Even in the tough times, you'll find it makes all the difference."

"Good advice, don't you think, Anya?"

"Yes, I should think that's very good advice. Thank you."

"You are most welcome."

"Anything else?" Danny asked.

She smiled. "Oh, I expect you'll figure it out along the way. Now, if you'll excuse me, I believe this is my stop."

As the train came slowed to a stop, Danny stood and helped her collect her things. She glanced back once more before leaving.

"Congratulations to you both. Enjoy your honeymoon." With a wink, she left them.

4

It was almost five in the afternoon by the time they arrived in their room at a lovely hotel in the West End. Danny placed Anya's bag on the folding luggage rack and dropped his small duffel bag on the floor beside it.

She sat on the end of the bed then immediately jumped up, as if she'd just perched on a bed of red hot coals instead of a floral coverlet. She was glad his back was turned so he didn't see her reaction. She'd felt her heart hammer a little harder with each passing mile on the taxi ride from the train station. She felt so foolish, letting her nerves rattle her like this. Heaven knows, she wasn't the first bride to be nervous about her wedding night.

"Wait," she said as Danny started taking off his uniform jacket. He paused, half in, half out of it. "I just realized I'm hungry. Quite hungry. Are you?"

He smiled as he slid back into his jacket. "Sure. You know me. I can always eat."

"Good. Then shall we?"

"Absolutely."

Moments later, they were seated in the hotel's restaurant downstairs.

A tall waiter appeared, dressed in black slacks and vest over a starched white shirt, his posture stiff. "Good afternoon. Might I ask what kind of tea you would like?"

"What would you suggest?" Danny asked.

"That would depend on your taste, of course, though I dare say most of our guests prefer our own house blend."

Danny looked her way. "How does that sound to you?"

"Yes. Fine. Thank you."

"Excellent," the waiter said. "And will we both be having the afternoon tea?"

Danny's brows drew together. "Yes. I just told you. The house blend."

The waiter's smile tightened. "I'm referring to the meal, sir. The afternoon tea."

"Sure. Yes. Why not? As they say, when in London ..."

Anya waited. "When in London?"

"Yes, who says what, sir?" added the waiter.

Danny shrugged. "It's just a saying. You've heard it, right? When in Rome you do as the Romans do?"

"But do *what*, Danny? What do the Romans do?"

"Never mind. Must be an American thing."

"Quite," the waiter answered. "Then am I to assume you'll both be having afternoon tea?"

"Yes," Anya answered. "Thank you."

"Very well. I shall return shortly with your tea." He bowed ever so slightly then left.

Danny raked his fingers through his hair. "You'd think the fact that both Brits and Americans speak the same language, we'd be able to understand each other."

"Sophie told me she often laughs at the strange way you Yanks talk."

"Like we say bathroom and they call it the lav or the privy?"

Anya smiled. "Yes, something like that."

"Or what we call a cigarette, they call a fag?"

"I've not heard that one before."

"Or the way they say, 'she's *in* hospital' instead of 'she's in *the* hospital'. Or '*at* university' instead of at *the* university."

"I have no idea, but at least you can pronounce their language," she teased.

"Point well taken. I trust you've noticed that I've avoided all attempts to speak Dutch since we arrived?"

"Yes, and I thank you for that, Lieutenant McClain."

"You're most welcome."

The waiter returned with a sterling silver pot of tea, and cups and saucers of china painted with violets and ivy.

"Let me ask you a question, my good man," Danny began. "Is afternoon tea just a fussy snack in the middle of the afternoon? Or is it the evening meal? Because I'll be honest, I could eat a horse about now."

Two lines deepened between the waiter's brows as he stiffened his back again. "I beg your pardon? I'll have you know we do not, and for the record, *never have* served horse meat."

Danny laughed as he raised his palms. "My apologies. I didn't mean to suggest any such thing! It's just an expression. It means I'm really *very* hungry as opposed to not wanting anything to eat."

"Quite. Then I shall explain. Our afternoon tea, dictated by the hour in which it is served, is a light meal of cucumber, egg, and salmon sandwiches, assorted scones served with clotted cream and jam, along with today's pastry selection, a delightful Victorian sponge cake. Not as hearty as horse meat, but I should think it might suffice."

"Perfect. Yes."

"I'm glad it meets your approval." Another half bow and he was gone.

Anya was grateful for the distraction as they chatted through their meal. Later, as the waiter removed their dishes, she felt the nerves creeping back in. "Would it be possible to bring us another pot of tea?"

"Anya, are you sure?"

She avoided Danny's eyes and confirmed her request with a smile and a nod to their waiter.

When he left, Danny reached for her hand across the table. "Anya, look at me."

She busied her free hand brushing crumbs from the linen tablecloth. When he squeezed her hand, she finally looked up. "Yes?"

"It's okay."

"What's okay?"

He didn't answer, just looked at her with the same adoring eyes she'd gazed into during their wedding.

"I know you're nervous. But if it's any help, so am I."

She felt the heat burning her cheeks and dropped her eyes to their joined hands. "Danny, I don't even know—"

"Neither do I."

Her eyes found his again. "What? You mean—"

"Yes. That's exactly what I mean."

The tightness in her chest lessened, at least a little. "You're not just saying that to make me relax, are you?"

"Much to the chagrin of my fellow crew mates, I promise you I'm 'not just saying' it."

A long, pent-up breath slipped through her lips as she found her smile again.

The waiter approached their table with a second pot of tea.

"Please forgive me," Anya said, "but I've changed my mind. It's ... been a long day."

"No problem, madam."

Danny gave her hand a final squeeze as he turned to the waiter. "Check, please?"

"I beg your pardon?" he asked.

"The check? The bill? Whatever you call it, bring it. Please."

As much as Danny had looked forward to their wedding night, he wasn't enjoying the prickly sensation of walking on eggshells as they returned to their room. He set the key and his wallet on the dresser and took off his jacket. As he loosened his tie, Anya set her pocketbook on top of the luggage she'd borrowed from Sophie, her hand shaking ever so slightly.

He pulled off his tie and tossed it on the dresser, then took a step closer and reached for her hand. "Come sit with me."

The lingering scent of her borrowed perfume wafted over him as they sat down, but he fought the urge to take her into his arms. There was no rush. She needed time, and he would give her however long she needed.

If only I could make her relax. If I could just make her laugh again.

An idea came to him. He leaned over and untied his shoes. "I have a question. What kind of advice do you think Frederic would give us about now?"

"Frederic?" Anya snorted, then covered her mouth at the sound of it. "Of all people, why would you think of Frederic at a time like this?"

"I don't really know. I guess I always had the impression he was some kind of playboy. A ladies man."

She rolled her eyes. "I'm not so sure he would be the one to ask."

"No?" Danny mimicked Frederic's unique posture and stilted English. "But he was so *suave* and so—how do you say —*debonair!*"

"What does this mean? Swa—"

"Suave and debonair?" he continued as Frederic. "It's— how do you say—someone who's charming and smooth. *Veddy, veddy* smooth." He dropped the accent. "Did you know he once said something to me about us?"

"Us? As in, you and me?"

"Yes. It was that day in the safe house when I first saw you, remember?"

"Yes. You were downstairs, laid out on the bottom bunk and looking rather pitiful, as I remember."

"Hey, *you* try jumping out of a B-17 in the middle of a war. I was lucky it was just my leg that got injured. I could've been shot out there or captured by Nazis, you know."

"Poor American flyboy. How well I remember."

He shook his head for her benefit. "Do you want to hear what Frederic said or not?"

"Go on. What did he say?"

"He had just come downstairs when you rushed off all mad or crying or something. I can't remember exactly."

"I was probably mad at you. I stayed mad at you often when we first met."

"And don't I know it? Anyway, Frederic came sauntering over to me after you left. He was puffing on one of those disgusting cigarettes he always smoked. What was in those things, rolled manure?"

"So awful, weren't they?" Anya wrinkled her nose. "You're probably better off not knowing."

"I'm sure you're right. So he comes over and takes a puff," Danny continued, acting out the part, "and he says, 'You Americans. You, how do you say ... fumble?' And I said, 'What do you mean?' And he says, 'You have Anya here,' and points his cigarette toward my bed and says, 'but now she's gone. So? You fumble.' He shrugged as if certain I understood."

"What did you say?"

"I said I didn't realize *football* was so popular in The Netherlands." At her confused expression, he added, "Fumble. It's when one team loses the ball to the other team."

"Oh, I see."

"You do?"

34

"Not really, but did he say anything else?"

"No, as I recall he walked off mumbling to himself, probably about how stupid Americans are when it comes to love."

"As if he'd know what love is? Frederic thinks he ... *thought* he was an authority on all subjects."

At that moment, Danny remembered the night Frederic and Eduard were killed by German mercenaries. Along with Anya, as part of the Resistance, they'd been transporting Danny and the other Allied crewmen out of the country. Anya was the team's sole survivor. An involuntary shudder passed over him as the flashback resurfaced. He'd watched Anya snap the neck of a German soldier who'd caught them escaping.

War memories. Great. I've done it again.

He could tell she was remembering that night too, and God only knows how many other nights just like it.

He took her hand in his. "I'm sorry. I didn't mean to bring all that up."

She shook her head and tried to smile. "It's okay. It was nice to remember how silly Frederic was."

"True. He provided some much-needed comic relief in the middle of the war, and that's always a good thing. But good grief, how that man could pass gas." Danny shivered. "Never saw anyone clear out a room full of people so fast."

"I know! Wasn't it awful? Sometimes, when the two of us were in the cab of a truck, it would be so bad, my eyes would water. They would literally water."

Danny laughed hard, leaning back on his elbows. "Yes sir, he was definitely a colorful guy."

Anya leaned back too, then turned on her side to face him, resting her head on her hand. He heard the thump of her shoes hitting the floor.

"I remember Frederic once telling me he wanted to go to America after the war to be an American movie star. 'Like the Clark Gable or the Lawrence Olive.' Not Olivier, mind you. But Lawrence *Olive*."

Danny chuckled and fell back on the bed, crossing his arms behind his head. "Just what Hollywood needs—another Don Juan."

"I could never get it through his head not to refer to people as '*the* Clark Gable' or '*the* Lawrence Olive—er, Olivier. Frederic was hopeless when it came to things like that. He imagined himself quite the sale ... slabe—"

"Celebrity?"

"Yes, that's it. He thought himself quite the celebrity. And more than worthy of attracting the attention of all those famous actresses."

"You mean, like *the* Greta Garbo? Or *the* Jean Harlow?"

"You're learning. Frederic would be proud."

"Yes, but there's one thing I've got that Frederic never had."

"And what might that be?"

He turned on his side to face her, then slowly traced his finger down her jawline. "You."

She was still smiling, though he noticed an almost imperceptible quiver at his touch.

"Yes, Lieutenant. That is one thing Frederic never had, though God knows he tried."

"I'm sure he did. No interest on your part?"

She pinned him with a glare. "What do you think?"

"Oh, I don't know. Maybe you're the kind of girl with a soft spot for the suave and debonair type. Which, now that I think of it, works out well for me. I'm sure you've noticed I'm the very essence of debonairness."

"That's not even a word, is it?"

"It is now."

She glanced away. "I must apologize if I ever gave you the impression that I found you debonair."

"Oh?"

"No, it was not your *debonairness* that first attracted me to you."

"No?" He wrapped a loose curl of her hair around his finger. "Then what was it that attracted you to me?"

"Let me think. Hmm. I guess it might have been your nose."

"My nose?"

She traced her finger down the bridge of it. "Yes, your nose. It's a good nose. A strong nose. As noses go."

"Why, thank you. I'm quite proud of it. Please—go on. What else attracted you to me? This is good. I like this."

"What else? Let me think. I suppose it might have been your smile."

Danny glammed a big one, turning from side to side. "My smile? It is rather captivating, isn't it?"

Anya laughed. "Capti ... what is that word?"

"Captivating. It means the sight of it arrests your complete attention. You're so stunned by its appearance that you can't help but stare, utterly enraptured by its beauty." He posed again, grinning as hard as he could.

She punched his shoulder. "You are the silliest man I have ever met, Danny McClain."

"Is that another one of my assets that attracted you to me? Or are you just saying that to be clever?"

She shook her head. "What am I going to do with such a silly man?"

"*Me* silly? I should remind you that the first time I ever saw you actually smile, you were acting utterly ridiculous."

"What? When? What are you talking about?"

"The night I first met you. It was later, when we had dinner in the safe house kitchen. You kept eating that awful stew—"

"The *dakhaas*. Oh, now I remember."

Danny winced, remembering the dark, lumpy stew. "That stuff was horrible! Didn't you tell me it was some kind of rabbit?"

"No, we call it roof rabbit, but it is actually cat meat."

"GAH! That's right! Now I remember." He shivered again, recalling how she kept eating the stuff, one spoonful after another, daring him to do the same. He'd kept up, spoonful by spoonful, until he couldn't stomach another bite. She'd exploded in laughter.

Anya laughed now, teasing him. "I remember how green your face turned, but you kept eating all those tasty morsels that were—"

"Stop!"

"—made from all those poor little kittens who gave their lives for you."

"Stop!" He wrapped his arms around her and pulled her close, tickling a rib. "I refuse to let you nauseate me at a moment like this."

Anya squealed. "No! Danny, stop!"

He pulled back to look at her. "How did I not know you're ticklish?" He playfully dug his finger between her ribs again and got the same response.

"Danny, STOP!"

"Okay! Okay! I stopped. See?"

She recovered with greatly exaggerated antics. "Oh, Danny, please don't ever do that again!" She gave a playful punch to his shoulder.

He raised his hands in surrender. "I said okay."

When she finally caught her breath and settled back, she took her time before glancing his direction. "What have I gotten myself into? I'm afraid I've married a crazy man."

He turned toward her again, propping his head against his hand. "Yes, that's true. You've married a man who is certifiably crazy in love with you."

Her face still flushed with laughter as her expression softened. She said nothing for a while, just gazed into his eyes as though searching for something.

Finally, he had to ask. "What is it?"

She shook her head, still silent. A moment later, she glanced away. "Nothing. It's nothing."

He gently nudged her chin back toward him. "Listen, Anya. I want to ... that is, I think you should ... maybe we should—"

She blinked. "Maybe we should what?"

He tried to swallow past the boulder stuck in his throat. He laced his fingers through hers and studied her eyes. "Anya, I love you ... *so* much. When you said 'I do' this morning, I thought I must surely be the luckiest, most blessed man on earth. And to be honest, I have to admit I couldn't wait for this moment ... to finally be alone with you. Here. Now."

He brought her hand to his lips. "But as much as I've looked forward to this, I need you to know I can wait. For as long as it takes."

"Danny," she whispered.

"I'm serious. I know it's a big step. For both of us. And if you're not ready, all you have to do is tell me."

A flicker of sorrow fell across her face. Her eyes glistened as she whispered, "Danny, I—"

"Shh, it's okay. You don't have to say a—"

She grabbed his face with a kiss so sudden, so passionate, he couldn't find a single breath. His arms wrapped around her as the hunger of her kisses rendered him helpless.

He whispered her name over and over. Then, "Anya?"

A moment passed. "Yes?"

Before he could say another word, her fingers slowly worked the top button of his shirt.

He paused. "Are you sure?"

Her hands stilled as she glanced up at him. A sly smile accompanied a tear that fell from her eye. Still, she said nothing, simply continued freeing the buttons.

"I'll take that as a yes."

5

9 June 1945

Anya sipped from the delicate teacup, savoring the warmth of its blend, as Danny drained the last drop of his second cup of coffee. They'd discovered the quaint café just around the corner from their hotel. Long past the morning rush, they had the place to themselves for the most part. They'd slept past eight, surprised to find the morning rays of sun slicing across their room. Danny suggested they order room service and stay in all day, assuring her they could surely think of something to pass the time.

But the lure of London tugged them out of bed, and here they were.

Unaccustomed to English food, Anya stared at the generous portions on her breakfast plate. Though London remained on strict rationing, Sophie had told her the pubs and restaurants maintained limited menus for paying customers. During the war years back home, she'd subsisted on little more than sugar beets, tulip bulbs, and an occasional stew if a rabbit or some other critter could be found. At least, that's all she remembered just now. Even after the Operation Chowhound food drops just days before the war ended, they were cautioned not to overeat after so many years of near starvation. Once they'd been reunited, Danny declared his intention to help her get healthy again. But her system had not yet adjusted, keeping her cautious with every bite.

Danny buttered a piece of toast. "Where shall we start? I'd hoped we could pop in to see the king, but my sources tell me he's busy, what with putting the country back together and all."

Anya didn't miss a beat. "Such a pity, as I'd hoped to return the tiara the queen loaned me for the wedding."

He barked a laugh, turning the heads of the only other couple in the café. He raised a hand in apology. "Sorry about that," he said, with a final chortle.

The couple smiled. "No problem," the American in uniform said. "It's nice having something to laugh about again, isn't it?"

"You can say that again."

Danny turned his attention back to Anya. "Didn't see *that* one coming, Mrs. McClain." He leaned toward her, lowering his voice. "Quite the comeback for a girl who didn't get much sleep last night."

She shushed him with a startled smile. "Mind your manners, will you?"

He broke off a slice of bacon. "I'll try. It won't be easy, mind you, but I'll try."

Anya took another sip of tea as she glanced at the other

couple, hoping they hadn't heard the exchange. Thankfully, she found them preoccupied with each other, holding hands across their table. The young woman looked to be about her age; a pretty girl with dark brown curls spilling beneath a navy blue beret. She wondered if she too was a war bride, as they were now being called, and what their story might be. She noted the silver bar on his uniform signifying his rank as a first lieutenant. Perhaps a pilot or co-pilot like Danny?

"Back to my original question," Danny said. "What sights would you like to visit today? I realize we only have a few days, so we won't be able to see everything. Anything in particular you'd like to see?"

"You forget I know nothing about London. Until the war, it was only a dot on a map in a school textbook."

"I see your point. But didn't your queen ride out the war here?"

"What do you mean, 'ride out' the war?"

"Just an expression, meaning she resided here in London instead of Holland once Germany occupied your country."

"Then yes, that's true."

"You told me she and her cabinet came here to avoid capture and having the government overthrown, which is what happened in so many other countries under Occupation. Sounds like one smart lady."

"Everyone loves Queen Wilhelmina. We were upset when we first heard she'd left us and taken the cabinet and national treasures with her. Then we listened by radio when she explained her actions. Safe over here, she could continue working with our allies to do what she could for the homeland. She literally saved our country."

Anya remembered listening to the queen's address on the radio her father had hidden in the wall. Tears had filled her mother's eyes at the news. Her father had wrapped both of them in his arms, holding them close in that tiny sliver of hope in the queen's explanation. And for that brief moment, for the first time since the Germans had invaded, she'd felt almost safe again.

Almost.

"Anya?"

She glanced up and found concern in Danny's eyes.

"It's nothing. I was just—" She shook her head and busied herself spreading jam on her toast. "You will have to choose where we go today since I'm unfamiliar with London."

"Then let's start at Buckingham Palace. It's not too far from here. We can pick up a map on the way so we'll know where everything is."

They finished eating, paid their bill, and stepped outside into the summer sunshine. Danny held her hand as they strolled along the busy footpath. Now and then they'd pass piles of rubble or deep pockmarks where bombs hit.

"Isn't it strange, all these people walking about as if nothing ever happened?" Anya said. "If not for the piles of rubble or craters where bombs fell, you would never know there'd been a war here. These Brits act like it's business as usual."

"Maybe it's their way of getting back to life and trying to put the war behind them. Though, if you ask me, they all look a little weary. Not too many smiles and certainly not much laughter. And look there at the long line at that produce market—or *queues* as they call them here. Those women look exhausted, and it's not even noon yet. I'd wager that kind of weariness comes from living in a war zone day in and day out for all these years."

"True, but still … it's as if life just goes on for them. Surely it can't be that easy, can it?"

"What do you mean?"

"How do you forget what happened these last five years? How do you forget everything that happened to your country? Your home? Your loved ones?"

"Are we talking about Londoners or people in general?"

"I don't know. It just seems odd to me, seeing everyone bustling about, going to work, queuing up at the market, taking a walk—"

"Anya." He wrapped his arm around her shoulders.

"Yes?"

"Look, I understand there are still a lot of things that don't make sense. It's only been a few weeks since the war ended. It's all strange and confusing, everyone trying to put their lives back together. But I have to believe they're all doing the best they can to figure out what that means. We've *all* changed. None of us are the same people we were before this war. But that doesn't mean we can't move forward and find a new path so we can go on living."

"I didn't say—"

"No, hear me out. All I'm saying is, these folks are doing what they have to do. Which is what you and I must do. And we'll do that when we get home. We will. But for these next few days, can we not worry about it? Not worry about these folks and why they're acting 'normal' after all they've been through? This is our honeymoon, remember?"

She took a deep breath and watched a squirrel skitter along the footpath then race up a nearby tree. "I know I promised to let it all go. I'm sorry. I know you're right, but I'm just having a hard time allowing myself to—"

"—live again?"

"Yes."

He kissed the top of her forehead. "Then will you let me give you *permission* to live and breathe again?"

"I suppose so."

"Good. Then off we go. The palace awaits."

The closer they drew to the palatial home of the British monarchy, they noticed the crowds ahead of them rushing along the road.

"What is it? What's happening?" Anya asked as they picked up their pace.

"I'm not sure, but let's check it out."

"It's the king and queen!" someone said. "Their motorcade is leaving the palace!"

Anya couldn't see much as she tried to keep up. Danny kept a firm hold of her hand as they bustled along with everyone else.

"There they are!" someone shouted. "They're coming this way!"

Like the parting of the Red Sea, everyone scurried out of the street, making way for the motorcade of automobiles coming their way. A roar of joyful shouts filled the air as people waved their hats and hands.

"Long live the King!"

"Long live the King and Queen!"

"Anya, look! Can you see them?"

Just then, she spotted the limousine slowly passing not two meters away from them. Anya saw the round jovial face of Queen Elizabeth as she raised the back of her gloved hand as if to wave, then simply held it there, stiff and barely moving. Brightly-colored feathers on her enormous hat matched the rich emerald shade of her coatdress. Anya caught a quick glimpse of King George's dark blue uniform with its gold-fringed epaulets, and the white peaked military cap atop his head. The increasing roar of the exuberant crowd rose as the vehicles moved beyond them.

"I guess no one told them we're here," Danny shouted, "or I'm sure they would have stopped for a quick hug."

"Of course they would," she teased.

"Not bad for our first day of sightseeing, is it?" Danny tucked her hand in the crook of his elbow as the crowd began to disperse. "Who knows, maybe Churchill will stroll by and invite us for a pint at his favorite pub."

Anya elbowed his ribs. "You're quite pompous today, aren't you?"

As they neared the palace, they spotted the Victoria Memorial and its surrounding platform filled with jubilant crowds. And just beyond it, the magnificent gates of Buckingham Palace.

Anya couldn't believe her eyes. Standing at the railing beside the gate, she tried to comprehend the enormity of the grand home of British royalty. "Why would anyone need such a large house? I can't even imagine it."

"I think it's more than just a residence." Danny stood beside her with his hands on the rails. "Apparently it's an actual working palace."

"I imagine it's beautiful inside, don't you?"

"I'm sure it is, though a bit formal for my taste."

She cast him a look and rolled her eyes before glancing back at the palace. "Doesn't look as if it was damaged during the war. I would think Hitler would have put a target on it."

"Actually, the palace was bombed sixteen times during the war, nine of them direct hits."

At the sound of the English accent, they turned to find the couple they'd seen earlier in the café. The American stood a full head taller than his young wife who smiled kindly at them, his arm draped casually across her shoulders.

"Oh, hello ... again," Danny said.

"I promise we're not following you," she teased. "We wanted to stop by the palace again before Jack leaves. This is where we first met."

"Here?" Danny asked.

"Yes, right here. I'd just introduced myself when the air raid sirens blew, of all things," he explained. "We rushed into that shelter over there and waited it out together."

"My friends couldn't believe I fell in love during a raid." She smiled up at her husband.

"You're leaving, Lieutenant? Heading home by any chance?" Danny asked.

"Yes, home to the good ol' USA. Just got my orders yesterday."

"Congratulations. Where do you call home?"

"Long Island. You?"

"Chicago."

"Sox or Cubs?"

"Cubs, all the way. And you? Dodgers, Giants, or Yankees?"

"Yankees all the way."

"Well, I won't hold that against you," Danny teased. He held out his hand. "I'm Danny McClain, and this is my wife Anya Ver—I mean, Anya *McClain*." He slipped his arm around her waist. "I still have to get used to that. We just got married. Yesterday, as a matter of fact."

The girl beamed. "Truly? Because Jack and I just got married four weeks ago."

Jack gave her neck a squeeze then kissed her soundly.

Anya thought Jack quite handsome with a ready smile, clear blue eyes, and neatly-trimmed blond-brown hair beneath his cap. His pretty wife looked up at him with adoring eyes, then turned her attention to them, her eyes sparkling with humor.

"You'll have to forgive my husband," she said.

"Forgive me for what? I'm not going to see you for months, so I've got to steal all the kisses I can."

"Fine, very well, love, but please give me a moment, will you?" She laughed, stretching out her hand to Anya. "I'm Sybil. Sybil Townsend. It's lovely to meet you."

"Nice to meet you, too."

"And when will *your* lieutenant be heading back to the States?"

Anya glanced at Danny. "We're not sure, are we?"

"My orders haven't come through yet. I'm hoping to stay behind and help close down the 390th so I can have more time with Anya."

"The 390th," Jack began. "That's near Framlingham, right?"

"Yes. Not far from Ipswich."

"I had a buddy back home who was stationed there a couple years ago. His Fort was shot down over Merseburg in '44."

"Sorry to hear that."

"I'm just thankful you made it through." Sybil glanced over at Danny. "And you too, Lieutenant."

"Where were you stationed?" Danny asked.

"Just up the road from you at Bury St. Edmunds with the 94th."

Sybil's tone brightened as she changed the subject. "Yes, well, what would you like to know about the palace? Consider me your personal tour guide. I've lived here all my life."

"Did you say it took nine direct hits during the war? It looks undamaged."

"Quite, but you see, most of the damage happened earlier during the Blitz, the worst of it in September of 1940. A German raider took aim at the palace and dropped five separate bombs, damaging the inner court and the Royal Chapel. Even right here where we're standing outside the forecourt, a delayed-action bomb left a crater more than ten feet deep and thirty feet wide. It was absolutely appalling."

Danny whistled. "You'd never know by the looks of it. I have to hand it to the reconstruction crews for repairing all that damage."

"Were the king and queen here when it happened?" Anya asked.

"Yes, but thankfully, they weren't injured," Sybil said. "The next day they were out and about viewing the damage and giving encouragement to the workers who were cleaning up the debris."

"Tell them what the queen said about the palace being

bombed," Jack prompted.

"She said she was actually glad the Germans bombed the palace because it helped her understand what the rest of London was experiencing. She said it made her feel like she could finally look the East End in the face, or something like that. The East End received a tremendous amount of damage during the war."

"But why were the king and queen still in residence?" Anya asked. "Why didn't they evacuate?"

"They sent the princesses—Elizabeth and Margaret—to Windsor Castle, but the king and queen insisted on staying; I suppose as a symbol of solidarity with their subjects. Whenever the palace sustained damage, they would both be seen about, taking a look for themselves to see what had happened."

Danny leaned against the railing. "I also heard they visited bomb shelters to encourage the people who found refuge there?"

"Yes. In fact, a couple of years ago I was trying to get home one day when the sirens went off, so I followed everyone to the nearest Tube station for shelter. The king and queen had been there visiting just moments before the sirens went off. I didn't get to see them, but everyone there was absolutely delighted by their visit. They said it was immensely inspiring to see the royal couple's genuine care and concern.

"Oh, but you should have been here when we heard the war had ended!" Sybil continued, her voice filled with excitement. "*Thousands* of people all around, as far as the eye could see! We'd all heard rumors, of course, and everyone was drawn here to the palace to wait for the announcement.

It didn't come until much, much later. We were beginning to think it was all a hoax until later that evening when Churchill made it official. We were told that the following day, the eighth of May, would be a national holiday—Victory in Europe Day!"

"It must have been so exciting," Anya said.

"Oh, it was the most glorious moment!" she continued, her hands in constant motion. "The RAF flew victory rolls overhead, and the church bells rang and rang. We were all dancing and laughing and shouting until we were positively hoarse from it all. We kept crying out, 'We want the king! We want the king!' We would have stayed all night had it not been for a ridiculous thunderstorm that kicked up just before midnight.

"But the next morning we were all back, then later that afternoon, the king and queen finally came out on that balcony. See it over there? The princesses were there too, then Prime Minister Churchill joined them, and the roar of the crowd was positively magical—"

"Sybil, these nice folks are—"

"Oh Jack, let me finish!" Sybil waved him off and continued, her eyes glistening with joy. "The day went on and no one wanted to leave. We were still so excited! Then later in the evening we looked up and saw the most magnificent sight —two brilliant searchlights coming from St. Paul's forming a giant 'V' for victory in the sky—" She hiccupped a tiny sob and held a fist to her mouth for a moment. "We'd been under blackouts for so many years, you see, so we all just cried and cried—"

"All right, honey," Jack said, digging a handkerchief out of his pocket. "Dry those tears. I think these folks have heard quite enough." He tucked his happy weeping wife beneath his arm and tossed them a wink. "Besides, I'm sure they have better things to do."

"No, please don't stop on our account," Anya said.

"Yes, please continue," Danny added. "Anya and I both missed the big celebrations that day, so it's a real treat to finally hear about it from someone who was here."

Sybil laughed, still dabbing her eyes. "Oh, now you're just being nice."

"No, it's true. Besides," Danny continued, "this is Anya's first visit to London, so I'm sure she's enjoying your firsthand account."

Sybil reached for Anya's wrist. "I've been trying and trying to place your accent, but you see, I'm horrible with such things."

"I'm from The Netherlands. Utrecht, to be exact."

"Ah yes, of course that's it. You're Dutch. But how do you speak English so well? Were you raised here in England?"

"No, but my father grew up here in England in a tiny fishing village called Port Isaac. We spoke both languages in our home."

"That explains it, then." Sybil's expression grew serious. "Oh, we heard such terrible things about the Occupation in Holland. I'm so very glad you survived. And now look at you— married and starting your happy-ever-after just like Jack and me. But you must tell us how you and your husband met?"

Anya and Danny looked at each other and smiled. "It's a long story, but we actually knew each other before the war," Danny began. "We hadn't met face to face, but we'd corresponded for several years. Then I guess you could say I quite literally dropped in to meet her when my crew had to bail out of our Fort over Holland."

"Were you shot down?" Jack asked.

"No, but badly damaged by shrapnel and engines on fire. We had no choice but to bail."

"Oh my goodness! How utterly romantic," Sybil trilled.

Jack shook his head and patted Sybil's head. "Sweetheart, somehow I doubt the lieutenant had romance on his mind when he jumped out of his plane. That was quite a harrowing experience. Glad to see you survived."

"Yes, and thank God for the Dutch Resistance workers who rescued me so the Germans couldn't take me prisoner. And that's where I met Anya—at a safe house. She was working with the Resistance—"

"Oh Anya, what a love story! Why, it must have been so exciting—"

"Sybil, pipe down, will you?" Jack laughed, cupping his hand over her mouth. "Let these nice people have some peace." He turned to face them. "You'll have to forgive my wife. She could chat up a tree stump."

She laughed, pulling his hand away. "That's not true!"

"No, it's actually quite nice to meet another war bride," Anya said, coming to her defense. "That's what they're calling us, isn't it?"

Sybil continued playfully fighting Jack's attempts to hush her. "Yes, and there are *thousands* of us. Strength in numbers, don't you think?"

"Yes, I agree."

"Well, it's been nice meeting you," Danny said, "We don't

want to keep you."

Jack peeked at his wristwatch then reached for his wife's hand. "Wow, look at the time, Syb. I've got to catch a train back to my base. I'm sure you understand—"

"But wait," Sybil said. "I have an idea. If you would allow me to see Jack off at the station, perhaps I could meet you somewhere afterwards and show you a few of the sights."

"We wouldn't want to impose on you like that," Anya said.

"No, it wouldn't be an imposition in the least. I'll be wretchedly sad once Jack leaves, and this way, you will give me something to do rather than shed rivers of tears."

"Are you sure?" Danny asked glancing at Jack.

"Don't look at me." Jack raked a hand through his hair before putting his cap back on. "Either way, we've got to run." He started pulling Sybil along beside him. She turned, walking backward.

"Wonderful!" she said. "Where shall we meet? At the foot of Big Ben over at Westminster? Take Birdcage Walk here and just follow it until you see the tower. Give me an hour?"

"Perfect," Danny said. "We'll see you there."

"It was nice to meet you fine folks," Jack said as he finally lassoed his wife with his arm. "Who knows, maybe we'll see you back in the States someday!"

With a final wave, they hurried away.

6

Danny and Anya took their time strolling hand in hand the short distance to Westminster, thankful for the clear blue sky above them.

"It's a little strange, don't you think? Agreeing to spend the day with a complete stranger?" he asked. "Do you think we blew it? We could be no-shows and stand her up."

"But that would be rude," Anya said. "It was kind of her to offer."

"She's a feisty little thing, isn't she?"

"Yes, but you used that same description for me not so long ago. And yet, here you are—married to me."

"True, and I couldn't be happier."

"She said it would give her something to do. It must be awful having to separate so soon after getting married." Anya stopped, her grip tightening on his hand. "I suppose I hadn't thought that far ahead, but will *we* have to separate? Will you have to go and send for me later?"

He noted a trace of angst in her voice. "What? How do you

mean?"

"When they send you home, will I go with you?"

"I think—"

Sybil suddenly appeared beside them. "Oh, I can't begin to tell you how relieved I am you're here!"

Danny uttered a silent prayer of thanks for the interruption as he turned at the sound of Sybil's voice. He blinked at the sight of her face; a blotchy, pale canvas beneath tracks of tear-smudged makeup.

"I stopped to freshen my face after Jack's train left, but I'm afraid it didn't do much good." She sniffled, dabbing at her eyes with a hankie. "And I was so afraid I might not get here in time. Or even worse, that you'd changed your mind after I barged my way in on the first day of your honeymoon. Jack says I've never met a stranger, and I suppose he's right. But I truly hope you haven't changed your mind. We could give it a go for an hour or so, then go our separate ways when you've had enough. If that suits you?"

He and Anya nodded in agreement. "Sounds good. We're grateful you're willing to show us around. The only other time I was in London was on leave, and I remember staying lost most of the time."

"Then I shall do my best to give you the finest tour possible." She straightened, puffing a cleansing sigh of relief.

Anya patted Sybil's arm. "When will you be able to join your husband?"

"That's just it. We don't know. We have to—"

"So what's the story behind Big Ben?" Danny blurted, desperate to change the subject. He dreaded the conversation he needed to have with Anya, but hoped they could avoid it until after the honeymoon.

"Oh yes, well then. I should probably begin by telling you that Big Ben is the name of the clock's great bell, *not* the clock itself, or even the tower, for that matter. Visitors always get that confused. When the war began, the lights of the clock faces were turned off to confuse the Luftwaffe pilots. The tower roof took a direct hit back in 1940 during the Blitz, damaging those two white hands you see up there, but the clock never stopped ticking through the entire war. Well, except for a few hours the following year when a workman accidentally dropped his hammer into the clock's works while repairing damage. But that was the only time. Otherwise, the clock kept perfect time for the duration of the war. Amazing, isn't it?"

"Incredible," Danny said. "You'd think Hitler would've targeted the tower from day one."

Sybil guided them down the footpath. "Funny you should say that. We always knew London was Hitler's primary target. And of course, we're rather proud of the fact that he failed. He tried and tried, right up until the end. But no matter how many times those buzz bombs and doodlebugs struck, and no matter how badly his Luftwaffe damaged segments of our city, we never let him break our spirit."

She lifted her arms. "Look—I have goose bumps." She smiled, rubbing them. "I can't help it. I'm so proud of my country and my city, and how we weathered all those brutal assaults, year after year, and never once let them defeat us."

"It's all so different from what I experienced up there." Danny pointed skyward. "We had a job to do, and we did it. But other than the time I spent in Holland after bailing out, I never saw the effect of our efforts at ground level. You actually *lived* it here."

"Yes, and I'm happy to say all the stronger for it."

They followed her along the walkway. "There isn't time to show you everything, of course, and it would be wise to avoid certain areas. I'm sure you've seen some of the homes and businesses that were leveled. I suppose it will take years for the rubble to be cleared so we can rebuild. We're all a bit anxious to see signs of reconstruction, but in reality, I'm sure it will take lots and lots of time."

Sybil continued her narrative as they walked alongside Westminster, the grand buildings along the banks of the Thames which once served as the palace for the royal family, now home to Parliament. She pointed out the empty hull of the Commons Chamber which had been destroyed by fire, its roof collapsing on the ruins. The House of Lords had been spared from any serious damage, though she told of a bomb which had passed clear through the floor, but thankfully never exploded.

Moving along, they crossed the street and approached the rear entrance of Westminster Abbey.

"Someday, when the dust has all cleared, you must come back and take a tour of the Abbey. It's quite magnificent. Most of the royal weddings have taken place here. King George and Queen Elizabeth were married here in 1923. Of course, the Coronation Chair and all the statues from the royal tombs were sent to the countryside, out of harm's way. And fortunately, the Abbey experienced only minor damage during the war."

As they made their way to the front entrance, Anya leaned

back for a better look at the ornate spires stretching high against the backdrop of the blue sky. "I can't comprehend all of this," she said quietly. "It's so different from home. The architecture, the height and expanse of all these buildings ..." She lowered her eyes to them again. "It's as if a whole world I never knew about has existed all along, and I'm too late ..."

She gazed intently into Danny's eyes, but clearly her mind was elsewhere.

"Too late for what, Anya?" he asked.

"Too late to grasp it." She turned, her eyes drawn back to the spires. "I see it, all of it, but it's as if my mind and my heart can't even comprehend what I'm seeing." She leveled her eyes at them again, a smile taunting her sad expression. "Oh, never mind me. I'm just the silly Dutch girl who keeps babbling every thought that crosses her mind."

"It must be quite strange for you, Anya," Sybil said. "But I'm so pleased to share my city with you."

Danny gathered his wife under his arm and kissed the top of her head. "Don't let it overwhelm you. Just relax and enjoy the sights, all right?"

She nodded. "All right. I'm trying."

For the next two hours, Sybil walked them by several historic landmarks. Danny was especially interested in seeing Number 10 Downing Street, home to the British government and residence of Winston Churchill. With its address in brass numerals on the shiny black door, the modest cream-colored entryway stood in contrast to the home's charcoal gray brick exterior. A uniformed guard stood at the door with his hands clasped behind his back.

"I'm surprised," Danny said, studying the building. "I

would've expected something bigger and more elegant. But here it sits in a simple neighborhood."

"Yes, but inside it's ever so much larger than it looks. Actually three houses in one, if I remember correctly. More than a hundred rooms, plus a nice garden in the back. I've never been inside, but I've seen pictures and learned all about it when I was a schoolgirl."

They passed the Horse Guards palace and Whitehall which housed the secret underground war headquarters, as well as the bunker where Churchill took his famous short naps. She walked them by the National Gallery in Trafalgar Square, telling them its priceless works of art had been moved to a specially designed hidden cave in a Welsh mountain for safekeeping.

"I found it actually quite funny because they took the paintings but left all the empty frames in place here at the museum. Then Sir Kenneth Clark would select one work of art from the hidden collection and have it brought here to be shown as the 'Picture of the Month.' If you can believe it, long queues formed as people gathered, anxious to see what it might be."

"Strange, in the middle of a war," Danny said.

"But that was the point, don't you see? An example of our tenacity to keep a stiff upper lip despite any enemy attacks. I visited the gallery several times during the war. You'd be surprised how inspirational it was to see a masterpiece, all by itself, lit up and framed in sheer isolation."

At Danny's suggestion, they stopped for a light lunch at an outdoor café where they shared a plate of cheeses, hardboiled eggs, and crusty bread.

"We'd all hoped the end of the war would mean no more rationing and no more queuing at the markets, but if anything, it's worse," Sybil lamented. "I must say I feel a bit guilty, dining out twice in one day."

"Please don't." Danny sliced a piece of bread for her. "It's the least we can do for taking your time."

"I must admit Jack spoiled me while he was here. He seemed to have wads of cash and happy to spend it. After living on rations for so long, it was lovely to have so many choices again."

"What will you do while waiting to join your husband in America?" Anya asked.

"I suppose I'll continue working at Rainbow Corner, though I don't know how much longer they'll stay open now that the war's over."

"That's one of the American Red Cross clubs, right?" Danny asked.

"Yes, have you been there?"

"Just once, on that same leave I mentioned earlier. Some of the guys had gone dancing there before and wanted to go. We didn't stay long because it was so crowded."

"Fancy that, we might have danced if you had."

Anya's eyes widened. "That's what you do there? Dance?"

"Yes! I love to dance, don't you?"

"No. I mean, I've never danced."

"You've *never* danced?"

Danny reached for Anya's hand. "You have to remember it was much different in Holland during the Occupation. Anya worked for the Resistance, primarily shuttling Jewish children to safe homes. There weren't many opportunities for things like dancing."

"We heard of dances now and then," Anya added. "Some were even held in bomb shelters. But there was never time for anything like that. If we weren't watching over the children or transporting aircrews to safety, all we wanted to do was sleep."

"You must think me so frivolous," Sybil said, her face filled with sympathy. "While you were saving lives, I was busy jitter-bugging with Yanks. I don't suppose I'd ever thought of it like that."

"Please don't," Anya said. "We all did what we had to do. I'm sure the Americans appreciated a chance to take their minds off the war, even for an hour or two."

"Absolutely," Danny added. "And if the Rainbow is like some of the others I've heard about, there was more to it than just dancing."

Sybil's eyes went wide. "I beg your pardon?"

"No! No, not *that*—"

"I should hope not!" Sybil joked.

"No! I only meant the clubs offered a lot more than just dancing. No, wait. That didn't sound right either. Oh, brother. I'm digging myself in deeper, aren't I?"

"Yes, so stop while you're ahead," Anya teased.

"I'm sure what you *meant*," Sybil said, "was that the Rainbow and other Red Cross Clubs offer other things like laundry services and first aid, and plenty of recreation like pool and pinball."

"What's pinball?"

Danny smiled as Sybil explained. "It's just a silly game played on a machine, shooting all these little steel balls around, trying to hit little targets and rack up lots of points. I've never understood the passion for it, but the Americans are enraptured by it, playing for hours and hours."

"Danny, do you play?" Anya asked.

"No, the two times I did, I was lousy at it. Never saw the point really."

"But the Yanks come to the club for all sorts of reasons," Sybil added. "We help the boys write home, play cards with them, or just listen to music. We've had some of the best bands play at the Rainbow. My

favorite was the American, Glenn Miller."

"Mine too," Danny said. "I still can't believe he's gone."

"What happened to him?" Anya asked.

"He joined the service so he could entertain the troops," Danny said. "He and his Army Air Force Band played all over England until just before Christmas last year when his plane disappeared over the English Channel. It was never found."

"I was working at the Rainbow the night it was announced," Sybil said. "We were all crying. You'd think we'd lost a family member, and I guess, in a way we did. It was such a shock."

"Was it ever," Danny added.

Sybil wiped her eyes again. "Don't mind me; I seem to be a never-ending bucket of tears today." She tucked the hankie back in her pocket. "There now. All better."

"Where to next?" Danny asked as they stood.

"That's any easy one. Follow me."

7

Stepping off the double-decker bus, Danny and Anya followed Sybil as she turned the next corner. Here and there, skeletal brick walls outlined empty foundations like so many ghostly footprints; the damage indiscriminate. As they rounded another corner, before them stood a magnificent cathedral beneath an enormous dome.

Sybil spoke quietly with reverence. "The Prime Minister said there was no greater symbol of British resilience during the war than St. Paul's Cathedral. He said it had to be saved at all costs."

"How could it survive when so many buildings around it were decimated?" Danny asked.

"To be honest, I know of no other explanation than divine intervention. The cathedral was damaged several times during the Blitz, and later as well. But thankfully, a group of men who called themselves the St. Paul's Fire Watch stood guard around the clock, remaining on alert, particularly during the long months of the Blitz. They had installed tanks of water and kept pails at the ready near the more vulnerable parts of the domed roof you see up there. It's quite extraordinary, how they protected the building and all its history."

"Still, if the Germans had targeted the cathedral for a direct hit," Danny said, "surely it would have been flattened like all these other buildings. I'd say divine intervention played a bigger part than those volunteers carrying buckets of water."

"You're right, of course. And that was true throughout the war, even after the Blitz." Sybil shielded her eyes from the sun as she studied the dome again. "But you have to admit it looks like a beacon of hope against all the destruction around it. That's why I wanted you both to see it.

"And here's the irony," she continued. "Before the war, you could never get a full view of the entire cathedral because all the surrounding buildings blocked the view. Only glimpses. But with so many buildings leveled around it now, you can see it from all sorts of angles and locations around the city. I was quite astounded the first time I saw it like this. Of course, it's bittersweet, I suppose, in light of all these other structures that were destroyed."

For the next half hour, they wandered down the wide aisles of the ornate cathedral, often gazing up at the colorful tiled mosaics on the ceiling. Sybil told them about the famous English architect Christopher Wren, who redesigned St. Paul's after the Great Fire of London in 1666 leveled it, along with so many other churches and buildings. She pointed out some of the damaged areas and the elaborate tombs in the cathedral's crypt, including that of Christopher Wren.

"It's very beautiful," Anya said, as they made their way back outside. "I've never seen churches like this one or Westminster Abbey. Are all the churches in London this big?"

"No, they come in all shapes and sizes. I'm not Catholic, so I've never worshipped here, but I love to visit. Especially now. It helps remind me that no matter what happens, life will go on."

"It seems we've lost our sunshine," Danny noted as they descended the steps outside. "Those clouds rolled in fast, didn't they?"

"Always, but just be glad you had a little sunshine. We're cloudy and gray most of the time, as you probably know by now. If you're up to it, there's one more place I'd like to show you. It's not far, but we'll want to catch another bus."

A few minutes later, they exited their bus after it crossed the Thames on the famous Tower Bridge. Anya couldn't take her eyes off the bridge. She'd seen a photograph of it in one of her school books, with its two towers connected by two parallel bridges. She realized it was the only structure she recognized from her school studies.

"Ah, London Bridge, right? Another one of Hitler's missed targets, I see," Danny noted.

"No, this is Tower Bridge. London Bridge is that one down there," she said, pointing at a rather plain bridge not far from them. "Visitors always confuse the two. Tower Bridge is named because of its location here alongside the Tower of London. Which isn't just a tower, as you can see, but rather a palace and all its buildings and grounds. It dates back to the year 1078, if you can believe it. Since then, it's been used as a residence for the royal family, a prison, a fortress, and let's see—what else ... oh yes, the royal treasury. This is where they keep the crowned jewels, though they were sent elsewhere for safekeeping during the war."

Danny blew a whistle. "Quite a bit of damage, I see. Devastating to see on such a historic place like this. Any direct hits?"

"Only one, and that was during the Blitz. You can see several of the buildings were either destroyed or severely damaged. But what I really wanted you to see is the moat. See that area outside the walls where you would normally find a moat filled with water?"

Anya looked at rows upon rows of vegetation. "It's all filled in. Are those gardens?"

"Yes! Isn't it brilliant? After the war started and food became so scarce, we were asked to plant gardens wherever we could. They were called Victory Gardens. You'll see them all over the country, some on golf courses or tennis courts, parks, just about anywhere. But this is surely the most admired and well-tended. I love to come by here whenever I'm in this part of the city. There's just something about it that cheers me so."

"Perhaps it's the sight of so much growth amongst all the rubble?" Anya said.

"I think you're right. Growth amongst the rubble. That's very astute, Anya."

They walked a little further as Sybil gave them a brief history of the events that had taken place here over the course of history. When a gentle rain began to fall, they took shelter under the eaves of a nearby bookstore.

"I suppose we should probably head back to the hotel

now," Danny said. "Sybil, you've been such a fantastic tour guide. Thank you again for showing us the sights."

"Oh, but you're most welcome. I've probably worn you out, but it's I who should thank *you*. You've no idea how lovely it's been, showing you my city instead of drowning myself in misery now that Jack's gone."

"Would you consider giving us a telephone number or an address?" Danny asked. "I'm only asking because it might be good for Anya to be able to reach you, in case she ... uh, well, what I mean is, if she has to—"

"Absolutely. I would love to stay in touch. Here, let me write it down for you. We don't have a telephone at home, but you can ring this number, and someone will get the message to me. It's my aunt's shop. We live just down the way from her."

Danny handed her his pen after she found something to write on in her handbag. When she finished, she handed the slip of paper to Anya.

"Please, any time at all." Sybil took a scarf from her bag and lifted it over her hair. "When you know more about your plans, feel free to let me know. And please stop by to see me at Rainbow Corner if you're in that area before you leave town. It's near Piccadilly Circus in the West End."

"We'd love to," Danny said.

"Well, then. Off we go. It's been such a delight," she said, giving Anya then Danny a hug. "And congratulations! Maybe Jack was right. Maybe someday we'll meet for tea in America. You do *have* tea in America?"

"Sure we do. It comes with lots of ice in a tall glass," Danny teased.

"You Yanks and your fondness for ice. Oh—I almost forgot. Will you be able to find your way back to your hotel?"

"Come to think of it, no."

She gave them easy instructions, then said her goodbyes.

The next morning, Anya awoke smiling at Danny's quiet snores near her ear. She was amazed how quickly he could fall asleep and envied him for it. With her back pressed against his chest, his arm around her waist, she felt the easy rise and fall of his slumber. Until their first night together, she'd never given much thought to sleeping in the same bed with someone before. Yesterday, on their first morning as husband and wife, she'd been startled to wake up with no memory of how she'd fallen asleep. She couldn't believe she'd stayed asleep all night, wrapped in Danny's arms. It was all so new and so different, the emotions crisscrossing her heart even now.

The sudden flutter of a snore tickled her ear. She smiled, careful not to stir, not wishing to wake him just yet. She still couldn't fully comprehend that they were married. She'd fought her feelings for him from the start, from the first moment she laid eyes on him at the safe house. Already the war had hardened her; the carefully laid bricks walled around her heart with fierce determination. The last thing she wanted was to feel anything for anyone again. She'd actually wondered if she might be cursed with everyone she'd ever loved somehow marked for death. To lose anyone else would surely undo her, and she wasn't about to let that happen. Never again.

Until Danny.

What a shock to see him there that first day; such a grown-up version of the American kid in the photograph he'd sent her brother. Tall and handsome; his close-cut hair and stubble a darker shade of brown than she would have expected. His strong jawline seemed to compliment his strength of character, even as his kind blue eyes pierced her soul that day. She remembered the deep dimples of his smile when he first realized it was her. That exact moment, it nearly broke her spirit. How desperately she'd wanted to rush into his strong arms and stay there until the nightmare of war was over.

Instead, despite his constant efforts to break down her defenses, always asking her to trust him, to let him watch over and protect her, Anya had kept him at arm's length for as long as she could. Until that day he came back to find her, and she could no longer resist the tug of her heart to trust his.

Even now, she struggled to allow herself the simple pleasure of his company. As if she didn't deserve such happiness. Her worlds had not yet blended. She wanted them to, needed them to. But a heavy blanket of sadness and despair seemed forever draped over her heart. And with it, a voice constantly taunting her, like a cruel and heartless version of herself who kept chiding her for daring to hope, then slapping her face if a single moment of goodness or happiness came along. As though she neither deserved it nor had any right to hold onto it, much less dream of a happily-ever-after life.

Yet here she was, wrapped in the arms of a man who loved her enough to marry her and vow to spend the rest of his life with her.

She pushed away the negative thoughts and tried to simply cherish the moment. She didn't want to think about the past anymore with all its ugliness and heartache. She chose not to dwell on the future and how much it terrified her. Instead, she closed her eyes and remembered the long hours they'd talked here in bed. Their laughter, their longing ... and the exquisite moments of intimacy they'd shared.

Anya smiled, thinking how silly she'd been to be so nervous about it. "These things have a way of working out," Sophie had told her. *Oh Sophie, how right you were.* She felt her face warm as the tenderness of their passion played through her mind. Never had she imagined such feelings, such complete oneness, such pleasure.

But as beautiful and surprising as it had all been to her, what mattered most was how wonderfully loved and incredibly *safe* she'd felt in Danny's arms.

If only this moment could last forever.

If only it would be enough.

Anya felt him stir as he awakened and felt the expanse of his chest against her back as he stretched with a slow and lazy yawn. She smiled at the strength of his arms when he pulled her closer still, and shivered at the warmth of his breath on her neck as he kissed her.

"Good morning," he murmured as he kissed the soft spot

below her ear.

"Good morning," she whispered.

If only this moment could last forever.

If only.

8

Danny and Anya spent that day and the next wandering around London at a far more leisurely pace. On Monday, after stopping for lunch at a pub in Westminster, Danny noticed a movie theater across the street as they exited.

"Anya, look!"

"What am I supposed to look at? The cinema?"

"Look at the marquee! They're showing *Winged Victory*! My flight school graduation ceremony was filmed for it. I'm *in* that movie! C'mon, let's see if there's a matinee."

Five minutes later, they were seated in the center of the small, partially-filled theater. On the way in, Danny insisted they splurge for a box of popcorn.

"But we just ate. How can you possibly be hungry?"

"I'm not. But you can't watch movies without popcorn. Which is strange considering all those years I worked in Dad's theater. After a while, even the slightest smell of the kernels popping at the concession stand got to me. I thought I'd never want another bite of the stuff for the rest of my life.

Yet, here we are, in London, at the movies—and we have to have popcorn, don't you see? And it's not just any movie—I'm actually *in* this one!"

She shook her head. "Don't be silly. You don't really believe you'll actually see yourself on the big screen?"

"You never know. It could happen." He placed a piece of popcorn between his teeth and waggled his brows. "Kith me?"

"No, I'm not going to—"

He didn't wait for her response, giving her a salty kiss and shooting the popped kernel in her mouth.

She batted his arm playfully, dissolving into laughter as she ate it.

He held a finger before his lips. "Shhh. The movie's starting."

As the red velvet curtain parted, a newsreel began. Its tinny narration over stilted music described the continued world-wide celebrations following the end of the war.

"Now, from Berlin to London, from the vanquished to the victor; outside Buckingham Palace, crowds cheered themselves hoarse."

As a symphony played a familiar merry tune, the camera panned the mass of humanity gathered around the palace, stretching as far as the eye could see.

He felt Anya's hand grab his arm. "It's just like Sybil said. Danny, look at all those people. Were you in a crowd like that when the announcement came?"

"No, I was riding a lorry back to the base. They'd sent us to Liverpool to pick up our gear that was sent there when we were MIA. We kept seeing flares shoot up from different bases we passed. Somehow we just knew the war had ended. Back at the 390th the guys got a little carried away as they partied and shot out some windows in the control tower. That was about it, I think. But I've never seen what happened here in London until now. Just look at all those people!"

The music played on as the camera showed a panoramic view of the millions gathered on May eighth, just a few weeks earlier. The narration continued.

"Seven times during V-E Day, the British royal family appeared on the balcony."

The king in his military uniform stood beside the queen, dressed in a coatdress and hat. Princess Margaret stood beside her father, while Princess Elizabeth, also in uniform, stood beside her mother. As the family waved, the crowds went wild, shouting and waving back. Later, Winston Churchill joined the royal family on the balcony sending the crowds there into a roaring, euphoric bliss.

Anya huddled close beside him. "I had no idea. It wasn't like this back home, at least not where I was. Until Sybil brought it up, I'd never dreamed there were celebrations like this."

The lump in his throat surprised him, as did the moisture blurring his vision. When Anya turned to look at him, he noticed her eyes were filled with tears too.

"Aren't we a pair?" he croaked, putting his arm around her.

He recognized the song playing over the next scene as the

same one played when he graduated from high school. "Pomp and Circumstance," wasn't it? Something about the nostalgic tune choked him up even more until he barked an unintentional sob. Thanks to the cheering audience, only Anya heard the pitiful thing.

The darkness did nothing to dissipate the throng of people celebrating on that night. People waved British flags. Others danced on top of vehicles and monuments; some even climbed to the top of street lights high above the crowd. The camera focused on a uniformed couple kissing passionately at the top of a street light as lines of soldiers and young ladies snaked through the crowds in long, wavy conga lines.

"We are living in the midst of many great events. We know that in the days when war seems remote and far away, these will be historic pictures. They will tell another generation how England celebrated Victory in Europe Day."

The movie audience cheered again as the newsreel continued then silenced when the screen filled with a massive German structure. At the infamous Nuremberg Stadium, the scene of countless Nazi party rallies throughout the war, a huge American flag was raised to cover the enormous swastika atop the massive building. Then, as it hid the hated Nazi emblem, an explosion destroyed the swastika in a symbolic gesture. Danny and Anya joined the loud cheers that filled the theater.

When the movie began, Danny could hardly contain himself. At one point, when the onscreen inductees began marching, they broke into song—the Army Air Force song. Danny sprang up out of his seat with a whoop and a holler, joining other airmen in the theater.

"Off we go, into the wild blue yonder!"

"Danny!" Anya tugged at his sleeve, her laughter accompanying his boisterous rendition.

He sat back down and watched the movie play on, more documentary than a regular story film, but Danny loved it anyway. He leaned over to Anya often to explain the training and drills and testing depicted, noting their accuracy.

"This is it! This is it, Anya!" He pointed at the screen and elbowed her at the same time. "That's our graduation. See if you can spot me."

"But they all look alike. With their caps on, you can hardly see their faces."

He scooted to the front of his seat. "Shhh! Just keep watching. Maybe they'll do a close-up."

The music played on as the precisely choreographed march of graduates filled the screen.

"There you are!" Anya shouted. "See? Right there, second from the left?"

The camera angle changed. "No! I didn't see me. Are you sure it was me?"

Her head bobbed. "Yes, I'm sure! Were you next to the end of your row or whatever they're called?"

He fell back in his seat. "Well, yes, but—"

"Then it had to be you."

He ignored the film, captivated by her smile, so wide and carefree. Such rare, unbridled joy on the face of his bride took every other thought from his mind. He'd never seen her more beautiful. Cupping her face in his hands, he kissed her passionately and didn't stop, even when she giggled.

As they watched the rest of the movie, Danny made comments now and then, mostly concerning the portrayal of life in the Army Air Force. When the movie ended and the lights came up, someone tapped Danny's shoulder.

A young man seated directly behind them looked at them with a sheepish grin on his face. "I couldn't help overhearing, and I simply must ask. Were you really in this film?"

"Just one of the cadets there in the graduation ceremony. That's all."

"I say, then! I've never met an American film star before. Would you be so kind as to give me your autograph? If it's not too much to ask?"

"But I'm not a star. I'm just a co-pilot for—"

"Well, then! Even better. A movie star *and* a war hero. We thought you Americans would never come join us, but once you did—well, I believe I'm safe in saying we couldn't have won it without you. So by all means, please, if you would—" He patted the pockets of his jacket to locate a pen, then rummaged through his trouser pockets for something to write on. "Here, my handkerchief. It's clean," he said with a wink to Anya. "I promise."

"Well, if you insist."

"Excellent. Here, use my back for a surface." He turned and leaned slightly over so Danny could jot his name on the handkerchief.

"There you go," Danny said.

"What was it like? Meeting all those famous people like Lon McAllister and Edmond O'Brien? And what about Jeanne

79

Crain? Is she as beautiful in person as she is on screen?"

"No, I never met any of the stars. They weren't there the day of our graduation. They must have added that scene later from a sound stage or something."

They started back up the aisle toward the exit.

"Really? Because it looked like they were right there," Anya said. "Why wouldn't they just film it there with all of you?"

"That's Hollywood for you. All smoking guns and mirrors."

Both the young man and Anya stared at him. Realizing their confusion, Danny explained.

"It's made to *appear* that they were there, but no doubt easier to control the sound and lighting on some back lot in Hollywood."

"Then what do mirrors and guns have to do with it?" Anya asked.

He waved her off. "Just an expression."

"Well, then. Thank you, sir." The young man carefully folded his handkerchief and put it in his pocket. "And thank you for your service during the war. The best of British," he said, extending his hand.

Danny shook his hand. "The best of British?"

The young man smiled. "Just an expression, as you say. It means the best of British luck to you."

"Oh, I see. Same to you."

As the lad made his way out of the theater, Anya leaned in. "Please, can I have your autograph, mister?"

"Yeah, that's a first. But who knows, maybe he's right. Maybe I was born to be in the movies." He dazzled her with his smile and danced his brows. "Well? What do you think?"

"I think you might be better suited for the circus."

"The circus? Now you're just being mean." He stole a kiss as they headed out of the theater.

Later, as they strolled through Hyde Park, they paused at the gates of Kensington Palace to view the visible damage to the home of the royal family. It seemed wherever they went, the city's scars of ruin and destruction surrounded them.

As much as the movie had lightened Anya's spirits, Danny could see traces of the haunting shadow drifting through her eyes again. He wondered once again what he'd been thinking to bring her here for their honeymoon. A wiser man would have hopped right back on the train and found some quiet coastal town, far from the constant reminders of the long war.

Maybe it wasn't too late.

He stopped to face her. "Anya, I have an idea. I don't know about you, but I think we've seen enough of London. Would you agree?"

"I wasn't going to say anything, but now that you mention it, yes. Why?"

"What if we go back to the hotel, pack our bags, and spend our last couple of days somewhere near the coast. I remember one of the guys in my outfit mentioning a little town called Aldeburgh. I'm not sure there's much to do there, but—"

She silenced him with a kiss, wrapping her arms around his neck. "Yes! Yes, please take me anywhere that doesn't remind us of war."

They arrived at the Victoria Apollo train station just after four-thirty that afternoon as the skies opened and drenched London in a heavy downpour. Anya thought it a fitting departure. It wasn't that she didn't like the city with all its historic sites and the constant hustle and bustle of people trying to put their lives back together. She simply felt overwhelmed by its size, its scope, and most of all, its miles and miles of damage and destruction. The presence of war still lingered here like a morbid residue shrouded over the city.

Even worse than the debris of war around them were the people they passed on the street. They all seemed exhausted from the long years of war. A far cry from the jubilant images they'd seen on the newsreel at the cinema. Would the ecstatic celebrations of VE Day ever fill these streets again with laughter, cheering and dancing? Would London survive? Would the scars of war eventually fade? Would Londoners overcome their sorrows, able to face the job still before them to restore their businesses, their homes, and their lives?

But deep in her heart, she knew she'd seen these faces before. She'd walked among them back home in Utrecht and all across her beloved homeland during the Occupation. She watched them drop dead in their tracks from years of malnutrition and hopelessness. With a shudder, she realized how precariously close she'd come to doing the same.

It made no sense, of course, to think London might have

survived without a scratch or expecting it to look exactly as it did in the pictures in her school textbooks. Wishful thinking? Perhaps.

Maybe that was why it overwhelmed her. Unrealistic expectations giving way to the harsh ugliness of war's ragged scars. Whatever the cause, she wondered if the world would ever be normal again.

She settled back in her seat by the window. "I'm so glad we're leaving."

Danny took hold of her hand. "Me too. We'll take a proper honeymoon when we get back to the States. But until then, maybe a couple of days at the coast will clear our sails."

"And you're sure this town we're going to wasn't bombed to bits during the war?"

He looked at her with such a blank face, she had to laugh. "You mean you don't know? You didn't ask anyone?"

"Well, now that you mention it, no. But not to worry. If we get there and it's nothing but a crater, we'll just skedaddle back to Framlingham and hide in our room above the pub. We'll just hunker down and order room service from Patrick. Fair enough?"

"Fair enough."

9

12 June 1945

Departing from London, they rode the rails northeast toward Ipswich where they transferred to the East Suffolk Line then on to Saxmundham. The ride mirrored the route they'd taken going the other direction on their wedding day. In Saxmundham, they boarded a bus that took them to Aldeburgh.

Danny and Anya found the quaint seaside town a welcome relief, especially as it appeared untainted by the war. The little village, situated on the River Alde on one side, the sea on the other, was quiet and serene. Perfect.

"We should have come here first and skipped London altogether," Danny mused as they approached the White Lion Inn. "Next time I'll let you plan the honeymoon."

"Next time?"

"Hey, this place looks nice, doesn't it? I didn't realize the inn was right across from the beach. I'm glad it finally stopped raining."

Anya smiled, ignoring the gray sky, simply grateful for the soothing sight of the waves lapping against the shore. "It's beautiful, Danny."

After checking into their room, they kicked off their shoes and relaxed for a while, lounging on the bed as they browsed through the town's tourist brochure.

"Look, here's that old building we saw across the street," Danny said. "It says here it's called Moot Hall. It's where the town council has met for over four hundred years. They still do. Can you imagine?"

Anya wrinkled her nose. "I would imagine it smells of mold and mildew."

"You're probably right. We won't bother. Let's see ... oh, here's something we might like to see. It's called the Martello Tower."

"Don't you have a neighbor by that name?"

"Yes, Mrs. Martello. Wouldn't that be a coincidence if there was some kind of family tie?"

"What kind of tower is it?"

"Apparently, there are a bunch of these all over Great Britain, and this one is the largest. They were built as defense forts during the French Revolutionary War and—"

"No. We came here to forget about the war, remember? Any war."

Danny winced and blew out a sigh. "You're right. Sorry. Okay then, let's find what else we might want to see."

She grabbed the brochure and sent it sailing over him and onto the floor. "Why don't we just put on our shoes and go? It's a small town on the beach. No more tourist attractions. Let's just go wherever our feet take us."

He wrapped his arms around her and kissed her soundly. "Good idea."

"But first we should eat. Are you hungry?"

"Starving. My buddy back on base said Aldeburgh has some of the best fish and chips in all of England."

Mischief tugged at her smile.

"What?"

"Did you know that your whole face lights up when you talk about food?"

"It does not."

"Yes, it does. It's one of those things I love about you."

"Well, then. We should talk about food more often."

"We always do."

"Then you should probably know there are millions of things I love about *you*. Like the way your eyes change color when you get upset."

"They do not. No one can change the color of their eyes."

He turned on his side to face her. "There, see? Right now. Your eyes are tinting more gray than blue. Whereas, when you're happy and laughing, your eyes look bluer. Much bluer."

"Danny, you are so silly."

"Or like now. The way you scrunch up your face when you're trying to think of a swift comeback."

She blanked her face. "I do no such thing."

"Or how your knee bounces when you're nervous. And how your voice gets raspy when you're feeling rather romantic ..." He dispensed with the chatter and kissed her neck just below her ear. "And that," he whispered in her ear.

"That what?" she said, her voice husky.

"The way you shiver when I kiss you here ... and here."

She said nothing more. He didn't expect her to.

They could see the sights later. At the moment, they had better things to do.

Later, they dined on fish and chips and immediately understood what all the fuss was about. The pub was cozy like most are in England, but here the air was heavier than usual with the aroma of deep-fried fish—a scent Anya found not altogether unpleasant as she might have supposed. She wasn't sure she wanted to try the battered fish and fried potatoes at first, but was glad she did.

"I've never cared much for fish before, but this is very good."

Danny grabbed a chip off her plate and ate it. "I had a hunch you might like it."

She stabbed a bite of fish from his plate and quickly downed it. "Stay away from my food, Danny McClain."

"Yes, ma'am," he teased with a laugh. "I have a feeling I might pull back a stump if I try again, eh?"

"You most certainly would."

"We call these French fries back home. Do the Dutch eat French fries?"

"Yes, but we call them *patat friets*. We eat *mayonnaise* with them—"

"Mayonnaise? On fries?" Danny faked a shiver of disgust. "Not sure I could stomach that."

She arched a brow and glared at his plate. "And yet you have no problem with tartar sauce?"

He stopped chewing, glancing down at the mound of the mayonnaise-based sauce alongside his battered cod. With his mouth still full, he gave her a sheepish grin. "Point well taken."

"Personally, I prefer them without. Or *patat zonder mayonaise.*"

"Interesting. I never knew them as anything but French fries until I read *A Tale of Two Cities* when I was in high school. Dickens called them 'husky chips of potatoes fried with some reluctant drops of oil.'"

Anya set down her fork. "How do you do that? How in the world can you remember something you read when in high school? I hardly remember a thing from school."

"I don't either, for the most part. Mine is more of a junk brain, so maybe it's the peculiar wording Dickens used. Maybe that's what stuck with me all these years later. Think about it— 'potatoes fried with reluctant drops of oil.' Who but Charles Dickens would come up with that? How can oil be *reluctant?*"

Anya smiled. "I see your point. But I could also ask, who but *you* would remember such a trivial thing? I remember how Hans used to read me some of the things you wrote about."

"He did?"

"We used to laugh so hard at—"

"What? Why?" he balked. "What was so funny?"

"I would have to say my favorite was in the first letter you wrote him when your teacher made the assignment to write a pen pal in a foreign country."

"You have no idea how much I dreaded that. I put it off as long as I could, until I realized I might get stuck writing a girl if I didn't hurry up and choose a name off Mr. Chesterton's list. That's when I picked *Hans Versteeg*. I thought it was the strangest name—*Versteeg*."

Anya lost herself in the memory. "He read me that letter the day he got it. He must have read it twenty times that first day."

"Okay, but what was so funny about it? As I recall it was pretty short. I didn't have a clue what to say to some kid on the other side of the world."

Anya pushed her plate aside. "Mostly, you rattled on about Chicago and those Cubs you love so much."

"No surprise there."

"Then you asked a lot of questions about The Netherlands and our windmills—things you were familiar with. But at the end, I remember you asking if Hans could speak English. You said you hoped so or your 'grade would be in the toilet.' We laughed so hard."

Danny chuckled at the memory. "Oh yeah, I did say that, didn't I? Well, I'm glad I was able to give the two of you a few laughs."

The smile remained on her face. "It's odd, isn't it? To think we're here now because of that first letter? It seems a lifetime ago. We were but children then."

He reached for her hand. "Those are good memories, Anya. I'm glad we share them, even if we were half a world apart."

"Yes. Good memories. Happier times."

She nibbled on another fry. "It's strange, everything so

different. Like food. So different from what I grew up eating. What about you? What kind of food does your mother make?"

An easy smile warmed his face. "She makes the most incredible fried chicken you've ever tasted. Crispy on the outside, juicy on the inside. And a pot roast that'll knock your socks off. And her biscuits?" He closed his eyes. "I mean, I've dreamed about those biscuits. They practically melt inside your mouth."

As he carried on, Anya's mind wandered down an unexpected path. She'd done her best to put aside any thoughts of life in America knowing it would only cause more worry. But she knew the time was coming soon when she'd meet his family, and most likely live with them until they could afford a place of their own. Such thoughts always tightened a knot in her stomach.

"Anya? Are you all right?"

She nodded, wishing away the intrusive thoughts.

"Are you sure?"

"Yes." She took a sip of tea, avoiding his eyes. She ate a couple more bites of fish, struggling to eat any more but keenly aware that he was watching her. "The sun will set soon. Do you think we might take a walk out on the beach when we're through here?"

"Sounds great."

A few minutes later, they left the pub. The breeze was cooler, and the sky had finally cleared with only a few clouds drifting over the water. Danny tucked Anya under his arm as they crossed the road and stepped onto the beach. She stopped, looking down at her feet.

"What is this? I thought beaches were made of sand."

"It's called a shingle beach," he said. "It's made of pebbles instead of sand."

She looked up at him. "They have these in America?"

"I don't think so. Why?"

"Then how did you know what it's called?"

"I read about it in the brochure while you were getting dressed for dinner."

"I should have known."

They continued walking toward the water, feeling the crunch of pebbles beneath their feet. "I have to say I prefer a sandy beach," he continued, "but there's a certain charm about these."

"It feels so strange. I'm not sure I could go barefoot on this."

"There's a shelter over there. Let's go sit and watch the sun set."

As they settled into the wooden structure shielded on three sides, Danny pulled Anya close beside him. "This is nice, isn't it?"

She nodded, taking a deep breath of the salty air as the breeze lifted her hair and danced it about. He leaned his head against hers.

"I love you, Anya." His long contented sigh warmed the side of her face. "I'm not sure I've said it enough. I never once heard my dad tell Mom he loved her, and I don't want a single day to go by without telling you."

She relaxed, nestling her head against the crook of his neck. "I love you, too."

They sat quietly watching the streaks of color splash from the west toward the water, changing before their eyes. The lingering clouds gradually transformed to a breathtaking palette of pinks, oranges, and purples, each shade deepening as they watched.

"I just realized something."

"What's that?" she said quietly.

"Look at that sky. See all those colors?"

"Yes?"

"It just dawned on me that without those clouds up there, we wouldn't see all those colors. The clouds give them a backdrop. A clear sky can't reflect color."

"I guess you're right. I never thought about it."

"Neither have I until now. But think about it. Without the clouds, the sunset would be rather boring." He leaned down, turning her chin to face him. "And without the clouds in our lives, we'd never see all those colors. It's not like we welcome the clouds into our lives—why would we? But the fact remains, once we've endured them ... once we've survived those darkest clouds, we have an entirely new backdrop. A new perspective to our lives. We can appreciate the simple fact we *survived*. We're forever changed; of course we are. But the depth has added a dimension to our character that we would never have known, had we not survived the dark clouds in our lives."

Anya said nothing, trying to comprehend his meaning. She hoped he wasn't suggesting she should somehow appreciate all the heartache and sorrows of the past five years. That would be ludicrous. Surely he was just trying to sound poetic and philosophical in his own silly way.

"Hey."

"Hey what?"

He shifted to face her. "You're so quiet. Did I say something wrong?"

"I don't know. Did you?" She couldn't help notice the concern pinching a crease between his brows.

"Anya?"

"Yes?"

"I wasn't suggesting that you—"

"Good. I'm glad." She straightened, turning to look back at the sunset, not quite trusting herself to say more.

"If I said something wrong, it was unintentional."

She nodded, her eyes following a seagull floating in the breeze just beyond them, perfectly still aloft some invisible air current. Then, just beyond it, as her eyes focused on the stunning sunset, she tamped down her insecurities, took a deep breath, and slowly blew it out.

"Ah, don't listen to me," he said, wrapping his arms around her again. "I'm just a blubbering fool in love on a pebbled beach in England."

"Yes, I believe you are."

"Just say you'll always love me, even when my foot is permanently lodged in my mouth."

"I wouldn't have it any other way."

10

Over the next day and a half, Danny and Anya relaxed in the charming seaside town, thankful for the slower pace and the simple pleasure of being together. They climbed the steps to the highest point in town and enjoyed the view of both town and sea. They visited the Aldeburgh Parish Church of Saint Peter and Paul, surprised how similar its interior design was to the Framlingham church where they married. Behind it, they wandered through the ancient graveyard filled with crooked and crumbling tombstones dating back to the seventeenth century.

"Look at this one, Anya."

Here lyeth the body of Thomas Cornwaleys gent
who married Y sole daughter
of Rich Farnsworth of Halesworth gent
and by her had Yssve 3 sonnes & 2 daughers.
He dyed Y 23th of Decem 1664.

"I wonder why his wife's name isn't included," she said.

"I don't know, but their spelling is atrocious," he teased with a smirk. "Must not have had any dictionaries on hand back then."

Anya rolled her eyes and punched him playfully. "It's almost three hundred years old, Danny. I'm sure the language was much different then."

"Look at this one over here."

> *In memory of Richard Longsworth*
> *who departed this life on April 12th*
> *in the 45th year of his life.*
> *Behold my friend as you pass by,*
> *as you are now, so once was I:*
> *as I am now, so you must be,*
> *prepare for death and follow me.*

"Rather bleak, isn't it?" she said.

"Yes, it is. Oh, look at this one. It has only one word—*Baby*. How odd."

"It's so old the rest of the engraving must have worn off through the years."

"I suppose." Anya laced her fingers with his. "It's so sad."

Danny squeezed her hand and tugged her along. They'd never talked about someday having children, but a baby's gravestone was hardly the place to have such a conversation. Still, he wondered again what their life together would look like if they'd met under different circumstances. If they'd met at school, or at a party like others. It was useless to spend time with such thoughts, but he couldn't help wondering if they would ever be free from all the sadness. He sure hoped so.

They visited shops selling seashells and handmade jewelry, hand-carved replicas of the historic buildings, and frequented the little bakery that served delightful cookies called chocolate digestives. The malty confection dipped in milk chocolate reminded Danny of a graham cracker. They bought two extra tins to take back with them.

Early the next morning, Danny and Anya took one last walk on the pebbled beach among the tiny boats pulled ashore, and the long rows of beachside villas, beautifully painted in a wide assortment of pastels.

Anya paused to look out across the water. "It's so beautiful here, I hate to leave. Seems like we just got here, doesn't it?"

"I was just thinking the same thing." He stopped and stood behind her, circling his arms around her shoulders, and resting his head atop hers. He loved the way they always fit together; loved the way he towered over her as if he'd been designed for the sole purpose of protecting her. He cherished the moment, wishing it didn't have to end.

"Do most people take long trips for their honeymoons?"

"They do in America. At least they did before the war. How about we plan on taking a real honeymoon once we get home? We could go somewhere special, like Niagara Falls, or maybe we could go to a *real* beach somewhere and squish sand between our toes. How does that sound?"

She nodded but didn't answer.

"Anya?"

She turned to look up at him. "Yes?"

"Are you okay? Did I say something wrong again?"

"No, not at all. It's just that ..."

"It's just what?"

She studied his eyes for a moment, then quietly whispered, "I'm still a little nervous about everything. And I hate feeling this way, like ... "

He brushed aside a strand of hair from her forehead. "Like what?"

She shrugged. "I don't want to ruin what little time we have left with any more of my silly worries."

"They aren't silly to me."

She glanced away. "I'm trying. Truly I am. It's just difficult for me to think of America as 'going home'." She looked up at him again. "But if I'm honest, it's not just about the idea of living somewhere so far away from my homeland. It's how I'll be going there. And when."

He couldn't avoid her eyes this time when the subject came up. He'd put it off as long as he could, but as her blue-gray eyes searched his, he knew it was time.

He smiled. "I suppose it's been the elephant in the room since we left Framlingham. No use putting it off any longer."

"What do you mean? What elephant?"

He chuckled. "You've never heard that expression before?"

"No. What does it mean?"

"Well, if we were back in our room at the inn, imagine an elephant standing right in the middle of the room. It would be impossible not to notice, right? So the expression refers to something rather obvious that, for whatever reason, we're avoiding. Like talking about how you'll get to America."

Her smile didn't quite reach her eyes. "Oh."

"To be honest, I haven't looked into it yet. I didn't want to jump that far ahead because ..." he paused with a sheepish grin, "well, if you must know, I wasn't sure you'd show up at the church to marry me."

"What? Why? Did you think I would change my mind?"

"The thought crossed my mind."

Anya placed her palms against his chest. "I would *never* have done that to you. I won't pretend I didn't have some second thoughts. But Sophie assured me that was perfectly normal."

"Good for her. Remind me to thank her when we get back."

Her eyes glistened. "You're all I've got now, Danny. Without you, I might never have gotten up off that dirty floor at home."

He took a deep breath and pulled her closer in his arms. "Then hear me when I say that I'll do everything I can to work all this out, getting you to America. Even if we can't go together, I'll pester them day and night to get you all the way to Chicago as soon as possible. Fair enough?"

She sighed with a sad smile. "I guess that means I won't be riding with you in one of those B-17s?"

"Pretty sure *that* won't be happening." He kissed her gently, softly. Then, pulling back he said, "But thanks for not fretting about it these last few days. Or at least not obsessing over it, especially after Sybil brought up the subject."

"Yes. I think perhaps that elephant has been with us ever since."

He kissed her again, tightening his embrace.

"Danny, it just occurred to me. When we get back to Framlingham, will you have to stay on base or can you stay with me at the pub now that we're married?"

Danny blinked. "Oh, I'll be staying with you at the pub," he asserted. "Wild horses couldn't keep me away."

"Horses?"

"Never mind."

15 June 1945

The short bus ride to Framlingham marked the end of their honeymoon. Anya spotted Sophie and Charlie standing beside Patrick's automobile in the parking area. As they stepped off the bus, Anya waved, thinking Charlie had seen them. Instead, he turned to say something to Sophie. Neither of them looked happy.

Danny joined her on the pavement, carrying both their bags. He followed Anya's gaze to the parking lot. "Whoa. I wonder what's going on."

Something churned in Anya's stomach as she watched the agitated conversation between their friends. "I was just wondering the same thing."

As they neared their friends, Sophie looked up and smiled. Anya hoped it was a good sign.

She gave Anya a hug. "Hello! How was your trip?"

"It was wonderful," she said as brightly as she could.

"Welcome back, buddy," Charlie said, giving Danny a hearty handshake. "Although it sure seems like we just put the two of you on that train for London."

"I had the same thought."

A few moments later, they settled into the car. "So? How

was it?" Sophie asked.

Danny and Anya looked at each other and smiled. "It was great. Really great," he said with a chuckle.

"Yes?" Sophie said, her eyes locked on Anya. "You had fun? Lots and lots of fun?"

"Yes, it was wonderful. London is such a beautiful city—or was, I should say. It's been terribly damaged, of course, but we were able to see Buckingham Palace, and even caught a glimpse of the king and queen as they passed by in a motorcade and—"

"And?" Sophie asked.

Anya stopped, glancing back and forth between Sophie and Danny. "And we visited St. Paul's Cathedral—"

"And?"

"Sophie, let Anya speak, won't you?" Charlie teased.

Anya pinned Danny with a look of desperation.

"Oh! Yeah, it was great," he said. "Then, we took the train to Aldeburgh. Beautiful little seaside fishing town. Much more relaxing. We should have spent our whole honeymoon there."

"Isn't it lovely?" Sophie said.

"What's happening at the 390th?" Danny asked. "Have I missed anything?"

A look passed between Sophie and Charlie before he spoke. "Oh, you know, just a lot of grunt work getting the base ready to close down."

Another look flittered between them.

Then a look passed between Anya and Danny.

"All right, Charlie, what is it? What's going on?" Danny asked.

"Nothing that can't wait," he said, with a quick glimpse through the rearview mirror.

Anya reached for Danny's hand.

"Seriously, Charlie. Out with it. What's going on?"

Charlie eyed him again through the mirror, then slumped a bit. "Your orders came through."

Sophie turned to face them. "For the record, *I* didn't think we should tell you yet. I didn't want to greet you with such news."

"Yes, and we see how well *that* worked out," Charlie countered. He put the car in gear as they got on the road, then reached over to squeeze Sophie's hand.

Anya looked from Charlie to Sophie, then over at Danny again. Whatever had churned in her gut earlier had solidified into a boulder on her chest.

"And what are my orders, Charlie?" he asked quietly.

He sighed again. "You'll be leaving Wednesday to fly a Fort back."

Danny gasped. "*Next* Wednesday? As in five days from now?"

"I'm afraid so."

Anya closed her eyes with a hushed groan, even as Danny threaded his fingers through hers with a tight grip.

"I'm sorry, buddy. The plan is to move all the planes out over the course of three days beginning Saturday."

"Wait—you said 'I'll' be flying out this weekend. You meant us, right? You and me?"

"No, just you, actually. Since I'll be staying here once I'm discharged, I won't be flying back to the States with you. One less seat to fill on flights home, I suppose. The paperwork came through yesterday."

Silence filled the car for several moments. Anya steeled herself against the fear washing over her. She freed her hand to press the bridge of her nose.

"Danny, surely you can tell them you're staying too, can't you?" she pleaded. "At least until we can figure out a way for me to—for *us* to fly to America together?"

"Sure, I can ask, but chances are they've already assigned me to a crew and a Fort."

"They have," Charlie said. "I saw the roster myself. You'll be flying with Sol Mancini's crew."

"But you'll talk to someone, won't you?"

"Of course I will, Anya. I just don't want you to get your hopes too high."

"But what about the colonel who helped you come back to Holland to find me? Maybe he can—"

"Moller's already back in the States," Charlie said. "There's a new CO here now."

"So ask him! You have to ask him. Surely he'll understand?" She winced at the desperation in her voice.

Danny put his arm around her and pulled her closer. "We'll see what we can do. Just take it easy, okay? I promised I'd do everything I can to work all this out, and I will. Just trust me, all right?"

Sophie reached over the seat and grabbed Anya's hand. "You won't be alone, Anya. Charlie and I will be right here with you. We'll get through this. Together. I hate that it's happening so soon, but we all knew it was coming. I'm just thankful there was time for you to get away for a few days."

"We'll do what we can," Danny said. "I'll try to see what

kind of arrangements we need to make for you. And you heard Sophie—she and Charlie will be here with you every step of the way."

Anya nodded, but much as her head might understand, her heart seemed to check itself then start a gradual descent toward numbness.

11

The next morning, Danny kissed his sleeping bride and slipped out of their room above the pub just as dawn streaked the sky. The scent of stale cigarettes and beer wafted around him as he descended the stairs. Moments later, Charlie joined him and the two made their way to the base in one of the 390th's Jeeps. Danny was determined to keep his word to Anya and do whatever he could to get his name pulled off the flight roster. His buddy did his best to encourage him, but Danny knew his chances were slim to none.

Three hours later, after talking to any higher-up who would listen, Danny had exhausted every possible avenue. Like it or not, he'd be heading back to the States with the rest of the crews that weekend. He was told in no uncertain terms to stop bothering the brass and join his crew at their hardstand to help prep the plane for the long flight home. He made his way to his quarters where he changed into his jumpsuit, his mind wrestling with the last remnants of hope.

"They wouldn't even let me register Anya's information to get on the list for passage to the States," he told Charlie as they walked the perimeter track toward his assigned bird. "Major Samford had a burr in his saddle from the moment I opened my mouth. What is it with that guy?"

"He's a pain in the butt. Always has been. But what's this list you're talking about?"

"I don't know much about it. A guy in line ahead of me at Samford's office told me about it. He said there are literally thousands of 'war brides' needing transport to the U.S. The Army Air Force is trying to figure out what to do with all of them, and in the meantime, they're supposed to put their names on some waiting list."

"Is that just for English brides?"

"I'm not sure. Anya has a visa from Holland, but I'm not sure what else is required. The guy in line with me starting talking about all these requirements, but by then my head was spinning."

"Did he have any idea how long it might be until these war brides ship out?"

"He wasn't sure, but he said someone else told him it could be next *year* before they go."

"Next year?! That's ridiculous. It couldn't possibly take that long."

"Yes, but what if it does?"

Charlie blew out a sigh. "I'm sure it will all work out."

"That's just it, Charlie. I'm not all that sure it *will* work out. Especially since I'm leaving Saturday. How am I going to tell Anya? She's already a bundle of nerves as it is. What's this going to do to her?"

"Hey, don't underestimate her. Look at how far she's come. She survived the Occupation for more than five years and fought with the Resistance. I'm guessing she's stronger than you think."

"She used to be strong, that's for sure. I knew how strong-willed she was from all those letters we wrote before the war. Even before that, her brother Hans used to tell me about all her antics and how she was always getting in trouble. Then when I first met her ... well, let me tell you, she was a pistol. I'd never met a female that tough before." He shook his head but smiled. "At least tough on the outside. But ever since she came here, she's ... different. It's like she's always right on the verge of having a breakdown or something. She's so fragile. Which, by the way, is a word I never thought I'd ever associate with Anya."

"Maybe so, but I bet that strong woman is still inside her. The war affected all of us in different ways. Give her some time, buddy. She'll come around. You'll see."

"That's just it. I don't have any time to give her. Two more days, and I'm outta here."

Charlie patted him on the back as they neared hardstand. "Look, at least Sophie and I will be here for her. We'll help out any way we can. We'll get her home to the States, even if I have to steal a plane and fly her myself."

"Don't think I haven't thought of doing that myself," Danny muttered.

"Patience, buddy. Hang in there."

When they joined the others, Danny greeted a few familiar faces, including Sol Mancini, a pilot from New Jersey. Sol introduced him to the other crew members.

"Hey Charlie, what are you doing here?" the navigator hollered from the rear of the Fort. "I thought you weren't going home since you married that English girl from the pub."

"I'm not. Just thought I'd lend a hand. Seems like the least I can do."

"Yeah? Well, grab a wrench and make yourself useful. We're guttin' this baby to make room for all our passengers. They said we could have as many as a dozen or more extras along for the ride."

"A dozen?!" Danny whistled. "All the way to the States?"

"That's what I'm hearin'."

"Just be glad we've got a front-row seat in the cockpit," Mancini said. "They'll be packed like sardines in this old bird."

For the rest of the afternoon, Danny and Charlie helped the others outfit the Fort for the trip home. While others stripped the interior of any non-essential equipment, Danny and the other officers helped simonize the plane, polishing the exterior to give better mileage. The crew laughed and joked as they worked; everyone excited about heading home to friends and loved ones.

But the only thing on Danny's mind was the image of Anya's face tonight when he'd have to tell her he'd be leaving come Saturday. Even worse, the disheartening news about that war bride list.

On Monday, with their husbands at work on base, Sophie suggested she and Anya should take a walk in the countryside on the outskirts of Framlingham. Anya reluctantly agreed, but once outside enjoyed the warmth of the summer sun on her skin. The fresh air helped tamp down the overbearing gloom that had taken up residence in her spirit. As they passed a farmhouse, the mooing of cows and the whinnying of horses both calmed and soothed her senses as nothing else could. The familiar scents and sounds reminded her of the Boorman's farm back home, and the many happy hours she'd spent there helping out with the chores after Wim broke his leg.

Wim ...

She'd not thought of him since coming here to England. Not even once. A strange cloud of guilt meandered through her, as though she'd betrayed his memory.

"Penny for your thoughts?" Sophie asked, reaching down to pick some wildflowers along the road.

"Danny asked me that once. Such a funny expression."

Sophie chuckled. "I heard it from Charlie. I guess we're both enlightened by these Yanks, aren't we?"

"I'll never learn all their expressions. Like the difference between a dog and a hot dog. I once told Danny I thought I'd like to eat a dog at Wrigley Field in Chicago, America. He laughed and laughed."

"Charlie told me about those hot dogs! Such a disgusting

name for something to eat, isn't it?" Sophie feigned a shiver. "Oh, these men and their strange American English. Whatever shall we do with them?"

Anya smiled. "But it does give us something to tease them about. And I love the sound of Danny's laughter. It's so carefree, as if the very sound of it could carry off all the cares of the world, and in that one moment, we could be happy."

Sophie handed Anya a handful of daisies. "I see your point. After meeting so many Americans in the pub these past few years, I have to admit I enjoy their more relaxed ways. We Brits are much more cultured and straight-laced, as they say. It's been fun getting to know the Yanks and their easygoing manner."

"Easygoing. That's a good description. I could wish it was ... um, I don't know the English word for ... *besmettelijk?* Like to catch—"

"Contagious? Like you could catch it from Danny?"

"Yes, that's it. I wish their easygoing manner was contagious."

"Me too. They are rather fun to be with, aren't they?"

Anya smiled, the thoughts peddling through her mind. "Sophie, I don't know what I should do. Always before, when problems came along, I knew what I needed to do, and then I did it. Now, I'm so far from home, and Danny is leaving, and I can't seem to make any sense of my thoughts." She shielded her eyes from the sun. "To be honest, I cannot stand living like this—always having to wait on someone else to act before I can do something as simple as buying a ticket on a boat to America. Why must I put my name on some list? Why must someone I don't know tell me when I may go? I don't understand."

Sophie nudged her elbow. "Let's go this way, down this lane."

They took the narrow dirt road under a canopy of trees. As their footfalls crunched on dirt and gravel, a breeze set the leaves dancing.

"Anya, I can't imagine how hard this is for you. If Charlie was leaving, and I couldn't join him for weeks or even months, I'm afraid I'd lose what's left of my mind. But I know I would be all right because this is my home. I'm here with my father, surrounded by people I've known all my life. Whilst you have left everything and everyone you've ever known behind, and none of them family. Try as I might, I cannot grasp what you must be feeling. Our situations are so different.

"But that doesn't mean I can't help you. Charlie and I want to help however we can. No matter if it's days or weeks or months, you'll have a place to live and friends who love you. In fact, Da asked if I thought you might like to work at the pub. We could use the help, and besides—it would give you something to do until you travel to America."

"That's very kind of your father."

"He's all gruff on the outside, but a real softie on the inside. Besides, Danny's been one of his favorites amongst all the Americans who've been stationed here, so he'd like you to consider it a favor on Danny's behalf."

"I would be honored to help however I can."

"He'd pay you, of course."

"No! I would not dream of it. As long as I'm able to keep the room upstairs, that would be payment enough."

"He's a stubborn one, my father, so I'll let the two of you work all that out."

"I should probably tell you I have never had a proper job before. At least not a paying job. I worked on a farm once, caring for the animals. Chickens and pigs and such."

"Then you'll be right at home because we serve a *lot* of pigs, if you know what I mean!"

Anya laughed at Sophie's giggle, which made them both laugh harder.

"Oh Anya, we'll have the most fun working together, won't we?" She looped her arm through Anya's.

A horn blared behind them as a military Jeep sped toward them.

"Charlie!" Sophie cried as the vehicle slowed. "What are you doing here?"

"Hello, ladies! Just out for a spin in my luxury car. Fancy, isn't it?"

Sophie leaned in to kiss his cheek. "Have you already finished work today?"

"No. In fact, you could say I'm on a mission."

"What kind of mission?"

He pushed up the bill of his cap. "Very hush-hush and top secret, I can tell you that much."

"But you'll tell me, Charlie Janssen, or I shall withhold all my kisses until—"

"Don't even think of it. I'm here to pick up Anya. And you, if you'd like to ride along."

"Me?" Anya asked. "Why me?"

"Danny finally got an appointment for the two of you with Major Samford. He's the CO heading up the transition, and his office is also in charge of processing forms for war brides needing transport to the States."

Anya struggled to swallow. "Did he say how long before I can go?"

Charlie shook his head. "Danny didn't know. He just asked me to bring you to the base to get registered. Hop on in, and I'll take you to him."

She gasped as she smoothed her wrinkled trousers. "I can't go like this! I should change into something nicer."

"Sorry, but no time for that. And remember, this is the Army. They aren't exactly fashion experts, if you know what I mean."

"Come along, Anya. You look fine." Sophie grabbed her hand and pulled her around to the passenger side. "We've got to get your name on that list!"

Anya studied the American major sitting behind the battered desk. The man clearly had no manners, or personality for that matter. The cigarette hanging precariously on his lip scattered ashes whenever he spoke, spotting the page as he studied it. He had an annoying habit of talking directly to Danny when his questions concerned her, never quite making eye contact with her.

"The problem is, your missus has no passport. And that visa won't get her stateside." He shuffled the papers. "Has she got a birth certificate?"

"Yes, but—"

"Yes, Major," Anya answered. "I have a birth certificate on file in the Utrecht Office of Records. But as you surely know, many of those files were destroyed by the Germans during the Occupation. There was no way for us to find out if mine was among those destroyed or whether it was still on file."

Still no eye contact. Another ash fell on the form. Samford brushed it away, leaving a gray streak on the page.

"McClain, you should've thought this out before wasting my time. How am I supposed to put her name on this list with no valid documentation?"

"But we were told the visa was all she needed, sir. Like she said, after the Occupation, all the government offices were in shambles. I doubt they've made much progress since we left."

Samford leaned back, his chair groaning in protest. "The problem is, if I put her on this list and don't supply the proper identification, then it's my butt they'll wanna chew." He took a long drag off what was left of his cigarette, then exhaled through his nostrils with narrowed eyes. "And if there's one thing I hate, it's having my butt chewed."

Anya shot a pleading glare at her husband. "Danny?"

He turned back to Samford. "Major, we have to get her on that list. How can we make that happen?"

Samford leaned forward to stub the butt of his cigarette in an overflowing ashtray. "Give me some time. Let me think about it."

Danny leaned in, shifting to the edge of his seat. "But sir, there isn't any time left. I fly out the day after tomorrow at 0600. But I'm not leaving until my wife's name is on that list."

Anya smiled, loving him for standing up to the pompous superior behind the desk. When Danny glanced at her, she noticed a slight shimmer in his eyes.

"McClain, I told you—"

"With all due respect, sir, do you have any idea what she's been through? Do you know what it's like to lose every single member of your family? Every friend you ever knew? Your home and all your possessions? My wife was part of the Dutch Resistance. She and her friends helped save the lives of thousands of our Allies who fell behind enemy lines, including me. She helped move children to safe houses ..."

Anya gently took his hand in hers as he paused to compose himself.

He directed his attention back to Samford. "Do you have children, Major?"

"I don't see what that has to do with—"

"Do you?"

He huffed. "Yes."

"How many?"

"Two."

"Girls? Boys?"

"Both girls. Look, McClain—"

"What ages? How old are they?"

"Six and eight."

"Then imagine yourself at a train depot surrounded by hundreds of young children being put on a train to God knows where. Your little girls are crying because they don't understand why you'd send them away to someone you don't even know. They're too young to know you're doing it to protect them, because you love them too much to risk having them stay where bombs are falling. And as the train starts to move, you see the faces of your daughters pressed against the window, sobbing, and pounding on the glass. And behind them you see someone like my wife here who tries to comfort your little girls and take care of them for you. And you have to trust her—this complete stranger—because otherwise you never could have let your daughters leave."

Danny took a deep breath and slowly blew it out. "And then, when the war ends and your little girls come home, you had better get down on your knees and thank God that someone like my wife here *cared* enough and was *brave* enough to keep them safe and sound for you."

Anya leaned over and cupped Danny's cheek with her hand, wiping a tear with her thumb. "Danny," she whispered. "I love you. Thank you."

"I love you more," he mouthed.

They took a moment to collect themselves. Samford's chair groaned again as he sat up, a forced cough clearing his voice. "The, uh ... well, you see—"

"Major, I want my wife's name on that list before I step a foot out of this office. From what I hear, none of these bride ships will be leaving anytime soon. We will get you the proper documentation long before you ever submit these forms to HQ. You have my word on that." He stood and reached for the pen on Samford's desk and extended it to him. "Do the right thing, Major. Put my wife's name on that list."

He stared at the pen for a moment, then snatched it from Danny's hand. "Oh hell, why not."

Anya jumped up and into Danny's open arms.

"Thank you, Major!" he cried. "Thank you."

"I need both your signatures," he said in the same no-nonsense tone. He turned the paper toward them and pointed at two blank lines. "There and there."

As he busied himself lighting another cigarette, Anya reached her hand across his desk. "Thank you, Major. I cannot tell you how much this means to me."

"I believe he just did." He nodded toward Danny and blew out a lungful of smoke as he shook her hand.

After signing their names, Danny straightened and threw a salute.

Samford returned the salute. "Now, get out of here before I change my mind."

12

The remaining hours flew by as Danny and his crew made final preparations for the flight home. He packed his belongings from the quarters where he'd lived since first arriving at the base last December. It seemed a lifetime ago. He could hardly remember the person he was when he first stashed his gear in the drafty Nissen hut on that freezing night. The stove at the center of the hut had done little to keep them warm despite their efforts to keep it stoked. How young and naïve he'd been back then, with his primary concerns focused on creature comforts, impatient to fly his first mission.

He thought of Dick Anderson, the pilot whose crew he'd been assigned to back home. Anderson didn't have an outgoing personality, but he was good at his job. His steady command of the crew and crackerjack abilities in the cockpit always got them back to base in one piece ... except, of course, the Hannover mission on 28 March. That day, *Sweet*

Sophie sustained massive damage from anti-aircraft fire on the return flight. Anderson was among those fatally injured; a piece of shrapnel slicing the aorta in his neck before Danny and those remaining jumped from the flaming Fort over a field in Holland.

The images of that day seemed forever seared in his mind, though he'd made a constant and concerted effort not to dwell on them. But now, as he gathered his belongings, he found those memories first and foremost in his thoughts. Why had he survived when others didn't? He'd always given his mother credit, knowing it was her prayers that had kept him alive. But what about Sully Thornton's mom in Atlanta? Or Shorty Lowenstein's mom in Pennsylvania, or Jimmy Foster's mom in Nashville? Surely they prayed for the safety of their sons just like his own mother had. Why were her prayers answered and theirs weren't?

Danny shook his head and raked his fingers through his hair. *Let it go. Just let it go. There'll be time to figure all that out later.* He made one last check to make sure he had everything, then closed and locked his footlocker as the door of the hut opened.

Corporal Higgins threw a salute as he entered. "Lieutenant McClain, if you're ready, I'll take your footlocker for you. We'll load it on the truck outside and make sure it's stowed on your Fort tonight, all set for your departure tomorrow morning."

Danny returned the salute. "Thank you, Corporal."

"You're welcome. ID information correct on the tag, sir?"

"Yes, it is. My home address in Chicago, along with my telephone number."

"Very good, sir," Higgins said. "Have a safe flight home."

"Thank you. When do you and the rest of the ground crews pack up for home?"

"We're not sure, sir. We'll stay as long as they need us here. Better here than Japan, the way I see it."

"Point well taken. Any of our guys sent over there yet?"

"None that I'm aware of, sir, but I'm not privy to that kind of information."

"Okay. Thanks, Corporal."

Higgins threw another salute then hefted Danny's footlocker onto his shoulder and left.

Danny looked around the hut one more time. He certainly wouldn't miss the place, but couldn't deny the strange and sad fondness for his memories here. A moment later, he placed his cap on his head, grabbed his small duffel, and left.

That afternoon, Danny kept his focus on his last remaining hours with Anya, making them as special as possible. When he returned from the base, he insisted she join him for a drive in the countryside to a spot he'd scoped out earlier in the day. Once there, he opened the trunk of Patrick's automobile where Sophie had stashed a picnic basket and a couple of quilts.

"What's all this?" Anya asked as he closed the trunk.

He handed her the quilts and kissed her cheek. "What does it look like? It's a picnic."

"But where did it come from?"

He took hold of her hand and led her through the grass. "I had a little help. Sophie put it all together for me. I thought we might enjoy some time to ourselves, away from everyone else." He winked at her before checking the sky. "At least as long as those clouds up there cooperate. I found a nice little spot under that tree just ahead."

They made their way through the grassy field to a gentle rolling hill sheltered beneath an enormous oak tree. "Nice, isn't it?"

She offered a tentative smile and nodded, then spread out the quilts near the tree. "It's lovely."

"I was hoping you'd say that. Have a seat and let's see what Sophie put together for us."

He unlatched the clasp and lifted the basket's lid on its hinge. "Get a load of all this food."

They both reached in, removing wedges of cheese, a thick slice of ham, a loaf of fresh baked bread, and two rather large cinnamon scones for dessert.

Danny chuckled. "There's enough here for an army. I hope you're hungry."

She set out the plates and utensils. "A little."

"Here's the knife. How about cutting us some slices of ham and cheese."

They chatted as they ate, making small talk about the view around them, the peaceful quiet surrounding them, the threatening sky, and anything else that didn't have anything to do with his departure the next day.

As they finished sharing one of the scones, Danny could stand it no longer. He brushed off his hands and reached back into the basket and found the small wrapped box he'd asked Sophie to hide for him. He slowly set it on the quilt before her.

"What is this?"

"What does it look like?"

She picked it up. "Some kind of gift."

"Go on. Open it."

She pulled the ribbon free and unwrapped the slender box, then opened the lid. She carefully lifted the silver bracelet and held it, admiring the charms. "Danny, it's beautiful."

"You like it?"

She paused a moment then said, "I can't imagine anything more lovely. Thank you."

He took it from her hand and clasped it onto her wrist. "I found it in one of those shops we visited in Aldeburgh. I slipped out that afternoon you were resting and went back to buy it."

"I'm beginning to realize that you can be a bit of a sneak."

"But a good sneak, wouldn't you say? Look at the charms," he said, pointing them out. "The windmill is to remind you of Holland."

She smiled, fingering the tiny windmill. "How did you find it here? They have windmills in England?"

"I have no idea, but the minute I saw it, I knew I had to buy it for you. The lady suggested putting it on the bracelet. I know you don't wear much jewelry, except for your wedding ring, but I thought you might like it. Then I saw this airplane and thought—"

"—it would remind me of you."

121

"Yes. It's not a B-17, obviously. I think it's a spitfire like the RAF boys fly, but I knew you'd get the idea. Then I figured we could add more charms along the way. Special reminders of our new life together."

She held her wrist before her. "Danny, I love it. Thank you." She leaned over to give him a kiss, then rested her forehead against his. "I'm going to miss you so much," she whispered.

Danny pulled her close, her head tucked against his shoulder as he leaned back against the tree trunk. "Not half as much as I'm going to miss you."

He could feel the beating of her heart against his side and wished the moment would never end. They sat like that for a while, neither of them speaking. He searched for the right words, anxious to stay optimistic even though they both knew it might be a long, long time before they'd be together again.

She turned to look up at him. "What will you do when you get home? We haven't talked about it much. Will you live with your parents until I come?"

He brushed a strand of hair out of her eyes. "That's my plan. Mom said she and Dad would love for us to stay with them until we find a place of our own. Which is good, because I'll need some time to figure out our finances."

"Will you go back to college?"

"I'm thinking about it. Would that be okay with you?"

Her brow crinkled. "Well, of course it would. Why do you ask?"

"Because these are things we should decide together. I would never do anything without first talking to you."

"Will you go back to Northwestern?"

"Probably, though I'd attend their Chicago campus instead of making the commute to Evanston. That way we could stay with my folks and save some money until we decide what we want to do or where we might go."

"How will we pay for it? For school?"

"The word around the base is that the government will pay for it."

"Really?"

"They're calling it the GI Bill. It was passed last year in Congress as a means to help all of us soldiers get back on our feet after the war. Supposedly, they'll even provide living expenses while I'm in school, and later, they'll help us on a down payment for a house."

"That's very generous, isn't it?"

"Absolutely. Depending how long it takes to receive the funds, we could actually get our own place sooner than I thought. But since I'll be in classes all day, it just seems to make more sense to stay at Mom and Dad's so we can save money, but also so you won't be all alone every day while I'm at school."

She didn't say anything, but shifted to lean her back against his side. He draped his arm across her shoulder, resting it against her chest as they looked out toward the horizon.

"You're awfully quiet, Anya. Everything okay?"

"I was thinking about your father."

He chuckled. "Well, that'll do it. My dad's been known to quiet legions of crowds by simply walking into a room."

"I believe you're exaggerating."

"A little, perhaps."

"I wonder ..."

"About what?"

She fidgeted, and he could almost feel her tensing.

"What if your father doesn't like me?"

"Are you kidding? What's not to like? He'll love you."

"Do you not remember all those letters you wrote? How mean he was to your mother and to you? And in the letters to Hans about how mad he was when Joey left to join the navy?"

"Oh. Those. I guess I forgot about those."

"I haven't. I'm not so sure I want to meet him. I have no patience with people who are mean to others. What if we get into a fight, your father and I? What if he—"

"Anya, stop," he said, turning her to face him again. "Don't do this. You're getting all upset without giving him a chance to get to know you."

"But if I'm to live in the same house, and he decides I'm not good enough for you, and—"

He placed his hand gently across her mouth. "He would *never* think you're not good enough for me. Trust me, honey. If anything, he'll say I'm not good enough for you."

With his hand still over her mouth, she rolled her eyes.

"He's going to *love* you. And so will Mom. I have a feeling you and Mom will become the best of friends. You'll love her. And then there's Joey and Millie—oh my goodness, I just remembered! Joey and Millie's baby is due in just a few weeks!"

"That's wonderful," she said, pulling his hand away and attempting a brave face.

"I'm just guessing, but something tells me Frank McClain

might mellow a bit when his first grandbaby comes along. Babies have a way of doing that, I hear."

She studied him, her eyes still reflecting the conflict bubbling inside her.

"But will they have room for us? All living in the same house?"

He exhaled, wishing he could make her see how pleasant it would be, having the family all together with a new baby in the house. "Sweetheart, you're just going to have to take my word for it. It will all work out. You'll see."

She looked away, taking another deep breath.

"Come here." He scooted away from the tree trunk and tugged her into his arms as they lay back. "You're going to be fine, Anya. We both are. So, no more worries about my dad or anyone else for that matter. Right now, all we need to focus on is getting you to America. I'll do everything I can on my end, and you make sure you're on that first ship to sail, okay?"

She nodded, but barely.

"The war's over, honey. We don't have to be afraid anymore. We've got a whole future ahead of us, don't you see?" He pulled her closer, kissing her, loving the feel of her in his arms and the softness of her lips.

"And one day," he whispered near her ear, his voice husky with pleasure, "we'll have our own home and fill it with love and happiness ... and lots and lots of babies."

She shivered then kissed him hungrily. He wanted nothing more than to share the love filling his heart and soul—but just as the desire rolled through him, a rumble of thunder in the distance stilled them both.

"Oh no," he groaned, sitting up to scan the skies. "We

probably need to make a run for—"

She yanked his tie, pulling him back down to her. "Not just yet, Lieutenant," she whispered. She threw the other quilt over them and picked up where they left off.

Later, in the afterglow of love, they gathered their things and made a dash for the car just as the sky unleashed its downpour. Shouting and laughing over the roar of the thunder, they piled in the car and headed back to the pub. There, they hurried up the back stairs to their room, soaked to the bone but too in love to care.

And as the logs crackled softly in their fireplace and the distant thunder continued to rumble, they spent their last night together.

Or so they thought.

For five long days, a thick fog clung to the islands of Great Britain scrubbing any chance for the anxious crews of the Eighth Air Force to start their pilgrimage home. The stubborn fog held fast even as the drenching rain soaked the entire country. With so many delays, the other stops in Iceland and Greenland got back-logged with planes, further complicating the rolling schedules as those airfields had weather problems of their own.

In Framlingham, nerves frayed with each passing day as the restless Yanks passed their time playing poker, reading the *Stars and Stripes*, and getting into more than a few scuffles and brawls. Adding to the angst was the glow of the red light in the Officer's Club each evening, banning alcohol to the majority of the 390th inhabitants as they waited. The few remaining Red Cross Girls brewed gallons of coffee instead.

For Danny, the extra days with Anya seemed bittersweet. They'd had the perfect day together on Tuesday. Even as he rose before sunrise on Wednesday, he'd left his wife in a good frame of mind. But with each passing day, as they'd say their goodbyes only to say hello again a few hours later, their shared anxiety began to take its toll. Danny was anxious to leave; tired of the constant limbo and stress it put on Anya.

Then, on Monday morning, 25 June, with a break in the clouds, it was finally his crew's time to go. He had once again kissed his sleeping wife, knowing with certainty that he would not see her for months. Then, as he and his crew rode the Jeep out to their hardstand, he glanced up at the partially clouded sky and prayed for more clearing.

It was odd to find so many men crowded around the Fort. A dozen others would join them for the three-day trip home.

"Looks like this might finally be the day, McClain," Mancini said, greeting him with a handshake.

"It's about time. Think we'll make it to Wales?"

"We will if I have anything to say about it. We're second in line, so hopefully we can blow outta here."

"Sounds good to me."

Danny scanned the skies one last time before tossing his duffel in and pulling himself up into the aircraft. After running through the preliminary checklist with Mancini, he waited with growing impatience for the flare signaling a go. When it arced from the control tower, he gave his pilot a thumbs up. Mancini returned the gesture with a broad smile and flipped the switch on his radio.

"Gentlemen?" He paused for effect, tossing Danny a wink. "What do you say we go home?"

Their raucous cheers filled the Fort, muffled only when the engines coughed to life. Danny thought he'd never been more thankful to hear the roar of those four mighty engines and feel their rumble. Flying second, it was only a matter of moments before they taxied down the length of the tarmac, made the final turn, and with another round of hoots and hollers, took flight.

When the cheering ebbed and they continued their ascent, the radio crackled to life.

"Tower to *O Sole Mio*, tower to *O Sole Mio*, come in please."

"This is *O Sole Mio*. What can I do for you?"

"I'm sorry, sir, but we need you to turn back to base. We just received a weather update of a nasty storm that just gathered in your flight path, so you'll need to bring her back to base."

"You've got to be kidding me!" Danny cried.

"Tower to *O Sole Mio*. Do you copy?"

Mancini flashed Danny another smile as he flipped the switch on and off rapidly. "What ... you say? ... breaking up. Must ... a short or ... I can't—"

"Tower to—"

With another wink, Mancini flipped the switch off. "Well, that's a real shame, isn't it?"

Danny smiled. "It certainly is, Lieutenant. But I'm sure we'll make the best of it."

"Copy that, Lieutenant. Let's go home!"

Part II

13

7 July 1945
Chicago, Illinois

Dear Anya,

I finally made it back to Chicago yesterday, and I'm missing you so much I can hardly function. It sure feels a lot longer than ten days since I last saw you, honey. I'll try to put a call through at some point, but for now I hope a letter will do. Strange, isn't it? You and I writing letters to each other again?

I thought we'd never get home with the weather dogging us all the way. We made it to Wales that first day only to get stuck there for five days! Can you believe it? The base didn't have enough housing for all the crews, so we had to sleep inside our Fort. Twenty of us! "Miserable" doesn't even begin to describe it. We couldn't even sack out beneath our Fort because of the driving rain. Then we took off for Iceland on Friday and got held up there for another three days. More driving rains with visibility almost zero. You've never seen so many cranky soldiers. Didn't help that the sun never set the entire time we were there. I never knew how much that can mess with your mind.

On Sunday afternoon, a bunch of us hitched a ride into Reykjavik. I have to admit it was really beautiful, even though all we wanted to do was go home. On Tuesday, we finally flew to Greenland, then made it to Bradley Field near Hartford, Connecticut the next day. It seemed a fitting homecoming as it was the 4th of July – America's birthday!

They put us on a troop train from there to Rockford, Illinois. Took two days, but at least it was more comfortable than the cockpit of a B-17. Rockford is only a couple hours northeast of Chicago. We had to turn in all our military gear there, and after doing so, I turned around and there were Mom and Dad! I was so shocked to see them! Mom couldn't stop hugging me and crying – "happy tears" as she calls them. Even Dad seemed glad to see me and actually gave me a hug. You have no idea how much that meant to me.

Since I have a thirty-day leave, they were able to drive me home. It was so great to see Joey and Millie, Anya. I've never been around someone who's pregnant, and all I can say is that must be one big baby she's carrying! Could be any day now, so they're real excited. Joey's walking without a cane now and manages just fine. By the look of him, you'd never know he'd been so severely injured at Pearl.

Funny, the things you appreciate after being gone so long. The house never looked so good, though I doubt it's changed at all since I left. The aroma of Mom's pot roast in the oven made my mouth water the minute we walked in the door. And you should've seen Sophie—she came flying at me, her tail wagging so hard I thought it might wag right off. I was actually surprised she remembered me since I've been gone so long. I can't wait for you to meet her.

We had a steady stream of visitors all afternoon and into the evening. My Aunt Lena brought one of her famous peach pies. Boy, was that a treat. I asked her to make one for you when you come. Most of the folks were from the neighborhood and church; all welcoming me home and wanting to know all about my beautiful bride. Your ears were surely burning because I couldn't stop talking about you. Millie told me she and Mom want to host a reception for us when you come. Apparently, that's a tradition when a couple is married out of town—or out of country, in our case.

My first night home I slept for almost ten hours. In fact, I only woke up because Sophie was standing on my chest, needing to go out. It was nice having her curled up against me again while I slept, but I sure wished it was you instead. I wonder how the three of us will sleep together. I've grown so accustomed to sleeping with you in my arms ... the scent of your hair, the rise and fall of your chest as you sleep ... well, I better stop right there, if you know what I mean.

I hope and pray everything is going all right there with you. How's the job at the pub working out? Don't let any of those Yanks or locals give you a hard time, okay? I gave Charlie and Patrick my permission to punch the lights out of any guy paying too much attention to you. Ha ha.

Charlie also promised to keep checking on your status at Major Samford's office. Let me know when you hear anything. Who knows, maybe even now you're reading this letter as you board one of those war bride ships. I sure hope so!

Anya, you're the best thing that ever happened to me, and just so you know, you're never far from my thoughts. Only every minute of every day. I miss you so much, sweetheart. Write me soon, okay?

Love,

Danny

On his third day home, Danny accepted Joey's invitation to spend some time with him at the theater. His mother promised Joey she'd watch over Millie, who was quite miserable these days, and said she'd call if Millie had any problems. They climbed into Joey's car, and as his brother backed out into the alley, Danny slung his arm across the top of the front seat.

"So what's it like, now that you're about to be a dad?"

"It's really strange, to be honest. I almost feel like I'm going into this completely blind, for lack of a better word."

"I bet."

"It's all such unknown territory, y'know? Why do you suppose men are never told much about a woman's pregnancy?" he asked with a chuckle. "From the moment we found out, Millie's been such a natural at it. Whereas I, on the other hand, feel like a bystander who's mostly just in the way. Shouldn't there be classes to teach you how to be a parent? Bringing a child into the world is a big deal, but it's like we're expected to just wing it."

Danny gave his brother's shoulder a pat. "Oh, I wouldn't be too worried. People have been having babies for thousands of years. You'll figure it out."

Joey gave him a quick glance. "Is that so? I'll be sure to remind you of that sage advice when you're about to have *your* first child."

Something quaked in the vicinity of his heart at the thought. "Whoa. I see your point."

"The good news is, since we're still living at home, Mom's always there to help. I've had a couple of heart-to-heart talks with her over the past couple of months."

"About what?"

Joey smiled, "I'm sure you'll find out soon enough for yourself once Anya gets here. But Mom helped me understand why women can be a little ... *testy* when they get to the third trimester."

"Trimester?"

Joey laughed. "Wow, you really have a lot to learn, baby brother. See, the nine months of pregnancy are divided into trimesters—three months each. By the time they get to the third trimester, the baby starts growing at a more rapid rate and moving around a lot more. I've gotta say, I love when Millie grabs my hand and puts it on her belly so I can feel the little guy kick." He shook his head with a crazy grin. "It's ... I don't even know how to describe how amazing it is."

"Little *guy*? How do you know it's a boy?"

Joey smiled. "Well, I don't, of course. Just a habit, I guess. From the start, I've thought it was a boy, and Millie assumes it's a girl, so we'll see. Anyway, once he—or she—started gaining all that weight, the pressure has been pretty intense on Millie. She's so uncomfortable. She keeps saying she feels like a beached whale. Especially at night. It's hard for her to get comfortable, so she tosses and turns all night. Even gets leg cramps. Sometimes she'll bolt right up in bed from one of those."

"Really? I had no idea."

"And then there's the irritability. Never saw it coming, I can tell you that much."

"Millie? Irritable? She seems like herself to me."

"Well, that's because she's Millie and never wants to be a bother to anyone. But behind closed doors? It's a whole other story."

Danny looked out the window at the houses rushing by. "You're right. No one ever tells you this stuff. Anya's had such a rough time these past few years, I'd sure hate to make her go through all that."

"Are you kidding me?" Joey looked at him like he'd sprouted a third eye. "I wouldn't trade it for the world. And neither would Millie. Mom keeps saying that once the baby comes, you forget all this other stuff. Otherwise, no one would have more than one, y'know?"

Danny chuckled. "Good point."

"Never mind me, I'm probably exaggerating. The thing is, Millie's still a doll, but it's such a stark contrast to see her so uneasy and always fanning herself and lugging herself around. But I'm telling you, she's still the greatest. I never would've made it through all my recovery without her. And I'm not just talking about the physical wounds. I read an article that said most of the guys who survived Pearl came home with a lot of junk to work through, so it's not just me."

"What do you mean?"

Joey tapped his temple. "Stuff messed up here. Even more, the emotional scars. I'm still in touch with some of the guys I knew on Pearl, and I see lots of others at the VA when I go for my checkups. So many of them are really messed up. Makes me realize how blessed I've been to have Millie helping me through all of it. Mom too, of course."

"And what about Dad?" Danny asked as they pulled into the parking lot behind the theater. "How's he been since I've been gone? He doesn't seem as crabby as he used to be."

Joey stopped the car and turned off the ignition. "He's better, I'd say. Still not the best dad on the planet, but I can see some changes, mostly for the better."

As they headed to the back door, Danny asked, "Do you ever wonder what kind of dad you'll be?"

"You mean, am I worried I'll be a jerk dad like he was most of the time?"

Danny laughed. "Well, yes, to put it bluntly."

Joey unlocked the door and opened it. "Yeah, I started

wondering about that the day Millie told me she was pregnant. But when I talked about it with her, she told me something really wise. She said we can become whoever we *want* to become. I don't have to follow Dad's footsteps, and neither do you. And if you stop and think about it, he's given us a lifelong example of how *not* to father. So any time he starts to aggravate me or pick on me, I just make a mental note to do the complete opposite when my little guy comes along."

"Good idea."

As his brother flipped on the lights, Danny looked around. "The place looks good, Joey." He inhaled deeply and let out a long sigh. "Before I left, I was so sick of the smell of popcorn, I thought I'd hate the stuff for the rest of my life." He breathed in again. "Well, I'm here to tell you I was sorely wrong. When Anya and I went to see a movie in London, all it took was one whiff, and I was suddenly homesick. Had to have some."

"What movie did you see?"

Danny slapped the heel of his hand against his forehead. "I can't believe I forgot to tell you! It was *Winged Victory*—the one they filmed when we graduated from flight school in Stockton. Did you see it?"

"Well, sure, but I had no idea you were *in* it. I just sent the reels back last week. Did you see yourself on the big screen?"

"No, but Anya thinks she did. It was that scene where the guys walk up and accept their wings, then turn and march toward the camera. She's sure she saw me, but I didn't. Hey, can you reorder those reels?"

"Sure. I'll make the call right now. Though I have to say that was one corny movie."

Danny followed Joey into the office. "And don't I know it."

They spent the rest of the morning chatting nonstop, stopping to do a few chores before the theater opened for its matinee. Danny loved hanging out with his brother. He'd always admired Joey, especially that night in 1938 after he graduated from high school. He and Dad had an ugly fight at the dinner table that evening. It wasn't the first time they'd quarreled like that, but Joey decided he'd had enough. He'd secretly enlisted in the navy earlier that spring, so he left in the middle of the night and reported for duty the next day.

Three and a half years later, on 7 December 1941, Joey was enjoying a leisurely Sunday morning on board the USS *Oklahoma* in port at Pearl Harbor, Hawaii when the Japanese attacked. Of the 429 officers and crew aboard the *Oklahoma,* Joey was one of only thirty-two who survived. He suffered a badly injured leg and burns to more than fifty percent of his body, but he survived.

Now, three and a half years later, Joey seemed to be doing great. He'd taken over management of the theater at Dad's request, and by the looks of things, he'd done a crackerjack job.

"So if you're running the theater, what's Dad up to these days?"

"He still stops by for a couple of hours every day. Probably just to let me know he's looking over my shoulder. But he doesn't hassle me like he used to. I've discussed the possibility of completely remodeling the place; primarily to install heat and air conditioning. We've lost so much business to our competition because of those ridiculous oscillating fans he attached to the walls years ago. They just can't keep the place cool enough. But you know Dad."

"Still griping about the Chicago Theater downtown?"

"Yep. He still thinks all that 'hoopla' is a waste of time and money."

"Oh yeah, the infamous 'hoopla' of big-name celebrities performing at intermission. Who could ever forget those rants? I suppose the Chicago is still packing them in?"

"By the droves. But like I keep telling him, we don't need to compete with the big boys downtown. Never have and never will. The problem is convincing Dad that a cooled theater in the summer and a warm theater in the winter will bring in more customers. But even when I show him the figures, he wants no part of it."

"That's our dad," Danny added with a chuckle. "Always a couple decades behind the times and no apologies for it. But here's a thought. What would happen if you bought the place from him outright? I mean, no offense, but as long as he still owns it, won't he always view you as hired help."

"Oh, trust me. I'm fully aware of that. He reminds me on a regular basis."

"So, what if you tell him you'd like to buy the Windsor from him? Let him retire, and you can take over lock, stock, and barrel."

"I'll admit I've thought about it, Danny. But with the baby coming, Millie and I will want to find a place of our own soon. I'd hate to tie up all our money right now."

"He'd probably let you make payments instead of plopping down the full amount up front. You've heard about the GI Bill, right?"

"Nothing specific. What do you know about it?"

"How about I buy you a cup of coffee across the street and tell you all about it?"

14

11 July 1945

Framlingham, England

Dear Danny,

I have missed you more than I ever imagined and long so desperately to hear from you. I have no idea how long it takes for our letters to travel, but it cannot be soon enough. After all you and I have been through, it's hard to believe we're once again writing letters, though I admit that taking pen to paper felt somehow familiar and wonderful. It will have to do for now.

I don't think I ever told you that of all the possessions I lost in our home in Utrecht, I mourned my stack of letters from you most of all. Not long after you returned to your base back in May, I had a dream one night about those letters. As I watched from outside the front window of our home, I could see the drunken Nazi thugs who'd taken over our home reading through all of your letters, laughing and making fun of all you'd written. I yelled at them to stop, pounding against the window until I broke it, cutting my hands and arms on the ragged glass. They couldn't hear me or see me, and I realized nothing I could say or do would stop them. I woke up crying and feeling so haunted by it all. Oh Danny, you will never know how much I despise these nightmares. Waking up in your arms seemed to keep them at bay. Now that you're gone, I must fight them alone again.

I told myself not to write dreary or whining letters, and yet here I've started off with a nightmare. Some things never change, I suppose.

Why didn't you wake me the morning you left? I can't believe I didn't hear you leave. I admit it was difficult—all those false alarms with so many rain delays and all those goodbyes. If I know you as well as I think I do, you probably decided to let me sleep, assuming you'd be back in a couple of hours like all the other mornings. I know we said our goodbyes the night before, but I should have seen you off. When I finally awoke and realized you were gone, I missed you so much I could hardly breathe. I miss you still.

Sophie has been wonderful. She's kept me busy teaching me how to cook everything on the pub's menu. She's very patient and always makes me laugh, even when I make a mess of things. The British are quite fussy about their tea, so she's trying to teach me how to make a proper "cuppa." Yesterday we made an

English pudding like the one we had on our honeymoon. Do you remember? I shall try to make it for you if we ever have a home of our own. Oh Danny, how I long for that day!

I've learned how to pull a pint without so much foam sloshing over and how to take orders from customers and serve them. On the first day I spilled an entire pint of ale on a poor fellow who was just passing through the village. It landed in his lap and made such a mess, it looked as though he'd wet himself! He was most kind, though I was terribly embarrassed, not knowing quite how to help without making a bigger mess of it and further humiliating myself. Sophie and Patrick couldn't stop laughing.

It's so different here, with so many of you Americans gone. Almost eerie. Before you left, remember all the hustle and bustle on base and around the village? All of you excited about the war being over and anxious to go home? When the last of the Forts took off, and not a single one could be spotted in the distance, we were overwhelmed by silence. It felt as though you could cut right through it, the absolute hush that fell over us.

There are still ground crews here, and they pile into the pub each evening, drinking to their hearts' delight. Only a few faces are familiar. Do you remember that odd fellow named Cosmos who stopped us on the street right after our wedding? How he jumped off his bicycle and let it crash to the ground while he gave you and Charlie a salute? He comes in every night and always asks about you. Charlie just rolls his eyes when he sees him coming, but I think he's rather funny. Did you know he plays the fiddle?

It's late and I must get some sleep. Every night I find myself fingering the charms on the bracelet you gave me, especially the airplane. Silly, perhaps, but they're such perfect reminders of you—of us—and the love we share. I can never thank you enough for such a thoughtful gift, Danny.

I miss you most of all late at night, here in our room. I keep wishing you'd slip through the door, fresh from your shower, and climb in bed to keep me warm. I never thought it possible that I could miss you so much that my heart literally aches. I know your mother is good about praying. Please tell her to pray that I'll soon come to you in Chicago, America.

With all my love,

Anya

"Anya, come walk with me," Sophie said as she looped the apron over her head. "I need a bit of fresh air."

Anya untied her apron and hung it with Sophie's on the peg by the back door. "I never thought I'd want to take walks again after so many years wearing out the soles of my shoes back home, but I do like the fresh air."

Sophie stretched her arms over her head as they headed

down the path. "It helps me think, getting out and walking a while. And I don't mind telling you, sometimes I just need a break from the kitchen. Gets a bit confining at times, don't you think?"

Anya shrugged, shoving her hands in the pockets of her trousers. "Sometimes, but I really enjoy the work. Learning to cook and bake, helping you and Patrick with this and that. It's been nice. Really nice."

Sophie hooked her arm through Anya's. "That's because it keeps you busy so you're not pining away for your flyboy in America."

Anya smiled. "Well, yes. I suppose that's true."

"I asked Charlie this morning if he'd stopped by Major Samford's office. Of course, I ask him every morning, and every morning he says the same thing. 'Yes I stopped by, and no there's no news yet.'"

"I'm trying so hard not to think about it. I keep telling myself if I don't think about it, that's when I'll hear something. Sounds a bit daft, doesn't it?"

Sophie smiled. "Are you kidding? I'd be losing my mind if Charlie had flown home without me. I think you're handling it fabulously." She tugged on Anya's arm. "Let's go this way today."

They headed down a different road in the direction of Parham. The sky was surprisingly clear and blue, a welcome break from the bleak gray skies that so often blanketed the area. Anya breathed in the scent of hay and earth and wildflowers.

"When I was a girl I used to ride my bicycle down these back lanes," Sophie said. "I've always loved living out in the country. Whenever I go to London, I enjoy being there for one or two hours, then all I want to do is come home. I suppose it's in my blood, the love for this land."

"Did Charlie ever ask you to consider moving back to the States with him?"

"We talked about it when he first proposed. To be honest, I was scared to death he'd insist on living in America. I couldn't imagine leaving Da, but my Charlie is quite perceptive. He must have seen it in my eyes or something. And since he has no family to speak of back in America, he said he'd be happy to live anywhere on earth as long as I was beside him." Sophie giggled. "I couldn't believe it, Anya. I was so stunned, I just stared at him. Couldn't think of a single word to say, so I just stared at those great big baby blue eyes of his. To me, that was confirmation that Charlie was the one. Right there, right then. I'd have married him that very moment if the vicar happened to stroll by."

"It's almost like a love story out of a novel."

"I know, isn't it? Of course, it's nothing compared to you and Danny—"

A horn blared behind them. "Hey, get out of the way, will ya?"

"Charlie Janssen, you scared us to death!" Sophie cried, jumping out of the Jeep's path just in time. "You stop doing that, do you hear me?"

He pulled up so close to the roadside, he simply reached out and tugged on her hand. "C'mere, Sophie girl, and give me a kiss."

"Not so fast. I've got to catch my breath again." Sophie fanned herself, pushing her hair out of her face.

"No? Well then, how about you, Anya? Got a kiss for your husband's best friend?"

Anya gave him a smirk. "I think not, Lieutenant. Don't you ever work? Or do you spend all your days just driving around these old roads looking for girls to kiss?"

"He'd better not!" Sophie entwined her fingers with his. "What are you up to now?"

"Actually, I have something to show you both. Climb in."

They paused for a second then climbed into the boxy vehicle "Show us what?"

"You'll just have to wait and see."

Anya pushed her hair out of her face as Charlie ground the gears and shifted the Jeep in motion. "Any news from the base, Charlie?"

He eyed her through the rearview mirror. "Sorry to say, but no. Samford was out of his office when I stopped by this morning. Any word from Danny?"

"No, not today. I put a letter in the post to him this morning. I can't believe how long it takes for our letters to get where they're going. You'd think with the war over, the postal service would be faster."

"Not the way I hear it," he said over his shoulder. "I think it'll be a good six months or more before things like that get back to normal. Much longer to rebuild the country, of course. Which brings me to this."

He pulled off the road and down a narrow lane. One more quick turn and they parked in a small gravel lot. Through a thick stand of trees, Anya could make out the skeletal remains of a building.

As they climbed out of the Jeep, Sophie asked, "Why have

you brought us to the chapel? What's this about?"

"Right this way, ladies," he said, passing through an old wooden lynchgate.

Once they cleared the gate and trees, the haunting skeletal remains of a bombed-out chapel came into full view. Crooked gravestones leaned here and there in the surrounding grounds, like so many ancient sentries standing guard.

"Anya, you probably don't know about the crash that took out this chapel," Charlie said.

"I think Danny may have mentioned it. What exactly happened?"

"It was 27 December of last year, early on a bitter cold morning. The conditions for flying that morning were dismal at best. We were blanketed with a freezing fog so thick, those manning the control tower couldn't even see the Forts taking off. Usually they ground planes when visibility is that poor, but the higher-ups sent them off anyway. The pilots had to fly on instruments since they were literally flying blind. Only seconds after take-off, Al Banning's plane crashed here. Back at the base, we could feel the earth trembling when it exploded."

"I remember," Sophie said with a shiver, folding her arms across her chest. "I woke up when the explosion shook my bed."

"When a Fort takes off on a bombing mission, it's packed to the gills with bombs and extra fuel tanks." Charlie shook his head. "Needless to say, none of the crew survived the crash. And as you can see, it wiped out the chapel and all those houses over there."

Anya shook her head. "How tragic."

"But I still don't understand why you brought us here?" Sophie asked again as they neared what would have been the main entrance to the chapel.

Charlie stuck a toothpick in his mouth. "Because I've been doing a lot of thinking here lately."

"Here?" Sophie asked.

He nodded, picking up a brick from the rubble. "I happened by here about a week ago, and for some reason I was just drawn to it. Almost like a magnet was pulling at me, you know? So I started looking around at all this damage, and thinking about that morning and those guys who lost their lives here in the blink of any eye ..." Charlie paused for a moment, fiddling with the toothpick, then cleared his throat. "And all of a sudden I felt a strong sense of purpose. Almost like a calling, if that makes any sense. And I knew immediately what I was supposed to do."

"I still don't understand, darling. What are you talking about?"

"I'm going to help rebuild. I don't know if the townsfolk plan to rebuild the church, but it doesn't matter. I think I'm supposed to help rebuild whatever's been damaged by the war. Here in Parham and Framlingham, the rest of Suffolk and anywhere else that needs help. That's what I want to do. That's what I feel called to do."

"How will you go about that?" Anya asked, looking around at the massive damage to the ancient church.

"Anya, you probably don't know, but just before Pearl Harbor was bombed, I graduated with a degree in architectural design from Washington University in St. Louis.

I'd always planned to build skyscrapers in some major metropolitan area. Then we went to war, and I enlisted and learned to fly. Got assigned to the 390th here." He draped his arm over Sophie's shoulder. "Luckiest day of my life, by the way, ending up here in Sophie's backyard."

He leaned over to kiss her cheek. "Married my girl and decided to stay here in England and make this my home. And like I said, about a week ago I found myself here on this sacred ground, and I just *knew*. This is what I'm supposed to do with my life now."

"I think it's a wonderful idea, Charlie," Anya said.

"I do too, love," Sophie added quietly, her expression warmed with admiration. "I think it's absolutely wonderful."

Charlie's toothpick moved to the other side of his mouth. "Seems like the least I can do, the way I see it. After all, we came flying in here, a bunch of boisterous free-spirited Yanks with our noisy planes and machinery, and basically moved right in on this land and made ourselves at home. Now, with the 390th ripping up stakes and heading home, seems to me folks around here deserve some help. And since I know how to design and build things, it just makes sense for me to lend a hand."

"How will you start?" Sophie asked, wandering along what was once the main aisle of the church. "You can't just start sweeping up and plastering bricks, can you?"

"No, I can't. But I've talked to a few people, discussed it with one of the engineers on base, and it looks like I'll be playing the role of a liaison, salvaging what we can from the base to use in the rebuilding of

the entire county. Working with local officials and those

from other American and RAF bases to help put England back on her feet. Pretty clever, huh?"

"Sweetheart, you're brilliant." Sophie stood on her tiptoes and planted a noisy kiss on his cheek. "But why didn't you tell me? I'm excited for you!"

"Excited for *us*," he countered. "I see this as a team effort." He turned to Anya. "Only wish I could have talked Danny into staying on with me. Though, last time we talked about the future, he seemed rather determined to finish college back in the States and start teaching."

"History, he tells me," Anya said. "He wants to make sure the future generations don't ever forget what happened these past few years."

"Good for him," Sophie said. "He'll be a fabulous teacher."

"Yes, I believe he will."

"In the meantime, there's work to be done, so off we go." Charlie herded them back toward the Jeep with an arm over both their shoulders.

As they climbed back into the vehicle, Anya glanced back through the trees toward what was left of the old church. She swallowed against the lump in her throat, wondering when the scars of war would ever stop twisting her heart. Or if they ever would.

15

12 July 1945

Chicago, Illinois

Danny joined his mother on the back porch where she was snapping green beans. Sophie followed at his heels, slipping out the screen door before it slapped shut. "Hey, Mom. Mind some company?"

"I'd love some, Danny. Would you like some lemonade?"

"No, I'm good." He dropped into the rocker next to hers and patted his stomach. "I'm still stuffed from lunch. I bet I've gained ten pounds since I've been home."

"I hope so. I never saw you so thin as the day we picked you up in Rockford. Just look how your shirt hangs on you." She "tsked" a couple of times for his benefit. "Guess I need to put an extra layer of icing on that carrot cake I made for dinner."

"You do that. You know I'm a sucker for your carrot cake, Mom. Or any other cake, for that matter."

She smiled, rocking slowly beside him, snapping away. "It's so good to have you home, son. Are you getting enough rest?"

Sophie sat at his feet, her tail swishing across the porch, her eyes locked on Danny's every move. "I would if it weren't for Sophie. She never used to bother me when I slept. Now she's spooning me all night. Which means I feel every movement when she's dog-paddling in her sleep or when she sits up for a good scratch."

She chuckled. "Oh, she's just letting you know how much she missed you. Your father would never let her sleep in our bed, of course. In fact, back when you left for college, he closed our door so she couldn't disturb us. But that didn't go over too well with Sophie, so she would lie down just outside our door and stick her paws under it, making such a racket on the hardwood floor."

"I bet Dad loved that," he teased. Sophie slowly moved in, then sat on her haunches, resting a paw on Danny's knee. He patted her head and scratched under her chin sending her back paw into a frenzy tapping against the floor.

"Oh, he tried everything. Even locked her in the kitchen, but she just howled and howled. So loud, I thought she'd wake the neighbors. He finally gave up and let her in our room, but not on the bed. Eventually, he made that bed for her to curl up in beside ours. She seemed to like that, and that's where she's slept until you came home."

"I should probably move the bed to my room and give it a try." He paused for a moment, scratching Sophie behind the ears. "Then again, dumb as it sounds, I'd probably miss having her up on the bed with me. But I've gotta tell you, not half as much as I miss having Anya sleeping beside me." He slid his eyes over at his mother and waggled his brows.

"Now, Danny," she scolded with a chuckle. "No need to tell me such things. A mother doesn't need to know everything that goes on in her son's life, you know."

He laughed at the rosy glow coloring her cheeks. "I'm just teasing." He gave Sophie a final pat on the head then leaned back and rocked his chair. "I sure miss her, Mom. She's all I can think about, even though I know I need to start making some decisions now that the war's over. But to be honest, all I really want to do is fly back to England and bring her home."

"I know, honey, but just give it a little more time. I'm sure those in charge want all those war brides sent over here as much as you do. While I was doing the dishes after lunch, I heard on the radio there are more than 70,000 war brides needing passage to America from Great Britain, and many of them pregnant or with small children. I'm afraid the news was rather dire because of all the paperwork to sort it all out."

Danny blew a long cascading whistle. "How hard can it be? They make a list, tell the ladies when to be at the dock, they put them on the ship, and off they go."

"Yes, but multiply that by tens of thousands, and you can see how difficult it must be."

"I guess. I just know Anya and how impatient she can be."

"We're praying for her, honey. We're all praying for her. In the meantime, we'll try to be patient ourselves and just take it one day at a time. That's all we can do."

They rocked in silence for a few moments. Then, snapping

the final bean, she set the pot on the table and brushed off her hands. "I've been meaning to ask you something. Would it be all right with you if I wrote a letter to Anya? I thought perhaps it might help her get to know us a little better so we won't seem like such strangers when she arrives."

"I think that would be terrific, Mom. I'm sure she'd love to hear from you."

"Good. If nothing else, it might give her something else to look forward to while she waits ... letters from her new family. I want her to know how much we're looking forward to meeting her and getting to know her; how much we've been praying for her. That sort of thing."

"I'm not sure about the praying part. Don't get me wrong. I'm glad you're praying for her. Millie and Joey told me they're praying too. But Anya ... well, she's a bit shaky on the subject of God. Though come to think of it, in her last letter she did tell me to ask you to pray. Obviously, I forgot."

"She did?"

"Yes. Something to the effect of knowing you pray a lot, so she wondered if you'd pray for her to come here as soon as possible."

"Well, that sounds like she still believes in prayer, right?"

He scratched his eyebrow. "Based on some of our conversations, I'm thinking it's more a matter of her believing that *you* can pray because she can't."

"She's still struggling with her faith?"

"Big time. The war pretty much shattered what faith she did have. And not just because of everyone she lost, but all the unspeakable things she witnessed. Things she had to do just to survive. She basically gave up on God, and who could

155

blame her after all that? Still, I can see some changes. Little glimmers of hope that she's trying to find her way back to God."

"That's good, son. I'm glad to hear it. And with that in mind, I promise I'll be sensitive when I write. Mostly, I want her to know how welcome she is into our family. We've got to start somewhere, and the way I see it, everyone likes to be cherished and made to feel welcome."

Danny reached over and placed his hand over hers. "You're the best, Mom." He leaned over and kissed her cheek. "I can't thank you enough for caring about her. I know it had to be hard, getting my telegram from a foreign country the day before I married someone you'd never met."

"Honey, Anya's not a stranger. My goodness, you've known her since you were still in high school."

"Yeah, but *you've* never met her."

"Yes, but I carried every one of her letters up to your room when they came, and you shared parts of them with me over the years. Anya and I may not have met, but I feel like I've known her for years." She squeezed his hand. "I couldn't be happier for the two of you."

He rose from the rocker. "One day at a time, huh?"

"That's right. One day at a time."

He gave her a hand to help her up. "I was thinking about walking over to Mrs. Zankowski's house and seeing what she has to say about me going back to school. I talked to Joey the other day about the GI Bill. It's supposed to help veterans financially now that we're home, including college tuition, down payments on homes, that sort of thing. He suggested talking to Mrs. Z and seeing what kind of courses I should take and what she thinks about the Northwestern Campus here in Chicago. Good idea?"

"I think that's a great idea. Lara is such a pleasure. I've enjoyed getting to know her better since Millie and Joey married." She picked up the bowl of beans and the paper bag of snapped ends and made her way to the screen door.

Danny and Sophie followed her inside. "I never dreamed my history teacher would end up being a relative. Joey says she's been a real godsend to Millie and him, especially since Millie got pregnant."

"Oh, she has. With Millie's folks still living in Boston, Lara has been a tremendous help to Millie and Joey—to all of us, in fact. You go have a chat with her, and tell her I said hello. I'll go upstairs and check on Millie. Be back in time for supper, all right?"

"Sure thing, Mom. C'mon, Sophie. Let's take a walk."

"Hello, Mrs. Smithson," Danny said as he passed his neighbor's house. When he was younger, he mowed her grass and shoveled snow for her. "I see someone's taking real good care of your lawn. Looks good."

"Well, hello there, Danny." She made her way down the porch steps and extended her hand. "I heard you were back from the war. I'm glad to see you made it home all in one piece."

He shook her hand, and noted the slightest hesitation as

she stepped back and folded her arms across her chest. "Well, I'm glad to be home in one piece, I assure you."

"I see Sophie has welcomed you home properly."

He reached down to pat the beagle's head. "Yes, ma'am, she certainly has. How's Mr. Smithson doing these days?"

"Oh, he's as ornery as ever, but otherwise doing just fine."

"Good, I'm glad to hear that." He tried to think of something else to say and went blank. "Well, it was nice to see you—"

"Danny, there's something you need to know, and I might as well just say it. It's why I didn't come to your welcome home party the other day. The thing is, I didn't buy any war bonds." She straightened her back and looked him straight in the eye. "Fact is, I don't believe in war. Never have. I think it's a crying shame Mr. Roosevelt sent all you boys over to fight someone else's war, and even though he's dead and gone now, I think he still has blood on his hands for every soldier and sailor who died. And not just them, but all the others who came home maimed for life. You and your brother Joey are the lucky ones, but you never should've been sent to fight this ridiculous war in the first place."

Danny froze. She'd never been the friendliest neighbor, but he couldn't understand why she felt the need to say such a thing. Then, as his thoughts took flight, he said, "Look, Mrs. Smithson, I don't mean to sound disrespectful, but it's *because* of guys like me and Joey that you're able to live in a country free from dictators like Hitler or Hirohito. It makes no difference to me if you did or didn't buy any war bonds, but the next time you encounter a veteran, take my advice. Skip the pacifist speech and tell him thanks. If not for us, you'd be *sprechen sie Deutsch.*"

She bristled, sputtering a response as he tugged on Sophie's leash. As he walked away, he looked back over his shoulder. "*Guten Tag, Frau Smithson.*"

Danny was still trying to calm his nerves when he turned to walk up the Zankowski's sidewalk. He knocked on the door and blew out a final grunt of disgust just before it opened.

"Danny!" she cried, opening her arms for a hug. "Oh Danny, I'm so glad to see you! How are you?"

"I'm good, Mrs. Z. How are you?"

"Fabulous, now that you're here! Come in, come in!" She stepped aside to let him enter.

"Oh." He looked down at Sophie. "Is it okay if I tie her up here on your porch?"

"Good heavens, no. Bring her in!" She gave the dog a good scratch beneath behind her ears. "Sophie and I are good friends, aren't we girl?"

"You are?"

"Well, sure we are. I'm down at your house all the time visiting Millie and Joey and your parents."

"That's right. I keep forgetting we're family now. Am I supposed to call you Auntie Lara now?"

"Don't be silly. Just call me Lara. I'm not your teacher anymore, and besides—you're all grown up now. And handsome as any movie star! Just look at you!"

"I doubt it, but that's kind of you to say."

"I was just about to call and see if I could come pay you a visit, so this is perfect timing. Come on back to the kitchen and let's have some lemonade."

Moments later, they were sitting at the kitchen table.

"I'm so sorry we had to miss your welcome home party. I was so disappointed not to be there, but we were up in Boston visiting my sister Gwen, Millie's mother. We just got home late last night."

"No problem. Millie told me you were out of town."

They chatted for almost an hour as Danny answered all kinds of questions about the war, his experience bailing out over Holland, and all about Anya. Lara caught him up on news of friends he'd gone to school with, and of course, the excitement of Millie and Joey's baby on the way.

Lara leaned back in her chair and folded her arms with a huge smile fixed on her face. "Honestly, Danny, I could sit here and grin at you all day long. I can't tell you how thankful I am that you're home and all in one piece."

He ran his fingers through his hair. "I appreciate that. Too bad not everyone feels that way."

"Really? Why do you say that?"

He told her about his brief conversation with Mrs. Smithson and his rebuke to her comments about the war.

"You *said* that?" Her eyes widened with her smile. "You said goodbye to her in German?"

"Yes, ma'am I did. I know a few other German words I could have added, but decided I better leave before I said something worse."

"That old battle-ax. I've had a few similar conversations with her until I realized she's too stubborn and bull-headed and not worth wasting my energy on. I'm so sorry you had to hear all that, but I hope you know how proud of you all the rest of us are. I guess you noticed we're all flying our flags for you and all the other American boys who fought for us."

"I saw that. Mom wrote when I first got to England to tell me about all the flags up and down the street. Sure helped knowing folks back here were thinking of me. And by the way, thanks for your letters. Mail call was a big, big deal on base, and I sure loved hearing my name called when I had a letter."

"It was my pleasure, Danny. So your mother mentioned you're planning to finish college. Is that right?"

"That's one of the things I wanted to talk to you about. Of course, who knows what will happen in the next couple of months. I'm still on leave with orders to report for duty on the eighteenth of August at Sioux Falls, South Dakota. For all I know, they could send us to the Pacific to help fight that war. So I can't register for classes yet, but hopefully our guys will take care of the Japs, and we can all get on with our lives."

"Oh Danny, I hadn't even thought about them sending you to the Pacific. I'm going to pray that doesn't happen. Can't imagine having to see you off again."

"No kidding. But I've still got to think ahead, especially now that I'm married. And with the promises they're making about the GI Bill giving us a free ride to college, I'd be a fool not to finish school now."

"Sounds like a good plan. Have you thought about what you'll study?"

"I want to teach history like you. I've told you before that you were my favorite teacher."

She grinned again. "Yes, but I never get tired of hearing it!"

"Well, it's true. And I want to make history come alive like you always did in class. I still remember all those historical characters you played; showing up in costume and staying in character through the entire class time. It made such a powerful impression on me, and I think it's why I have such a passion for history."

"I still love surprising my students like that. But I should probably let you in on a little secret."

"What's that?"

"The idea wasn't original. I stole it from *my* favorite teacher, Mr. Stonewall. Isn't that a great name for a history professor? The first time he walked into class dressed as Benjamin Franklin, we all laughed. But he never broke character, and taught us things about Franklin that I still remember to this day. He would show up in character once a week, though we never knew when. Which meant we never wanted to skip class for fear of missing out, of course. Genius. The man was pure genius. And that's when I caught the passion. That's when I knew what I wanted to do with my life. I wanted to teach American history and pass along that same passion to my students just like Professor Stonewall."

"Apparently, his legacy lives on, doesn't it? So tell me. Where do you think I should go? I'm thinking of North-western's Chicago campus. Isn't that where you went?"

They'd been talking for another half hour when the telephone rang. Lara excused herself and stepped into the hall to answer it.

"What?! Really?" she cried. "Danny, it's your mother. She says they're heading to the hospital. Millie's in labor!"

16

13 July 1945
Chicago, Illinois

Dear Anya,

Happy news from America! Millie gave birth to a beautiful baby boy last night! She was in labor almost ten hours, but delivered the little guy just before midnight. He weighed in at eight pounds and two ounces, and has a thick head of hair the same auburn shade as Millie's. He's the cutest little thing you ever saw. Joey got to hold him for a couple of minutes before he was whisked off to the nursery, and you've never seen such a proud dad. He got all choked up when the nurse placed him in his arms, and naturally, the rest of us got a little misty-eyed as well.

They named him Joseph James McClain, and they plan to call him Jimmy after Joey's best friend on the

USS Oklahoma. Jimmy Linden didn't survive the attack on Pearl, and Joey wanted to honor his memory. Millie and Jimmy will stay in the hospital for the rest of the week.

When I got up this morning, I heard Dad working down in the basement, so I grabbed a cup of coffee and went downstairs. He was startled to see me, but glad I wasn't Joey since he was putting the final touches on a cradle he'd made for the baby. It's so beautiful, Anya, and something I never expected from Dad. We talked for a while as he worked, then he finally pulled up a stool and took a break. We haven't had a chance to talk one-on-one since I've been back. Or, should I say, he hasn't made himself available to me that way. He's still such an odd duck, and chances are I'll never really understand him or how his mind works. But as we talked, I realized it was the first time I ever felt like he respected me as a man, not just his son. That may not make much sense to you, but it meant the world to me. He asked a lot of questions about the day-to-day routine while I was stationed in Framlingham, and what it was like to fly a B-17 above enemy territory.

I guess we'd been talking about half an hour or so when it occurred to me to ask him about his service in World War I. At first, he locked his jaw and shook his head. "Nothing to talk about," he said. But I pressed him on it. It took him a while, but then he told me.

He said he hated his father. Would have done anything to leave home. And when Woodrow Wilson got America in the First World War, he saw his chance. He enlisted the next day. He said the only friend he ever had was a kid in his unit from Idaho; a wiry little guy they nicknamed Spider. Dad felt like it was his job to keep Spider's back, look after him. Next thing he knew, he was in a mud-soaked trench in France begging God to keep Spider alive ... Dad's hands were holding the kid's intestines together; waiting for a medic who never came.

He swallowed hard, and it was a long time before he could speak again. When he did, he looked me in the eye and said there's not a day that goes by that he doesn't think of Spider and the day he let him down. I started to say something, and he stopped me. Said I was never to speak of it again.

Anya, I know you understand more than I do how something like that changes a person. It explains so much to me, after all these years, to piece together why he's always been so gruff and moody, never had any friends, never let anyone get close to him. Sure made me look at him in a different light.

Not sure if I should have shared that with you, but I can't stop thinking about it. Enough of all that for now.

I was actually visiting Mrs. Zankowski when we got the call about Millie going into labor. Before the call, we had a good talk, and she gave me some valuable information regarding my return to school. If it's all right with you, I'm going to proceed with enrolling at the Northwestern Campus here in Chicago. The way I see it, if the U.S. is willing to foot the tab for me to *finish school through the GI Bill, I'd be ridiculously stupid not to take advantage of it. Especially since I can live at home and help out at the theater from time to time. I figured I'd at least get started, then once you come, we can sit down and discuss a plan.*

Don't mind me ... I guess I'm a little carried away right now, thinking about our future. Seeing little Jimmy melted something inside me, and I'm missing you so much. To think that one day you and I might have a baby of our own ... wow.

I'm sure you'll be delighted to hear (ha ha) that the Cubs are having a great season so far! We're 43 wins, 29 losses, with one tie game—best record we've had in years. I keep thinking this could be the year we go all the way. One more reason to get you home soon so you can go to Wrigley with me and cheer for our Cubs!

I sure hope to hear from you soon. I'm so hungry for news from Framlingham. Has my buddy Cosmos been by the pub again? Oh! That reminds me—I can't wait to try some of those dishes you and Sophie have been cooking up. Mom will be thrilled to have some help in the kitchen!

All for now. Write soon.

Love,

Danny

1 August 1945

"There's a sight you don't see every day!" Danny hollered after rounding the corner onto his street late on Wednesday afternoon. Coming toward him on the sidewalk, Millie walked beside Joey, who was pushing Jimmy in the stroller. Leading the procession was Sophie, leashed to the stroller's front rail.

Danny chuckled. "Will you look at that strut? She must think she's the grand marshal of the St. Patrick's parade. Don't you, Sophie girl?"

At the sound of her name, Sophie finally noticed him ahead and bolted in his direction with a round of excited barks.

"Hold on there, girl!" Joey shouted, his hands firmly on the stroller's handle. The halt stopped the beagle in her tracks with a yelp. "You know better than that, Sophie."

As Danny joined them, he knelt beside her, scratching behind her ears as her tail wagged like a wild metronome. "That's my fault. I shouldn't have called to her." He leaned in for a peek at Jimmy. "I'm telling you, that little guy could sleep through the roar of a B-17 taking off. How does he do that?"

"Gets it from his grandfather," Millie said with a laugh. "Which may be why he gets along so well with Frank."

"You're probably right about that. First time I saw Dad doze off while Jimmy slept in his arms, I couldn't believe it. I had no idea the old man had a soft spot like that."

Just then, Jimmy stretched with a yawn, his tiny pink lips in motion as his eyes fluttered open.

"Well, hi there, little buddy," Danny said, gently tickling his tummy. Jimmy smiled with a coo.

"He sure loves his Uncle Danny," Millie said. "Have you noticed how he lights up whenever—"

A ferocious bark snapped their attention as a beast of a dog barreled toward them from across the street. Millie snatched Jimmy out of the carrier just as Sophie tore across the street in a flurry of angry barking; the carrier dangling and bouncing along behind her. Danny raced to grab her leash, shouting for her to stop ... just as the squeal of brakes obliterated all other sounds.

The car came to a stop after it slammed into both dogs with a sickening thud. Their injured cries rose in a harrowing disharmony, jolting Danny's heart. He rushed to Sophie's side, falling to his knees.

"SOPHIE! Oh no, no, no! Sophie girl, I'm here, I'm right here. I've got you, girl."

Her wails turned sorrowful as Danny examined her, searching her body for injury. As he felt down her back and around her hip, she yowled an octave higher and twice as loud.

Mrs. Smithson opened her car door and stepped out. "Oh my stars, oh my goodness! What happened? I never saw them! Are they dead?"

Danny looked up, only then realizing his eyes were filling with tears. He made no effort to respond, turning his attention back to Sophie.

Joey took a knee beside him. "Where's she hurt? Can you tell?"

"It's her lower back or hip, or maybe it's her spine. I can't tell, but we've got to get her to the vet."

"I'll get the car." Joey dashed off and took the porch steps two at a time, passing his parents as they hurried out.

"What's happened?" Betty cried, following Frank down the sidewalk. "Oh, honey, it's Sophie—"

"Danny, what happened?" his father yelled. "Is she hurt?"

"Oh dear," the elderly woman said as she rounded them to check on the other dog. "I don't think this one's going to make it."

They looked over at the huge dog and saw blood pooling below its head. His enormous paws quivered as his body shuddered once, twice, then a third time before it stilled.

"Whose dog is that?" Mrs. Smithson asked.

"What does it matter?" Frank cried. "You get behind the wheel of that old tank and can't even see over the steering wheel! How many dogs have to get killed before they take your keys away, Edna? I guess you won't be satisfied until you run down someone's kid, will you?"

She blanched. "Why, Frank McClain, that's a terrible thing to say—"

"Just leave, will you? Frank growled. "Betty, go get a blanket and tell Joey to hurry with the car!"

She started to take off just as Joey pulled the car up beside them. Danny gently draped the blanket around Sophie and lifted her onto the backseat of his dad's car, heartsick with each cry and whimper as they rushed to the veterinarian's office.

Danny refused to leave the vet's office, though there wasn't anything for him to do but wait. His father took Joey to the theater then came back to wait with him. After a preliminary examination and x-rays, Dr. Lister told them Sophie had suffered a broken hip, but fortunately had sustained no internal injuries. Surgery would be required. As he explained what needed to be done, Danny clenched his jaw knowing there was no way Frank McClain would ever consent to surgery for a pet.

"I'll pay for it, Dad."

"What?"

"I'll pay for the surgery."

His dad searched his eyes, though Danny couldn't discern what he might be thinking. He grew uncomfortable with the awkward silence but kept his eyes fixed on his father's.

"I'll let you two talk it over," the vet said, heading down the hall. "I'll be back in a few minutes. I need a decision one way or the other. Soon."

"Dad, I have the money. I've still got—"

Frank took a seat in the waiting area. "Don't be ridiculous."

"Ridiculous? You know how much Sophie means to me! I'm not about to let you just take her out back and shoot her like some injured racehorse."

"Son, take a seat."

"No, Dad. It's not up for discussion, so you might as well just—"

"Danny. Sit. Down." Frank closed his eyes.

He obliged, dropping into a chair across from his father, bewildered that he could fly bombers all over Europe and jump out with nothing but a silk parachute strapped to his back, yet come home and feel like a ten-year-old kid again when his father ordered him to sit. The thought irritated him, but he shoved it aside to make his case.

"Here's the thing," he began. "After all we've—"

"I said it's ridiculous because I don't want you to spend money you and Anya will need. I'll pay for Sophie's surgery."

Danny blinked. "What?"

The vet returned. "Well, gentlemen, what's your decision?"

"You fix what needs fixing, Doc," Frank said. "Whatever it takes."

"That's all I needed to hear." The vet gave him a thumbs-up and turned to go.

Stunned, Danny looked at his father. "Dad?"

His father pulled off his glasses with a loud sigh and gave his face a rub. "Son, I know how much Sophie means to you. I've known that from the first night you brought her home after she showed up behind Chaney's grocery store. She was nothing but skin and bones. And you took real good care of her. I was real proud of the way you took responsibility for her." He put his glasses back on. "But what you don't know is how much that dog means to *me*."

He waited, curious at his father's remark.

"You remember me telling you about the dog I had when I was a kid?"

"Yes, sir. His name was Barney, right?"

"That's right."

"You said he was a beagle mix like Sophie."

"He was. Looked so much alike she could've been from the same litter of pups."

Danny realized the connection. "Barney was hit by a car."

171

Dad nodded. "That's right. Hit by a neighbor who was speeding down our street."

Danny shook his head. Quite a coincidence, even decades apart. "So you understand."

"I do. Barney was killed instantly. I was so upset, I punched Mr. Winkler's nose and broke it." He clucked his cheek against his teeth. "I got a whipping for it later, but I didn't care. I loved that dog. I know it sounds silly, but he was the only friend I had as a kid." He sniffed hard and shook his head. "You never met my father. He died before you were born. But your grandfather was a mean ol' cuss. He'd take his belt off and beat me just for something to do. Didn't need a reason. And I learned early on how to stay out of his way.

"Then one Christmas, my mother gave me a puppy. Had to do it when Dad was out of the house, and she made me promise to take care of it and keep it out of sight. Best Christmas I ever had as a kid. I loved that silly ol' dog from the minute I laid eyes on him. He followed me everywhere. Smart, too. Real smart. I trained him to hide under my bed whenever Dad was home, quiet as a church mouse. Hard to believe, but he'd slink under there and never make a sound.

"That dog was my best friend ..." He looked up and offered a sad smile. "Fact is, he was my *only* friend."

Danny struggled to imagine what that must have been like. He never knew about his grandfather or why he was so mean, but it sure explained a lot about his dad. He felt sorry for him; sorry for the lonely kid with a dog named Barney.

"Then you brought home this scrawny little pooch you named Sophie. And when you went off to college, she took a liking toward me. Can't say as I minded. We got used to each other, I guess you could say."

"I remember," Danny said with an easy smile. "I was pretty jealous the first time I came home and noticed how you two had bonded in my absence."

"We sure did. Truth be known, kind of seemed like I was getting a second chance after losing Barney all those years ago. Didn't realize it at the time, but looking back, I can see the connection. Then after I got mugged behind the theater and spent all those months recovering once I came home, she started sticking to me like Elmer's glue. Rarely let me out of her sight, except when you were home.

"Then you went overseas, and Sophie kept me company. Especially on those long nights when you were missing in action—" He snorted this time and winced at the sound, turning his head away as he cleared his throat.

Staring out the window, he continued. "Sometimes, late at night when I couldn't sleep, worrying about what had happened to you ... wondering if you were still ... I'd go downstairs to the basement and sit in my easy chair for hours. Sophie would climb up my lap and rest her head on my chest, looking up at me with those big brown eyes. And it helped. It helped having her there, knowing I didn't have to say anything. I've never been good at ... I mean, sometimes ... well, I couldn't let your mother see me like that. All torn up."

Danny slowly moved to the seat next to his father and rested his arm across his shoulders. Frank sniffed a couple more times and nodded. Moments passed.

"So you see, Sophie means a lot to me too, son. And that's why we'll do whatever it takes to make her walk again."

This time, it was Danny who couldn't find his voice. He squeezed his father's shoulder and nodded. His father patted his knee and nodded in return.

Like father, like son.

17

5 August 1945

Framlingham, England

With each passing day, Anya grew more restless. She fought the clouds of depression all day, every day, and well into the night. Danny had been gone six long weeks, and the distance between them felt like a chasm growing wider by the hour. Their letters traveled at a snail's pace which only made it worse.

Most days, she could rally her spirits enough to put on a good face, though the underlying angst rendered even the simplest task exhausting. But Anya was a fighter. Even as a young girl she'd never been afraid to stand up for herself, no matter the situation. She'd always prided herself for never backing down from a challenge. Such an attitude proved indispensable while working for the Dutch Resistance. But when the war finally ended, it seemed as if all her defenses came crumbling down, often leaving her in another puddle of tears. And nothing aggravated her more than those tears.

Three days ago, they'd gathered at Wickham Market Station to see the ground crews and headquarter staff of the 390th depart for Southampton where they would board a ship for America. For Charlie, the departure of his remaining squadron was cause for celebration. He and Sophie cheered the giddy Americans finally on their way home, hugging and shouting as the last crew mates crammed onto the railway cars, hanging on for dear life.

For Anya, the scene was bittersweet. With members of Danny's squadron still in town, she'd felt a kindred spirit with those who'd served alongside him. Most likely, few of them actually knew Danny by name or had so much as a single conversation with him, but nonetheless, their presence had comforted Anya.

And then there was Cosmos.

Not long after Danny left, the young stump of a sergeant visited the pub late one afternoon and asked if he might have a word with her. Since the usual evening crowd had not yet gathered, she agreed and took a seat on the chair he pulled out for her.

With a nervous smile, he put a fist to his mouth and coughed politely, before folding his hands on the table. "Mrs. Lieutenant, I know it must be most difficult for you, remaining here in this small English village with your husband so far away. I know also that Lieutenant Janssen and the lovely Mrs. Janssen have taken you under their wings until such a time as you will make your way to America to be reunited with your betrothed."

Anya pressed her lips together as she listened to Cosmos's

generous dose of flattery. "Yes, Charlie and Sophie have been wonderful."

"But you see, I too feel a particularly strong bond with Lieutenant McClain, for he served as co-pilot on my inaugural flight just a few months ago when those of us who comprise the ground echelons were invited to fly on the Chowhound missions."

Anya brightened. "Yes, I remember meeting you just after Danny and I were married. You mentioned the Chowhound mission that day. Did you know I'm from Utrecht? I was there that day when—"

"Utrecht?!" he cried, reaching his hands across the table to clasp over hers. "Oh bless the Lord! My dear, precious friend—do you *realize* what this *means*? While you were below, no doubt gazing up into the sky at the flock of Fortresses dropping off their payloads of food and medicine— and dare I say, hope? —I, Cosmos Francis Benedetto, was above you, in the belly of a mighty Fort, awestruck at the sight of such an unforgettable mission of mercy."

He paused, unable to continue as tears pooled in his eyes. "I'm sorry," he mouthed as he pulled a handkerchief from his pocket. He blew his nose, a great honk echoing against the low ceiling of the quiet pub, then wiped his eyes.

Anya wasn't quite sure how to handle the display of emotion, but was moved by his tender heart. "How very kind of you to care so deeply, Sergeant. It was such a difficult time for all of us in The Netherlands, and those food drops *did* give us hope. We were so tired and so very hungry." Anya shook her head with the memory. "I will never forget that day. The planes coming one after another, flying so low to the ground, then dropping those pallets on the white crosses marked for them. I still remember the smiles and the sound of laughter. It had been such a long time since we laughed."

He gripped her hands. "Oh, Mrs. Lieutenant—"

"Please, you must call me Anya. I insist."

"Anya." He smiled so warmly she thought he might choke up again. "Such a beautiful name for a truly beautiful young woman. But it is I who must insist upon calling you *Mrs. Lieutenant* so that all will know I am fully aware of your marital status, thereby dismissing any possible misconception by those who might see us together. It would literally break my Italian heart if word got back to Lieutenant McClain that his lovely bride was seen in the company of Cosmos Benedetto and thereby raising suspicion of a duplicitous encounter."

Anya stared at him. "I'm sorry, what did you say?"

He patted her hand then refolded his hands on the table again with a chuckle. "My apologies. My mother always says I have a propensity toward literary expression when I speak, and I suppose she's right. But what I am trying to say is, due to my utmost respect for your husband, I shall practice the most chivalrous methods by which our friendship may be seen as aboveboard, honest, and completely platonic."

Anya fought the urge to snicker as he sat back, finished and quite pleased with his declaration. She knew Cosmos was sincere and appreciated his respect, but couldn't help thinking how Danny would react to such a declaration.

"As I was saying, Mrs. Lieutenant, knowing what I know now, that we shared a truly historic moment that day in Utrecht, I am honored to extend my promise to keep an eye out for you, assisting Lieutenant and Mrs. Janssen as they take care of you in the absence of your husband. And I shall do so with the utmost humility."

"Thank you, Sergeant. That means a lot to me," she said, meaning it.

True to his word, he checked on her every night, always close by but never hovering. On more than one occasion, he came to her rescue when a drunken soldier crossed the line. Anya could take care of herself, but she rather enjoyed having Cosmos handle the difficult patrons. Afterward, she would shake his hand and offer a pint on the house. Of course, he'd never accept.

On the last night before his squadron left Framlingham, Cosmos went through a pocketful of handkerchiefs. In a constant state of emotion, he made the rounds to say his goodbyes to the locals and especially the staff at Quincy's. Later in the evening, he stepped up on the pub's hearth and asked for everyone's attention. Not an easy task as the crowd was fairly tanked by then, but eventually the place quietened.

"My friends, my friends, as we share our last evening together, though happy at the prospect of heading home, we must also thank our dear friends here at Quincy's. We thank you for your many kindnesses and unmatched hospitality toward us these past few years. I cannot imagine how we would have survived without you through the darkest days and bleakest nights of this war—"

"Oh brother, here we go," Charlie groaned under his breath, earning an elbow planted in his ribs and a glare from his wife.

"And with that in mind, I would like to play for you a song

of farewell. May you remember us kindly, and may the good Lord bless you for every pint of ale, every morsel of each and every meal, every kind deed, and every listening ear."

He placed his worn fiddle beneath his chin and raised the bow. The tune was not one Anya recognized, though all the Americans immediately joined in.

Should old acquaintance be forgot,
And never brought to mind?
Should old acquaintance be forgot,
And old lang syne?

The voices grew stronger as everyone draped their arms on those beside them, then swayed in rhythm to the chorus.

For auld lang syne, my dear,
For auld lang syne,
We'll take a cup of kindness yet,
For auld lang syne.

Anya smiled, enjoying the camaraderie of those around her, knowing she would miss them all, good and bad alike. When the song ended, the noisy chatter returned, but only for a moment.

"My friends! My friends! If I might play for you just one more song?" His eyes found Anya's as he pointed his bow in her direction. "This one's for you, Mrs. Lieutenant."

Charlie groaned again, silenced immediately by Sophie's glare.

Heads turned as Cosmos played the first notes of a song that evoked a surprising sadness in Anya's soul. The crowd hushed again, yielding attention to Cosmos whose eyes closed, his expression reflecting the emotion drawn by his bow across the strings. Then, once again, the richness of the men's voices filled the room as Sophie slipped her arm around Anya's waist.

Oh, Danny Boy, the pipes, the pipes are calling,
From glen to glen, and down the mountain side,
The summer's gone, and all the roses falling,
It's you, it's you must go and I must bide,
But come ye back when summer's in the meadow,
Or when the valley's hushed and white with snow,
'Tis I'll be here in sunshine or in shadow,
Oh, Danny Boy, oh Danny Boy, I love you so!

Anya thought she'd never heard anything so moving in all her life. Her tears flowed freely as they continued to sing. When the song ended and the cheers began to subside, she made her way to Cosmos and gave him a heartfelt hug, thanking him over and over.

The next morning, as they gathered to say their goodbyes at Wickham Station, she spotted Cosmos weaving his way through the crowd toward her. She was surprised at the lump in her throat as he neared, her eyes stinging.

"Mrs. Lieutenant, there's one more thing I must ask of you."

"What is it, Sergeant?"

"I cannot bear to think I will never see you or Lieutenant McClain again, and to that end, I wonder if you would be so kind as to write down the address in Chicago where I might find him when I return to the United States of America. If that meets your approval, of course."

She smiled at the thought. "Why, Cosmos, that would be wonderful. I know Danny would love to see you if you're ever in Chicago. Here, let me write it down for you."

Naturally, he had an index card at the ready and a pen which he extended toward her. She jotted down the address which she'd known by heart for years. "Here you go."

He pressed the card against his heart. "Eternal thanks, Mrs. Lieutenant. And if I might be so bold, I too have prepared a card for you with my own address and telephone number, in case you or the lieutenant are ever in New Jersey."

"That's very kind. Thank you."

"ALL ABOARD!"

"Well, that's my call," he said, his chin trembling as he held out his hand. "So I shall say goodbye until we meet again."

Anya looked at his hand for only a second before giving Cosmos Francis Benedetto a hug instead. "Take care. And thank you for being my friend."

He stepped back and nodded as his tears continued to fall. "Goodbye, Mrs. Lieutenant." Then, straightening, he offered a salute, snapped his arm down, turned sharply on his heel, and walked away.

At that precise moment, Anya had an idea. As she watched him jostle through the crowd until he was out of sight, she tried to imagine the look on Danny's face when he opened his door to find the Italian standing there.

"What's with your loopy smile?" Charlie asked, coming to her side. "What was that all about?"

She shook her head and pressed her lips together again.

"Oh, nothing. Just a little surprise for Danny."

"Huh?"

She chuckled. "Never mind."

Moments later, as the final car disappeared down the tracks, the crowd who'd gathered to see them off reluctantly dispersed.

Then three days later, they gathered one more time to see off the last of the 390th crew members. This time, as they watched the train pull away, the resulting silence enveloped them with an immediate sadness so deep, Anya could physically feel it. Charlie wrapped his arm around his wife, his other around Anya's shoulders, and held them firm in his grasp.

"Am I the only one who feels like we're the only three people left in all the world?"

"I feel it too," Sophie said, leaning her head on his shoulder.

"Me too," Anya added quietly.

"Well, I don't know about you, but it's nothing a good Sunday roast can't comfort," he said, turning them to go. "Shall we?"

18

Along with the departure of the 390th and the vacuum of utter silence left in its wake, came a more sobering reality. Major Samford, no doubt halfway home by now, had gladly rid himself of Anya's "situation." With the base shutting down, all future contacts regarding her status as a war bride would be handled by the American Embassy in London. Just as well, since he'd made it abundantly clear that she and the other local war brides were no longer his problem. Still, having no one there in town to cut through what he called "miles of red tape" frustrated her beyond words.

Her last meeting with him had not gone well.

"Mrs. McClain, you don't seem to understand. And quite frankly, with as many visits as you've made here over the past weeks, I would've thought you would accept the fact that I can only do so much since you are not British. It's hard enough getting the forms filed for all these local gold diggers. The fact that you're Dutch makes it—"

"Excuse me, what do you mean by 'gold diggers'? I'm not familiar with these words."

He busied himself, focusing on the messy stack of papers on his desk. "It's just an expression. Nothing more."

"Yes, I assumed so. But what does it mean?" she asked again, her words slow and measured as if speaking to a child.

He lifted his shoulders in a shrug. "It's what we call the English girls who want a free ticket to America. We've all met their kind. They're a dime a dozen. They chat up some lonely GI, convince him to marry them—maybe even pop out a kid or two—just so they can escape this war-ravaged country with a free pass courtesy of Uncle Sam."

Anya dismissed the mention of this relative called Sam and stood abruptly, the chair scraping against the floor behind her. "How *dare* you. What a despicable thing to say! Do you have any idea what it's been like for those of us whose homelands have been practically destroyed by war? Do you? Have you even been on the battlefield, Major? Have you lived through the horrors we have experienced? Of course not because you sit here in your comfortable office, shuffling papers and acting like some kind of god making judgment on people you know nothing about, choosing who will go and who will—"

"Look, Mrs. McClain—"

"I am not finished! Do you think I like having to crawl in here week after week, begging you for a chance to somehow, some way put me on one of those ships to America, and all the while wondering why it is you don't seem to have even a trace of understanding of what it's been like for people like me? Do you think I *like* having to pin my every hope for a chance to see my husband again on the likes of you and all your mightier-than-thou arrogance when all the while—"

She stopped abruptly, her heart racing and eyes prickling, as she suddenly realized her mistake. Losing her temper and mouthing off to him could destroy any chance of passage to America.

What have I done? What have I done!

She closed her eyes and took a deep breath before risking a glance.

He yanked off his glasses with a dramatic flair and pinched the bridge of his nose.

She lowered her head and tried to slow the beating of her heart. "I'm sorry. I shouldn't have spoken to you like that."

He eased his glasses back on, once again refusing to look up from his work. "Look, I've done all that I can. From here on, you're the embassy's problem, not mine. As you can see, we're packing up to leave, so if you don't mind, I have a mountain of paperwork to sift through before we go."

She waited, watching him scribble notes on a paper as he dismissed her. Without saying another word, she left the room.

Just outside the door, a young corporal put a finger to his lips then motioned silently, inviting her to follow him around the corner. She recognized him as Samford's assistant who manned the desk outside the major's office. He showed her into a vacant office then quietly closed the door.

"Ma'am, I couldn't help but overhear what you just said to Major Samford in there—"

"I'm so terribly sorry. I was totally out of line and should never have—"

"No! That's why I wanted to speak to you. I've had to work with him for two long years, ma'am, and I've wanted to chew him out pretty much every single day. Course, if I did, I would've been court marshaled and sent to the brig for the rest of my life." His face warmed to a lopsided smile as he held his hand out to her. "I just wanted to thank you. It was a real pleasure hearing what you just said to him. And he sure deserved to hear it."

She shook his hand though still concerned. "Yes, but don't you see? He'll never put my name on that manifest now. For all I know, my file has already been tossed in his trash bin, never to be seen again."

"Oh, don't you worry about that," he said with the same goofy smile as he folded his arms confidently across his chest. "Major Samford thinks he runs the show, but fact is, nothing happens here unless *I* send the paperwork through."

"I don't understand."

"Ma'am, I'm sure it's all very confusing, but let's just say an officer like the major is only as good as the corporal who does all his grunt work. He'll hand those files over to me today to send to the American Embassy in London. And I feel it is my duty as a patriot to make sure *your* file is at the top of that pile. The way I see it, once Lieutenant McClain flew back to the States, Samford took a disliking to you. And just so you know, that's got nothing to do with you, but everything to do with his high opinion of himself. You were right when you said what you did. He thinks he's more powerful than the Almighty, if you know what I mean. And for whatever reason, he decided to give you a hard time."

"But what did I do to make him dislike me so? I've made

every effort to be as polite as possible in all my encounters with him. Well, until today."

"Absolutely. But the fact that you've stopped by here almost every day could in itself be the problem. I'm guessing he just got tired of being bothered. Which, no doubt, was how he perceived all your visits."

She blew out a slow breath, hoping the young corporal was right. She looked at his shock of red hair, the freckles across his nose, and eyes the color of a springtime sky back home, and knew she could trust him. "You really think you can do what you said? Put my file on top?"

"Not a problem. He'll never see it again after he hands it over."

"I can't thank you enough, Corporal—"

"Werthan. Corporal Christopher Werthan. But heck, I'm the one who should be thanking *you*, Mrs. McClain. Besides, I always liked your husband. A lot of flyboy officers who pass through here think they're too good to be nice to someone of lower rank like me. Lieutenant McClain was always respectful, always said a kind word after returning my salute."

"That's nice to hear. I'll be sure and tell him how helpful you've been."

"Good, and I hope you can tell him in person real soon. You don't worry, Mrs. McClain. I'll make sure you get on one of the first ships that sail for America."

She held out her hand for a shake, her voice graveled. "Thank you, Corporal. Thank you so much."

He gave her a firm handshake in return. "My pleasure, ma'am."

Something changed. She had felt it almost immediately as

she began her walk back to the pub. A renewed sense of hope lightened her step. Finally—*finally*—someone had taken her seriously. Someone who could do what needed to be done to send her to America.

Walking along the long, dusty road back to town, Anya made a decision. Telling off Samford had felt good. *So* very good. And even though she'd been terrified, thinking she blew it, she had to admit it felt good to stand on her own two feet again. It felt familiar. Like the Anya of old, straightening her backbone, and speaking up for herself, no longer intimidated. If she could master her blasted emotions before crossing the ocean, she might actually make it to Chicago, America and have a genuine chance for a good life with Danny.

No more tears. No more gloomy thoughts. No more sadness.

When she entered the pub, Patrick called to her from behind the bar. "Ah, Anya, I'm glad you're here. A letter just came in the post for you. From America!"

She rushed behind the bar, snatched the letter from his hand, and planted a kiss on his rosy cheek.

"Well then, off you go up to your room. I know you'll be wanting to read your letter."

"Thank you, Patrick!" she called, already halfway up the stairs.

She tossed her things on the dresser and stretched out on the bed, opening the envelope. Only then did she realize the handwriting wasn't Danny's.

My dearest Anya,

It seems I've known you for years, even though I've never had the honor of meeting you in person. It's been

many years now, but I still remember the joy of finding
your letters in our mailbox because I knew how much
Danny cherished them. I always had a smile on my
face when I left them on his pillow. It seems so long
ago, doesn't it? In many ways, a lifetime.

And now, here we are, all these years later, and
we're family! How I would have loved to have been
there for your wedding. I know I would have cried
buckets of tears—all of them happy, I assure you.

Dear Anya, we are so excited that you'll be joining
us soon! Danny knows I'm praying for you, asking God
to clear the path of any obstacles that would hinder
you from coming. I have prayed for you these many
years. What a joy it shall be to finally welcome you
into our arms, our home, our lives.

Until then, be well and know that we are counting
the minutes until you arrive.

With all my love,
Mother McClain

Anya set the letter aside, trying to imagine what Danny's
mother looked like. What did her voice sound like? How did
she react to Danny's father and his many tirades? Try as she
might, she couldn't quite imagine what her life would be like
living with these people. Would Mr. McClain be aloof toward
her? Would he grumble in her presence or make her feel like
an intruder? Would Joey and Millie accept her? Would the
house be crowded with all of them living under one roof?

She blew a strand of hair off her forehead and tried to stop
the litany of questions and doubts. Where was that new

resolve she'd just made on her way back to the pub?

Anya closed her eyes, doing her best to let it all go. Moments later, she read Mrs. McClain's letter again. There, toward the end, the words she'd skimmed over the first time practically leaped off the page at her ... *I'm praying for you, asking God to clear the path of any obstacles that would hinder you from coming.*

Her biggest obstacle? That was easy. Major Samford's indifferent shrug filled the picture screen in her mind. Then, in a blink of the eye, that image was replaced by the kind, lopsided grin of Corporal Werthan.

Could it be? Was it possible God just answered Betty McClain's prayer for her path to be cleared of any obstacle?

Goose bumps pebbled across her skin as she tried to grasp the significance of what just happened. Something strangely familiar chased those goose bumps away, though she wasn't ready to acknowledge anything—or *Anyone*—just yet.

18 August 1945
Sioux Falls, South Dakota

> *Dear Anya,*
>
> *Greetings from Sioux Falls, South Dakota! Couldn't believe my leave was already over last Friday. Sure went fast. I had to report to Camp Grant to board a troop train headed for South Dakota. Mass chaos*

seems to be the order of the day with all the rumors following Japan's surrender earlier this week. I'm not sure what to make of the atomic bomb situation. Like everyone else, I'm thrilled the war with Japan is finally over, but concerned about this new bomb and its potential if it ever got into the wrong hands. I sure hope President Truman knows what he's doing.

Regardless, I still had to report for duty. There are thousands of us here, and no one seems to know what to do with all of us. We're on pins and needles wondering when we'll be able to go home for good. They have to discharge us at some point, but right now it's just a guessing game. There are all sorts of betting pools on what day the war would be declared over and what time of day it would be announced, when we might be discharged, and a thousand other fodder for gamblers. What else are a bunch of restless soldiers going to do?

Unfortunately, I can answer that question myself. With nothing to do, the guys are all edgy and getting on each other's nerves. Some keep pulling rank, doing stupid stuff like punishing subordinates for not saluting when their vehicle passes—then making them march in circles for an hour, just for something to do.

It's so strange, Anya. Some of the guys are actually nervous about leaving the military, even wishing they'd send us back to England. The other day at mess, a guy from Michigan was all jitters, talking crazy about nightmares he keeps having. Another guy said he couldn't stand being home when he was on leave. Couldn't relate to his wife and kids anymore.

Sure makes you wonder, doesn't it? Since I've never had any of those thoughts cross my mind, I had no idea what to say.

Word around base is, it could take up to a year or more to sort through all the red tape and get us set up for the benefits promised through the GI Bill. There's been a lot of confusion about what the government will or won't do. I keep hearing about something they're calling the "52-20 Club." Best I can understand, they're supposed to pay us $20 a week for up to 52 weeks to help out with expenses until we get a job. Not sure how that would work with me going back to school, but if it's available, I'll sure take it. Maybe we can put it into savings for our first house. We'll see.

I'm happy to say Sophie (the dog) is doing much better. I went to visit her before I left, and Dr. Lister said he'd release her in a couple more days. I hoped she might be home before I left, but at least I'll know she'll get lots of TLC from Dad in my absence. I'm still so thankful she didn't die. Mrs. Smithson called a few times to see how she's doing. It's a good thing Mom answered the phone. I'm not sure I could be civil toward her.

Turns out the other dog had been picked up by the dog pound but escaped. Apparently, it attacked one of the dog catchers then took off. I guess I should be thankful he never got close enough to attack Sophie. She wouldn't have stood a chance. That mutt had to weigh at least a hundred pounds, and all of them mean.

What a relief to hear Corporal Werthan came to your rescue! I remember him always being friendly and courteous. Sure would like to shake his hand for helping you out. Have you been in touch with the American Embassy yet? I'll bet it's as chaotic there as it is here, what with so many brides wanting to get passage to the U.S. Have you thought about making a trip down to London to make a personal visit? Maybe Charlie and Sophie would go with you. Just a thought. Let me know when you hear anything. I keep dreaming about the moment I see you at the pier. It can't happen fast enough!

Lots to look forward to once I get discharged. I'm anxious to get registered for my classes, so I've asked Mom to go ahead and send in my forms since I hope to be home in time for the start of school.

But more than anything else, I'm looking forward to having you come home to me. Anya, I'm so excited about the life we can have together and all the plans we might make, but mostly I just want to hold you in my arms and give you a thousand kisses. Until then, just know there's a guy over here in the good ol' U.S.A. who misses you so much, he thinks he just might lose his mind.

Loving you always,

Danny

P.S. I forgot to tell you my uniform felt mighty snug after four weeks of Mom's cooking! She was pleased, needless to say.

19

1 September 1945

Framlingham, England

Dear Danny,

Only today did I receive your letter of 18 August, so I'm taking a chance and sending this to your home in Chicago instead. If you're not yet home, surely you will be soon. I didn't want to risk it getting lost in Sioux Falls, South Dakota. I had to look it up on the map downstairs on the pub wall. Such a strange word— Sioux. I couldn't imagine how to pronounce it, but Charlie said it for me. After locating it on the map, I felt even farther apart from you, and wondered how much longer it might be before we are reunited.

We're still trying to adjust to the strange silence here in Framlingham since the base was closed. We *keep thinking we'll get used to it, but we haven't yet. Of course, everyone here is happy for those who've returned home now that the war is over, but at the same time we miss the sights and sounds of all you American soldiers. The other day Sophie and I walked over to the base, and the silence was "deafening" as we've heard others say. Already weeds are creeping through the pavement on the runways. Charlie said the runways and much of the perimeter track would eventually be torn up to restore the farmland, but who knows when that might happen. We've also heard rumors that the farmers wish to use the control tower to store fertilizer—something I would normally laugh about, but it struck me as another sad reminder that all the Americans are truly gone for good.*

I do have a bit of news to share. I received a post yesterday from the American Embassy in London. They've requested I come for several interviews and instructed me to bring a number of documents with me —including a sworn statement from you that you can support me when I arrive in America. Since you will be a full-time student, I don't know if they'll approve it.

I was also asked to send them your home address. They will send your parents a form to complete for my file. They must also supply a statement about their finances, and agree to sponsor me as their "child" and support me as long as necessary in case you are unable to. Danny, I <u>hate</u> this! I do not wish to impose on your parents and their financial privacy! But I have no choice. I only hope they will not be offended by this.

It's all so confusing.

When I go to London, they will make appointments for me to undergo several physical examinations and get the required inoculations. I am already dreading the trip and wondered what might happen if I refused to go. But I know that would mean I might never travel to America.

The letter stated that I will be notified at some point to move to a place called Camp Tidworth near Southampton. Sophie told me it's located on the southern coast of England about 75 miles southwest from London (about 300 miles from here). That is where they will assemble all of us "war brides" to await passage. I only hope it's a short stay. I'd rather wait here in Framlingham until it's my turn to sail.

I forgot to mention previously how much I appreciated the letter from your mother. From what you've always told me of her, and from her letter, she seems to be such a kind person, and I'm looking forward to meeting her.

That was such a tragic story you wrote about your father losing his young friend in World War I. Yes, it certainly accounts for why he is the way he is. That and the story about his dog Barney. It is very hard for me to imagine him any way other than gruff and unfriendly. Still, I was touched to hear of his concern for you while you were MIA and for Sophie's recent crisis, so I shall try very hard to think of him in kinder ways.

I wrote to Helga again—my mother's friend back in

Utrecht—asking once more if she had any luck finding my birth certificate. I've only had the one letter from her; the one with my visa which I received before you left. I can only assume the post is delayed because of all the reorganization efforts across Europe since the war ended. I hope she responds before I have to report to Camp Tidworth.

I miss you so much, Danny. With you so far away, it's as though a hollow place in my heart grows wider every day, and I've no way to stop it. I can't tell you how many times a day I touch the charms of my bracelet and long for you. I miss you so much at times I can hardly breathe. If only I could count the days until I see you again, but I have no idea when that might be. Is it too optimistic to hope for Christmas?

Please let me know when you've returned to Chicago.

Love,

Anya

7 September 1945

London, England

Anya was relieved when Sophie insisted on accompanying her on the day trip to London for her appointment at the American Embassy. They chatted nonstop on the early train ride down to London, which helped calm Anya's nerves tremendously, especially as they neared the city. The bombing damage devastated her at first sight, until she steeled herself against the images, focusing on the task at hand. Once they arrived at Victoria Station, they hopped aboard one of the double-decker buses which delivered them to Grosvenor Square.

Though the day was still young, Anya's dress already clung to her despite the mild temperature. As they approached the long rectangular building, the sight of the American flag fluttering high above gave her pause. But any hesitance was soon forgotten when they joined the long queue at the embassy gate. Sophie's ever-present optimism kept the mood light; at least until she was told she could not enter the compound with Anya.

"It's no problem. I'll be waiting right over there on those benches."

The guard pushed up the bill of his cap. "I hope you brought a long book to read. Your friend here will be inside most of the day."

Sophie gave Anya a hug. "Then I shall pop into that book shop we passed and treat myself to a cup of tea while I'm there. Don't you worry about me."

"I'm sorry, Sophie. I had no idea it would take so long."

"Not another word. I haven't been to London in ages. It'll do me good to take a walkabout. If I'm not here when you're done, just wait for me at that bench, all right?"

With a wave, Anya turned on her heel, took a deep breath, and followed the other women making their way into the embassy. A few moments later, someone called her name.

"Anya? Is that you?"

She turned and searched the crowded hall. There, standing on tiptoe and waving at her stood Sybil, the English girl they'd met on their honeymoon. The relief at seeing another familiar face was so comforting, Anya rushed toward her.

"Sybil!" Before she could utter another word, Sybil engulfed her in a hug.

"Oh, it *is* you! I can't believe it!" Sybil laughed, still hugging her. "I was so hoping to see you again, and here you are!"

Only when she pulled back did Anya see the pronounced tummy beneath her frock. "Oh my goodness, I didn't know you were—"

"Neither did I!" Sybil set a loving hand on her stomach and laughed. "That is to say, I didn't know I was pregnant the last time I saw you. I was so surprised and literally shocked when I found out. Had to ring Jack clear over in America to tell him the good news."

"He must be thrilled to find out he's going to be a father. I'm so happy for you."

"Thank you, and aren't you kind to say so? But enough about me. How have you been? Is Danny here with you—that is your husband's name, isn't it? Danny?"

"Yes, Danny. But no, he flew to America at the end of June."

Sybil squeezed Anya's hand. "Oh, isn't it the hardest? I often wondered if you all thought me quite the fool for the way I carried on that day after Jack left."

"Not at all. I couldn't imagine it at the time, how hard it was, and now I know."

"Isn't it? But somehow we'll get through this together.

Where are you staying? Are you living here in London now?"

"No, I'm still staying in Framlingham with our friends. I'm here for the day to meet with the liaison for war brides. Is that why you're here?"

"Yes. You, me, and the other thousand women here today. Honestly, the queues for seeing these officials are endless. It's so hard not to get discouraged. Sometimes I think I'll never see Jack again. Do you feel that way too?"

Anya's heart ached in response. "Yes, and I think about it constantly." She glanced around them. "And so much worse now, after seeing all these women. How will they ever manage all of us? Have you heard anything?"

Sybil grabbed her hand. "Come with me, and let's join the queue before it gets longer."

The line snaked around a corner and down a long corridor of closed doors. Anya bit the side of her lip, fighting the frustration. For more than six hours, they waited with all the others. Women cradling babies in their arms. Toddlers restless and whining. Cries of despair from brides who hadn't heard from their American husbands, wondering if they were forgotten. Angry rhetoric, inciting others to protest against the shoddy manner they'd all been treated.

The comments danced all around them.

"They told me it could be up to a year before they let us cross the ocean."

"I heard the Americans want us last on the list. They want all their GIs home first."

"Makes me wish I never married the Yank. Got me pregnant and off he sails for home. Fine kettle of fish this is."

"How am I supposed to feed my baby?"

"They're saying there are 50,000 of us war brides! The rate they're going here, we'll never see our men again."

"I heard it was 70,000. Maybe more!"

"Have you had your physical yet? Never been through anything so humiliating in all my life."

"Did you see that headline in *Stars and Stripes?* Said we 'war brides' were giving Uncle Sam a headache. Well, I say we give him more than just a headache if he doesn't do something soon!"

"I've got half a mind to divorce the Yank and be done with it."

Anya wished for cotton to stuff in her ears and wondered if all this was worth it. As the hours ticked by in the stifling heat of the endless embassy halls, Anya knew one thing for certain. She would have given up hours ago had it not been for Sybil's optimism and cheerful banter.

"Don't fret. Once we finally get in to see these officials, they'll be so weary, they'll whiz us through just to be done for the day. You'll see."

Helga had finally sent Anya's papers from Utrecht, though no birth certificate had been found. The Dutch government offices had sustained massive damage throughout the war, and could only issue unofficial papers verifying her birth from some records found in Amsterdam. Would that suffice? Was grouchy Major Samford right when he told her it was hard enough to sort through all the English brides, much less those from other countries?

With only moments to spare before the offices closed for the day, both Anya and Sybil finally had their turn. As Anya approached the officer sitting behind the small desk, she hoped—and even prayed—he wasn't like Major Samford. On a lark, she decided to borrow Shakespeare's concept and kill him with kindness as she handed over her documents.

"You must be exhausted from all this," she said with as gentle a smile as she could muster.

He looked up from the papers and studied her face. He was quite handsome; not at all what she'd expected to find sitting behind a desk doing such menial work. With a slight sigh and a weary smile, he nodded. "I am, but do you know you're the only one who's offered such a comment? Most of these brides come in here with a bone to pick, berating us for all the red tape, but we're just doing our job."

He studied her a moment longer, slowly setting her papers on the desk. "It's all quite frustrating, trying to help all of you. Don't get me wrong—I want to help." He looked around cautiously before leaning toward her, lowering his voice. "It's just that we're so ill-prepared for this. Unfortunately, that makes it difficult for all of you, having to wait and wait, and filling out all these forms."

"I can't imagine," she said. "In the queue, some said there were as many as 70,000 of us applying for passage to America. Is that true?"

He nodded and rolled his eyes. "Before it's all over, I'd say it will be closer to twice that many, if you include all the rest of Europe." His eyes narrowed a bit. "Your accent. Dutch?"

Her heart fluttered. "Yes, but I've been here for several months. My husband was stationed with the 390th in Framlingham."

He waited for more. She hesitated.

"It's a long story."

He chuckled. "They all are. Okay, let's see what you have and what you need." He looked over the documents she'd provided, then shuffled through his files. He pulled out a folder with her name typed on it as well as Danny's military documentation.

"Well then, Mrs. McClain. I see Corporal Werthan from the 390th has requested special attention be given to you."

"Corporal Werthan. Yes. He was extremely helpful."

"Good. Let me just look through your file and make sure you've got all we need."

A few minutes later, he continued. "Yes, it looks like Captain Werthan did most of my work for me." He pressed a stamp into the ink pad then stamped all her forms. "Which means you're all set."

"All set?"

"All set. I've provided the forms you'll need for your physicals, and since you've already received approved VIP status thanks to Werthan, you're good to go."

Anya blinked in utter shock. "Thank you. Thank you *so* much."

"You're more than welcome."

She gathered her file and purse and stood to go. Then, without thinking, she held out her hand and gave him a firm handshake. "Thank you for your kindness, Lieutenant—"

"Powell. Phillip Powell."

She smiled. "Lieutenant Phillip Powell. I can't tell how much I appreciate your help."

"It's my pleasure, Mrs. McClain." He squeezed her hand again then let go. "God bless you on your journey to America."

His words rendered an instant wave of calm through her from head to toe. She smiled, unable to speak, but knowing without question that the American who'd held her hand was another answer to Betty McClain's prayers.

She couldn't wait to share the good news with Sophie.

20

12 September 1945

Chicago, Illinois

Dear Anya,

I'm on the train heading downtown for classes. One week in and I'm already behind in a couple of my courses. I don't remember this much reading, but I suppose that goes with the territory for a history major. These professors could learn a lot from Mrs. Zankowski about making the material more interesting, but overall I like most of them.

I feel like I'm a hundred years old compared to the other kids in my classes. Makes sense because it sure feels like that long since I was in school before the war.

I know you're not a big Cubs fan (yet!), but I have to tell you what happened the other day. Joey got to know a guy named Marv who's been a regular at the theater for the past few months. Real nice guy who lost his son at Pearl Harbor, so obviously he took a liking to Joey. Turns out he's a ticket-taker at Wrigley Field where the Cubs play! So Joey asked if he could get some good tickets for us to a game or two. (I can't remember if I told you that uniformed servicemen get in free at Wrigley – I guess as a gesture of support of the troops.)

Anyway, he said it would be his honor to give Joey a couple of complimentary tickets for as many games as we want! Isn't that great!? He even said he'd make sure we'd have seats for the World Series games if the Cubs keep playing as well as they are. How about that!

All that to say, I'll definitely take you to some games once you come home! Now, I'm sure you're probably rolling your eyes about now ... but I promise you'll enjoy going. Everyone here has Cubs fever! Well, except for the White Sox fans, of course. I'm not kidding when I say this could be our year! Now if we can just get you on that ship before the season ends.

Otherwise, we've fallen into a routine around here. I'm helping at the theater when I can, plus I've applied for some jobs on campus. It's so different from the Evanston campus where I used to go, but I'm getting used to it.

You wouldn't believe how much little Jimmy has grown. I had no idea babies develop so fast. Joey is determined to make me change one of Jimmy's dirty diapers, but Mom always comes to my rescue. She says I'll have plenty of opportunity to learn when you and I have our own kids. Have to say I'm already looking forward to that. Especially if we have a little girl as pretty as you.

Let me know if you've heard anything or if they've given you a departure date. I know the waiting must be so hard, but I'm glad to hear Sybil is there with you through the process. Who would've imagined on the day we ran into them in London that you and she would become good friends?

Everyone here sends their love. Tell Sophie, Charlie, and Patrick hello for me. I sure miss all of them, but nowhere near as much as I miss YOU. The nights are the hardest. "Sophie-the-dog" is doing much better, though she still requires lots of help. She keeps me company at night, but she's no substitute for my beautiful wife. In case you wondered.

With all my love,

Danny

Danny filed out of his *European Civilization* class with the other students and headed across campus. He had an hour break before his last class of the day at 11:00, and usually camped out in one of the study nooks at Schaffner Library.

But with the weather so nice, he opted to stay outdoors. He found a bench near the pond not far from his classroom and dug an apple out of his satchel.

It still felt odd, being back in school. Almost like he didn't belong. Last year at this time, he hadn't yet made the trip across the Atlantic to his base in Framlingham; hadn't yet flown a mission, and didn't have a clue that one day he would parachute out of a B-17 into Occupied Holland. It all seemed so distant now, more like a dream than reality.

Yet here he was, back in school on a busy college campus with no visible evidence of the war they'd just fought and won. He wondered how many guys on campus here were like him—veterans getting their education thanks to the GI Bill. He'd surely passed them in the halls, fairly confident he could tell which of them had seen action overseas. Something in their eyes. Loss of innocence, perhaps? Memories from the battlefield still fresh in their minds? Prolonged grief for lost friends? Didn't matter. They all shared a distinct maturity beyond their years.

He took another bite of his apple and opened his textbook as a stiff breeze whipped his bookmark and sent it sailing.

"I've got it," a voice behind him called.

As he stood and turned around, he locked eyes with her.

"Danny?" she gasped.

"Beverly?"

She'd changed her hair, wore it shorter now. But otherwise, his college sweetheart looked the same. He swallowed hard. "What are you doing here?"

"I can't believe it's you! I work here on campus." She blushed as she handed him the renegade bookmark. "I never expected ... I mean, after all these years? What are you doing here?"

"I'm back in school. Finishing my degree, thanks to Uncle Sam."

"The GI Bill?"

"Yes."

"I knew you were in the Army Air Force. Co-pilot, was it?"

"Yes, but how did you know?"

"Friends. Friends of friends. That sort of thing."

He felt his face warm. "Well, yes, I flew B-17s. Co-pilot. Stationed in England." He cleared his throat, hating the nervous quiver in his voice. "You?"

"Me?" She smiled. "No, I didn't fly B-17s. Or any other plane, for that matter."

"No, I meant Ron. Or was it Ronnie? I can't remember."

She looked away with a shift in her countenance. "Ronnie was in the navy. He was a fighter pilot on the USS *Princeton.*" She looked back in his direction, her eyes moist. "Last October, the *Princeton* was part of a task force trying to take back the Philippines. Ronnie's ship was destroyed by a single Japanese bomb dropped on the flight deck. He'd just returned for refueling."

She pressed her knuckle to the corner of one eye then the other. "I keep thinking I'm done with these pesky tears, and then here they come again—"

Without so much as a thought, he dropped his apple and moved to her side. She stiffened, hesitating at first, then relaxed her head against his shoulder. It felt so familiar, and yet—different. He startled, realizing what he'd done and took an awkward step back.

"I'm, uh ... sorry." He dug out his handkerchief and offered it to her.

She looked at him, her brows pinched together as she took it. "No, I'm sorry. I shouldn't have—"

"No, I'm the one who's—"

She gulped a chuckle then let it go, dabbing at her eyes. "Look at us. A regular couple of clowns, aren't we?"

He scratched his eyebrow. "Yeah, sorry about that. I think it was just seeing you again so suddenly, then hearing about Ronnie ... look, why don't we sit down. Do you have time?"

"Yes, I'm on my break." She took a seat as he sat a safe distance from her.

"What do you do here?"

"I'm the assistant director of public relations for the university. We do marketing, publicity, recruitment. That sort of thing."

He nodded, looking out across the pond. "Sounds like the perfect job for you."

"Oh, I don't know. Mostly it just pays the rent these days."

He looked over at her again. "Listen, Beverly, I'm really sorry about Ronnie. I lost friends too, but I can't imagine losing someone you love."

She took a deep breath then slowly let it out. "It's been hard. Really hard. One minute, I was saying goodbye to my handsome husband, all decked out in his dress whites. The next thing I know, a car pulls up to my house and two very somber naval officers knock on my door. No one ever prepares you for that."

She wiped at her eyes again, then folded the handkerchief and handed it back to him.

"No, you keep it. I've got plenty of others."

Beverly nodded then turned to face him. "Thank you. But I'm glad to know you made it through the war and came home. I'm sure your family was relieved and happy when you returned. What about your brother Joey? Has he recovered from his injuries?"

"Joey's doing fine. Married to a great girl and they just had a baby a couple of months ago."

"That's nice. Good for them. And what about you? Is there a *Mrs.* Danny McClain?"

"Yes there is. Her name is Anya. In fact, I think I once told you about her. Remember the pen pal in Holland I had in high school? His name was Hans and he died—"

"—while trying to save a young girl who was drowning. Of course I remember. It was such a tragic story."

"Yes, it was. Anya is his sister who wrote to tell me what happened. Then she and I started writing and became friends."

"Okay, I remember her too, but I'm confused. As I recall, you never heard from her again after the Germans invaded Holland, right? How in the world did you meet her?"

"You wouldn't believe it."

For the next few minutes, Danny explained the complicated story; told her about their wedding in England, and how anxious he was for her to sail to America. He even pulled out his wallet and showed her the picture from their wedding.

"She's lovely, Danny. Such a beautiful love story. I'm truly happy for you."

"Thanks, Beverly. I appreciate that."

They sat in silence for a couple of minutes until Danny remembered the time and checked his watch. "I've got class starting in ten minutes, so I need to go." He stood and gathered his books.

"It's good to see you again," she said, standing.

"Yes, for me, too. Quite a shock after all these years, but nice."

As he turned to go, she caught his arm. "Danny?"

"Yes?"

"I probably shouldn't ask, but ... would you meet for coffee sometime?"

He felt his eyebrows arch and tried to work them back down. "Uh, well, I guess—"

She looked away. "It's just that I'd like to ... well, there are things I need to say. If you would allow me?"

He glanced at his watch, stalling. "Uh, well, I guess that would be okay. I'm only on campus on Monday, Wednesday, and Friday, so—"

"Then how about Friday? Day after tomorrow?"

"Okay. My break starts at 10:00."

"Good. Then I'll meet you at the campus coffee shop."

"Okay."

"Okay. Friday at ten. I'll see you then."

She turned to go the other way as Danny made his way to the sidewalk. His heart stuttered as he wondered what in the world he was thinking to agree to a coffee date with his college sweetheart.

His *ex*-college sweetheart.

Now a widow.

Never mind that I'm a married man.

21

"You're kidding, right?"

Danny felt the heat creeping up his neck as the porch swing moved slowly back and forth. "I know, I know. I'm an idiot. But I just couldn't say no to her, Joey. She seemed so, I don't know, needy? Or something. And she was never like that before. Never."

Joey's rocker creaked with each movement as he chewed on a toothpick and studied his younger brother. The scrutiny caused Danny to look away, turning his gaze across the front lawn.

"Back up. Tell me again why you agreed to meet Beverly for coffee."

"Look, it's no big deal. Maybe I felt like I owed it to her since she lost her husband in the war. Or maybe I'm just curious what she needs to tell me. I don't know. I just felt like I couldn't say no."

"Wasn't this the same girl who broke your heart a few years back?"

"Of course it is. And if anyone has something that needs to be said, it ought to be me. I'm the one who got dumped."

Joey kept rocking, his eyes glued on Danny. "I guess it's none of my business, but if you think you have to meet her, then make sure it's the *last* time you meet her. Got it?"

"Absolutely."

"Meet who?" Millie asked, letting the screen door slap behind her. She handed Jimmy to his father whose face lit up when the little guy cooed a smile.

"Did you miss your daddy, little man?" Joey tucked his son against his chest. "How about you and I have a nice little rock here on Grandma's porch?"

Millie took the other rocker. "Who's this you're meeting, Danny? Anyone I know?"

"No, just an old friend from school."

"An old *girlfriend* from school," Joey added.

She stopped rocking. "What? You're seeing an old girlfriend?"

"It's nothing. Really."

"Nothing, huh? Then you'll be writing Anya to tell her, will you?"

Danny swallowed over the baseball-size lump in his throat. He coughed as a wave of guilt swept through him, then faked another one. "Of course, I will. I hide nothing from my wife."

"Well then. Good for you." Millie gave him a wink.

"Good for you," Joey echoed. "Hey, Cubs are playing the Phillies on Friday. Dad said he'd work the theater so you and I could go. Will that work for you?"

"Sure! I'll just meet you at Wrigley after my last class. I'm done at noon. Game starts at 1:30 so I should be there by 12:30. Just let me know where to meet you."

"Will do. This could be the year, brother."

"This *is* the year, brother!"

14 September 1945

Chicago, Illinois

Danny awoke with a serious case of the jitters on Friday morning. He looked himself in the eye while shaving and asked for the umpteenth time why he'd agreed to meet Beverly for coffee. And, for the umpteenth time, he told himself he was overthinking the whole thing. He'd written Anya the night before, primarily to keep himself accountable and completely aboveboard. He felt sure she'd understand.

Well, mostly sure.

He wrote about everything else he could think of before adding a brief note about Beverly.

You won't believe who I ran into on campus. Remember Beverly, the girl at Northwestern who dumped me for a football player? I had no idea she was working at the downtown campus. Really weird seeing her again. I found out her husband was killed in action last fall when his aircraft carrier was bombed

*by the Japs. I told her all about you and showed her
the picture from our wedding day. She seemed really
happy for us.*

*Anyway, we're having coffee on Friday. She said
there's something she needs to tell me. Seeing her
again only confirmed how lucky a guy I am to be
married to you and how much I love you. I feel sorry
for her losing her husband, but mostly I'm just glad
she dumped me. Otherwise I might never have enlisted
and crossed paths with you in Holland. In a strange
way I guess I should thank her for that, huh?*

The problem was, no matter how legitimate it looked on
paper, he couldn't help wondering if it would upset Anya. On
and on, the argument battled through his mind. By the time
he got to his first class, he'd made up his mind to meet
Beverly, then explain why he couldn't stay.

As he entered the student union coffee shop, she waved
him over to a corner table.

"I would have bought you a cup of coffee, but I wasn't sure
you'd come."

"That's okay, because I'm afraid I can't stay."

Her expression fell, and he felt like a jerk.

"It's just that, as much as I try to convince myself
otherwise, I know Anya would not be comfortable with me
seeing you again. No matter how innocent. And I'd never do
anything to hurt her. I hope you understand."

"Oh. Well, I ..." She looked away but said nothing more.

He pulled out a chair and sat down. "Beverly, I'm sorry. I
just didn't want to give you the wrong impression or
anything."

"No, I understand, Danny. Honest I do. But I'd never do anything to interfere with your relationship with your wife. I would hope you know that."

He held her eyes for a moment before she continued.

"The thing is, I simply wanted to apologize for what happened between us, back before the war. I was young and stupid, if you must know, and I was a fool for hurting you the way I did."

"It's okay. Besides, that was a lifetime ago, so—"

"I know, but I made a vow to myself that if I ever had the opportunity, I would apologize to you. Because in choosing Ronnie, I made an enormous mistake. Not long after he shipped out to the Pacific, I found out he'd been seeing someone. I knew because she came to me about a month later and was quite pregnant. Apparently he'd been seeing her off and on for quite some time. I didn't believe her at first, and certainly didn't think the child was Ronnie's, but she had pictures of the two of them together. She showed me a handful of letters addressed to her in his handwriting. I was so stunned, I quite literally couldn't comprehend all of it."

"I'm so sorry."

"No, I'm the one who's sorry. I know you, Danny McClain, and I know *you* would never do such a thing. You're a good and decent man. Which is why I've wanted to ask for your forgiveness. And the thing is, I've always known that I needed to say it more than you needed to hear it. Especially now, after saying you wouldn't do anything that might hurt Anya's feelings. Because I know that feeling all too well." She pressed her lips into a trembling smile.

Danny folded his hands together and studied them, his

mind a jumble as he searched for the right words.

"Beverly, um ... well, thank you. But you don't owe me an apology. Seriously, you don't. We were *both* young and stupid back then. I think everyone is at that age. Yes, you broke my heart, but like most things that happen to us along the way, I learned from it. I never wished you ill, or that Ronnie would hurt you like that." He shook his head. "I guess I'll never understand why people do the things they do. When I was overseas, guys were always getting those 'Dear John' letters everyone talked about. It's hard enough waking up each morning wondering if today would be the day you die, but getting a letter like that? Brutal. And like it or not, it always affected the whole crew.

"But at the same time, I saw plenty of guys cheating on their wives. With lots of beautiful English girls around, and all of them smitten with American flyboys—well, it just happens. But I just don't get it. Never did, never will. Guess I'm just too old-fashioned."

"No, I think you were raised with a solid foundation of morals. I noticed that about you from the first time we met."

The mention of it flashed him back to the fall of 1941. He was working behind the counter of The Grill at Northwestern, a popular soda shop on the Evanston campus. "Hi there, Danny," she'd said. She ordered a cup of coffee and a brownie, and he'd fallen for her head over heels.

"Danny?"

He blinked, dismissing the memory. "Oh, well, I should probably go." He checked his watch then stood and grabbed his satchel. "Thanks for understanding, Beverly. I'm sure I'll see you around campus, but—"

"Not a problem, Danny."

He glanced at her once more, then made his way out the door and up the stairs to the campus post office where he mailed his letter to Anya.

And prayed she'd understand.

22

Wrigley Field, Chicago, Illinois

Danny spotted Joey waiting at the appointed gate when he arrived. He introduced him to his new friend, ticket-taker Marvin Clancy, who vigorously shook his hand and thanked him for his service during the war.

Marvin slipped the tickets out of his shirt pocket. "Great seats, only five rows up behind the Cubs dugout," he said with a broad smile. "And I'm sure you know we're playing a doubleheader today since we got rained out yesterday. These seats are yours for both games."

"Marv, you sure we can't pay you for these?" Joey asked.

"Get outta here. Your money's no good to me. Besides, you're both veterans so you get in free anyway. These just give you better seats."

Danny extended his hand a second time. "Thanks so much, Mr. Clancy."

"Call me Marv. And you're welcome. Have a good time, boys."

Joey wove his way through the crowded tunnel with Danny right behind him.

As they made their way to the third base side of the stadium, the powerful aromas of popcorn, hot dogs, and grilled burgers ushered back memories of years gone by when he and Joey came to the beloved park with gloves in hand. Their pockets filled with change, Danny and his brother came ready to buy snacks and sodas from the vendors. Double-headers dictated a splurge for hot dogs, and over the years, they'd decided that no hot dog tasted better than those eaten at Wrigley during a ball game.

"Never like this before the war," Danny shouted. "I can't believe this crowd."

"I know, isn't it great? Dad and I came to some games earlier this season, but they were nothing like this. Only goes to show you what a winning season can do. Here we go. This is our entrance."

They walked back into the sunshine and began their descent to the sectioned box seats behind the Cubs dugout. As they located their seats on the aisle, they looked at each other with grins so big, they had to laugh.

"Doesn't get much better than this, little brother!" Joey said.

"Wow—I forgot they painted the scoreboard and bleachers green last year. That'll take some getting used to, don't you think?"

"Lots of fans have been bellyaching about it, but that'll end once we win the pennant. Hey, look," Joey said, pointing toward the dugout. "There's Derringer making his way back from the bullpen. He must be pitching today."

"Still the flashy dresser with a hot temper?" Danny asked.

"Flashy as ever, still smoking his pipe in the clubhouse, and always ready for a fight," Joey said with a chuckle. "But he started the season as the winningest pitcher in the majors, so Grimm puts up with him."

Joey waved over a vendor and bought two bags of peanuts and two sodas, insisting on paying. "Hey, I'm the one with an income, so these are on me."

"You think you're a regular Rockefeller, don't you?"

"Hardly. Just happy to have my kid brother back at Wrigley with me."

"Happy to be here, big brother." Danny clapped him on the back. "Hey, is that still Roy Nelson playing the organ?"

"Sure is. Have to say I was surprised when other ballparks around the country started installing organs like ours here. Never thought baseball fans would go for it."

"Maybe, but you have to admit if Nelson weren't playing, it would seem awfully quiet now that we're so used to it."

"You're probably right."

As the team headed back to the dugout, Danny asked about the Cubs' beloved manager, Charley Grimm.

"They never should've let him go back in '38. Everyone was thrilled when Wrigley brought him back last year to replace Wilson. The team loves him, and wow, that makes *all* the difference in the world."

"Attention! Attention please!" cried the familiar voice over the PA system. "Have your pencil and scorecards ready, and I'll give you the correct lineup for today's first game!"

"Ol' Pat Pieper's still calling the games, eh?" Danny laughed as Joey nodded. "Do you remember Dad telling us how, back in the old days, Pieper used to run up and down the lines lugging his big megaphone to call the game?"

"Yeah, I heard him interviewed on the radio the other day. Said he always lost seven or eight pounds a game, especially in the dead heat of summer."

"PLAAAAAAAAY BAAAAALLLL!" Pieper roared.

The crowd cheered the Cubs then booed the Philadelphia Phillies as they took the field.

"I still can't believe we're having such a great season," Danny said, "especially with all the latecomers trickling back from the war."

"No kidding," Joey added. "Supposedly, out of the 600 or so major league ball players, about 360 were drafted into active service back in '41. Pretty much gutted some of the teams. Course, that gave a lot of the 4-F players a chance to shine."

"But how could those guys be fit enough to play ball, but culled from active service? Like Phil Cavarretta. He's been a powerhouse for years, so how come he didn't get drafted?"

"Some kind of hearing problem, I think. A lot of the 4-F guys had issues like that—problems that had no real impact on their playing. High blood pressure, ringing in the ears, color blindness, that sort of thing. And before the attack on Pearl in '41, guys who were married with kids didn't have to serve since the government didn't want them to leave their families with no income. Course, as the war dragged on, a lot of those guys were drafted anyway to do desk jobs on the home front."

"Didn't you tell me only nine guys showed up at the start of spring training down in French Lick?"

"Yeah, weird, huh? It was so bad, they had to hire some semi-pro players, and even some high school kids to play. Which was pretty funny since they could only play on weekends because of school. Can you imagine? And there was a 53-year-old coach who showed up to play at third." Joey shook his head and laughed before taking another swig of his soda. "I can't even picture what that team must have looked like. Oh, and get this—they were stretched so thin on the mound during some of the early spring training games, they had to borrow pitchers from the opposing teams."

"Unbelievable. Especially when you consider they started the season like that. And yet here they are, close to snatching the National League pennant!"

"Yep, that's our Cubs. And during a war, no less. But they had their challenges just like all the other clubs. Like traveling. Back in '42 when Roosevelt wrote his 'Green Light' letter, allowing baseball to continue during the war 'for the good of the country'—that was easier said than done. Since the troops had priority over the rails, the teams got bumped all the time which messed up everybody's schedule. The Phillies ended up in a baggage car once because there were so many soldiers on board."

"Couldn't happen to a nicer team," Danny teased.

"Got that right."

"So what's the situation with the lights? In one of your letters, you wrote that Wrigley finally bought some for night games, but handed them over to the navy once the war started. Think we'll get lights anytime soon?"

"He made a good call on that, since none of the stadiums could use lights during the blackouts. But I haven't heard any more about it. Guess the money's still tight even though the war's over."

About halfway through the game, Joey suddenly elbowed Danny. "I can't believe I forgot to ask you. Did you meet Beverly this morning?"

"Yes, and I'm glad I did. Mostly, she wanted to apologize for dumping me for Ronnie. Turns out he'd been cheating on her before he left for the Pacific. Not only that, his pregnant girlfriend showed up on Bev's doorstep."

"Ouch. That had to hurt."

"No kidding. So she not only lost her husband in the war, but she has to live with the fact he'd been unfaithful to her. I think that's why she wanted me to know how sorry she was for hurting me. And I'll be honest. As rotten as it was to hear how all that turned out for her, it felt kind of good when she admitted she'd made the wrong choice, picking him over me."

"Well, there you go. Nice to hear her say it, but no need to see her again. Right?"

Danny watched Phillies pitcher Andy Karl throw another strike. "What did you say?"

"I said there's no need to see Beverly again, right? Now that you heard what she had to say?"

Danny shrugged. "I'm sure I'll run into her on campus from time to time, but otherwise, no. And just so you know, I wrote a letter to Anya and told her all about it. Mailed it right after I met with Bev. So that's that."

"Here's hoping."

A pop fly sailed over their heads as fans scrambled to catch the foul ball.

"Here's hoping?" Danny asked. "What's that supposed to

mean?"

"Well, look at it from Anya's perspective," Joey began. "She's thousands of miles away, frustrated with all the delays of getting over here, and now she'll get a letter mentioning your old girlfriend who you've now seen *twice* and you're bound to see now and then on campus? Put yourself in her shoes. Wouldn't that make you a little jealous?"

Danny glanced at him, then shelled another peanut and tossed it in his mouth. "I see your point, but it's a little late now, don't you think? And let's not forget it was Millie who suggested I write Anya about seeing Beverly, just to keep it on the up-and-up."

Joey slurped more of his soda. "Oh, no you don't," he teased. "You got yourself into this. Don't be dragging Millie or me into your problems."

"Who said anything about problems?"

"Riiiiiight," Joey mused as the inning ended.

Danny arched his back as the Cubs took the field again. After warming up, Derringer threw his first pitch.

"I still can't get over the change in Dad. I keep waiting for the grumpy old guy to light into me or have an outburst at the dinner table. He's a lot more subdued than he used to be."

"Hey, considering what he used to be like, I have no complaints. In fact, it's been a real kick watching him with Jimmy. I doubt he ever cradled you or me like that when we were babies. Seems like when we were kids, all he ever did was try to make us as miserable as possible."

Danny laughed. "Well, it's obvious he didn't inflict too much harm. You make a pretty good father yourself, at least from where I'm sitting."

"Hey, it's easy when you're married to a great girl like Millie. She's smart and lovable, no matter what she does or has to put up with. To watch her, you'd think she was a pro at this parenting thing. And it's obvious Jimmy picks up on her confidence. Course, he's got us both wrapped around his little finger most of the time."

"You can say that again."

Their conversation ebbed and flowed as the game stretched on. In the seventh inning, the Phillies rallied two runs as Derringer lost his steam. Grimm sent in two relief pitchers, but the damage was done. The Phillies won 4-3.

"Sure hope we didn't bring them bad luck," Danny said, standing to take a stretch.

"We'll get 'em next game. Are you hungry?"

"Starving. The hot dogs are on me. Let's go stretch our legs and buy some on the way back."

Twenty minutes later, they'd wolfed down two dogs each and washed them down with a second round of soda. Back in their seats for the second game, they cheered as the Cubs and Phillies once again took their respective spots on the field.

"Glad Passeau is pitching this one," Danny said, happy to see number 13 take the mound. "I was hoping to see the old man pitch today. He's got to be nearing forty, right?"

"Nah, he's only thirty-six. He was another deferment. That gunshot wound to his left hand when he was a teenager must've scared off the draft board, but lucky for us it's never affected his pitching."

"Or his hitting. Didn't he start the season as one of the majors' best hitting pitchers?"

"Yeah, his bat has been on fire these past few years. He's racked up hits and home runs like you wouldn't believe. Cubs got their money's worth with Passeau."

"Sure hope he can give us a win this game. I'd hate to spend this many hours at Wrigley only to see them lose both games."

Thankfully, the Cubs romped the Phillies 6-0 in the second game as lucky number 13, Claude Passeau, pitched the shutout for his seventeenth win of the season. The Cubs were now 87-52-1 on the season, and the McClain brothers couldn't be happier.

23

20 September 1945

London, England

Anya made numerous trips to London, most of them by herself since Sybil would be with her once she arrived. On a trip in mid-September, she and Sybil endured the dreaded physicals. Anya received the required smallpox immunization, but since pregnant women were excluded from the requirement, Sybil didn't have one. Afterward, Anya felt feverish and her arm ached for hours, both common side effects of the immunization. She was grateful for a chance to rest that afternoon at Sybil's flat.

Sybil stretched out on the loveseat beneath a window and fanned herself. "I don't know why you don't go ahead and move in with me here and save all these trips back and forth to Framlingham."

Anya took a seat on an overstuffed chair. "I suppose at some point I will. Maybe it's childish, this attachment to

Sophie and Charlie. Patrick too. But when I'm with them at the pub, so close to the base, I feel closer to Danny, strange as that may sound."

"No, I understand. That's why I still go to Rainbow Corner a few nights each week. There's a reason that section of London is called 'Little America.' You can feel it when you walk in the door, even though most of the Americans are gone now. Still lots of personnel here, but mostly we see them on weekends. I've seen some of those boys from the embassy there. Nice fellas. Polite. We should go."

"What?"

"You and me. We should go. You're staying over tonight, so let's pop down to Piccadilly and see what's happening at the Rainbow. I can't believe I didn't think to take you before."

"But I feel awful right now. All clammy and my arm still hurts."

"Then take a little lie-down and let's see how you feel later. I promise you'll have a good time."

Against her better judgment, Anya agreed to accompany Sybil that evening to the famous American Red Cross Club at the corner of Shaftesbury Avenue and Piccadilly Circus. The busy footpaths and bright lights of the area evoked a strange beating of Anya's heart, as though she was encountering another world she'd never even imagined.

The blue bunting over the windows and the numerous red, white, and blue flags branded the corner building as distinctively American. Horns honked, buses sped by, and all around them people jostled one another as they made their way along the crowded footpaths.

Anya tried to take it all in. "I can't believe all this. Is it always this crowded?"

Sybil laughed. "Oh, Anya! This is *nothing*. Imagine ten times as many people, most of them in uniform, all trying to get through these doors. Probably more like twenty times as many."

Even from outside, Anya could hear music pulsing through the lobby. Big band, they called it, and she finally understood why everyone loved it so. She was disappointed to find the music originating from a gramophone piped through the club's public address system. She'd never seen a live swing band, though Danny had talked about them. Still, several couples danced to the raucous beat making the most audacious moves she'd ever seen.

"It's called the jitterbug. Isn't it great?" Sybil shouted, giggling at the silly expression on Anya's face.

"I've never seen dancing like that before."

"You must have a go! Let's find you a dance partner—"

"No!" she cried, grabbing Sybil's arm. "I wouldn't dare. I've never danced before!"

Sybil stopped in her tracks. "You've *never* danced? Not ever?"

Anya shook her head. "No. And I'm *not* going to dance with anyone but Danny."

Sybil grinned as she gave in. "Well, I suppose I see your point. Then come with me. I'll give you a tour."

She followed Sybil through the crowded halls, surprised so many Americans were still in London. She wondered what it must have been like before the war ended. In a corner on one of the floors, she saw what looked like a shooting gallery with Adolf Hitler's face as the target. A long row of machines banked one entire wall, most of them attended by clusters of men in uniform.

"Pinball machines," Sybil explained as they passed by. "Like arcade games. Very popular in America. And over there, you see the billiard tables which are also extremely popular."

Overhead, Anya noticed strings of triangular flags in red, white, and blue crisscrossing the rooms. She followed Sybil to an upper floor designated for hobbies. "They can draw, paint, and sculpt—all sorts of artwork, as you can see. Seems terribly deserted now, but not long ago it was positively bustling with Yanks. Many of the pictures you see on the walls of the club were painted right here in this room. Scenes from home and images from the war—like that one there of planes flying in formation. It's a creative outlet for them."

On another floor, they peeked into rooms with rows upon rows of beds provided for those on leave. "Most of the time, we'd be at capacity and have to provide cots for the boys to sleep in nearby bomb shelters."

Anya couldn't imagine it. "You mean all of these beds were filled?"

"Oh my yes. We often had 25,000 visitors a day, so we couldn't possibly provide enough beds for all of them."

Sybil shared a steady stream of memories about the club in its heyday, conjuring up all kinds of images in Anya's mind. She showed her the large and cozy library filled with books and stacks upon stacks of newspapers. "Those hometown newspapers were the lifeline for a lot of the boys. See how wrinkled they are? The boys would devour them."

Sybil explained the various roles of the Red Cross volunteers, from helping the Yanks write home, to sewing buttons on uniforms, providing first aid, or arranging sightseeing tours of London. All sorts of services.

"And of course, the dancing! There were times you could hardly move on that dance floor, it was so crowded."

"Must have been a lot of fun for you and the other girls meeting so many Americans." So different from her war years back home.

"The most fun I've ever had in my entire life," Sybil said. "Especially when we had live bands playing. Glenn Miller and Cab Calloway were by far the most favorite. When those horns would start playing and the drums pounding, and everyone singing along and dancing ... it felt like electricity crackling through the air. Honestly, most of the time you couldn't hear yourself think in the ballroom for all the music and chatter. It was wonderful!"

She led Anya to another staircase. "Let's head downstairs to Dunker's Den and get something to drink. Have you ever had a Coca-Cola?"

"No. What is it?"

"It's a bubbly beverage they call a soda. You'll love it."

A few moments later as they descended the basement stairs, Anya couldn't believe the vastness of the room coming into view. Obviously designed like a restaurant, yet completely different.

"Why do they call it Dunker's Den?"

"I have no idea, but if I had to guess, I'd say it's the strange way they dip their doughnuts in their coffee."

"What is a doughnut?"

"It's a pastry. A round confection with a hole in the middle that's deep fried. Really quite good, especially if you have a hankering for sweets like I do."

"We have something like that in The Netherlands called *oliebollen.* They're round, like fritters, and we serve them sprinkled with powdered sugar."

"Sounds heavenly. You'll have to try one of our doughnuts. I'll show you how the Yanks dip them in their coffee."

Anya looked around at the enormous room filled with tables and chairs and booths. "I've never seen anything like this before."

"It's a re-creation of the corner drug stores they have back home. Quite popular amongst the younger crowd in America. They serve hamburgers and French fries, which are potatoes similar to our chips. And they drink lots and lots of Coca-Cola. Let's take a seat over there at the counter."

As they made their way through the room, Anya marveled at the shiny chrome and red vinyl booths, some filled with uniformed Americans and English girls, tables covered with plates and cups and ashtrays, the air hazy with cigarette smoke. They passed a group of soldiers gathered around a strange piece of furniture that played another big band tune.

"It's called a jukebox," Sybil said. "Ever seen one before?"

Anya shook her head. "What is it?"

"It's like a gramophone that plays different records. You select the songs you want to hear by punching a few buttons. The Americans adore them."

Soldiers greeted Sybil warmly by name, and she laughed and teased with them as Anya followed her to the long counter. Following her lead, she took a seat on one of the round red stools tucked alongside the counter. A young woman wearing a white apron over her gray Red Cross uniform stood at a tap filling a chilled glass mug.

She looked over her shoulder and smiled. "Sybil? I didn't expect to see you here tonight."

"Just popped in for a bite with my friend Anya. This is her first time at the Rainbow. She's a war bride too. Anya, this is my friend Kate Miller. "

Anya blinked as the young woman turned to face them, her abdomen easily twice the size of Sybil's. "Oh my goodness, when is your baby due?"

"Not soon enough," she groaned, "but one more month according to the doctor. Nice to meet you, Anya." She placed the mugs on a tray which another volunteer picked up and carried away.

"Nice to meet you too, Kate."

"Anya's from Holland," Sybil explained, "but her husband was stationed with the 390th in Framlingham up in Suffolk."

"Well, then. Welcome to Rainbow Corner. Give me just a moment then I'll join you. It's time for my break. Let's sit at that table over there so I can put my feet up. What do you fancy this evening?"

"You sit down, Kate," Sybil insisted. "I'll pour some Cokes for us."

"Oh, thank you, dear." Kate eased herself onto a chair with a grateful sigh and propped her feet up on an empty chair.

Sybil returned with a tray and set three chilled mugs on the table along with a paper-lined basket of fried potato strips, then took her seat. "I don't understand why you're still working, Kate. We have plenty of help and not that many Yanks about tonight. Why don't you go home and get some rest?"

"Because being home alone is ever so much worse. At least here, the time passes a lot faster. It's too depressing at home and makes the waiting all the harder. Plus, the old man who lives in the flat next to mine plays music all hours of the night and day and refuses to turn down the volume. Might as well be here and doing something worthwhile. But enough about me. Tell me about yourself, Anya. How did you and your husband meet?"

"AAACK!" Anya blinked and sputtered after taking a sip of the fizzy beverage, her hand flying to the bridge of her nose.

Sybil and Kate laughed. "We forgot to warn you!"

Anya's eyes watered. "It's prickling up my nose. What's *in* this? And why is it so cold?"

"Carbonated syrup," Kate answered. "The carbon is what makes it bubble. As for the cold, the Yanks want all their drinks icy cold. Which I find extremely odd, don't you?"

She nodded, dashing the corners of her eyes with her fingertips.

"But it's actually very good, don't you think?" Sybil took a sip from her straw.

Anya smiled with a nod. "Well, yes, I think so. Very sweet, but good."

Sybil handed her the small basket of fried potatoes. "Now try one of these."

Anya took a tentative bite of the narrow potato slice. Salty and crisp on the outside, soft on the inside. "This reminds me of our *friets*."

"All right," Kate began, "now that you've had your first Coca-Cola and a taste of American snack food, tell me how you and your husband met."

Anya gave an abbreviated version of the long history she and Danny shared. The three chatted amicably, noting many of the same feelings about their long wait to go to America and the idea of moving to a country so different from their own.

"I must say it's helped having a chance to work here, surrounded by all these Yanks and their strange ways," Sybil added. "Might've been too much of a shock finding ourselves uprooted to a land where everyone talks with such peculiar accents and eats all this fried food."

Kate fanned herself with a menu. "Anya, where does Danny live in America?"

"He lives with his family in Chicago. Have you heard of it?"

"Yes, sure I have. My Joe lives in Long Island, same as Sybil's Jack. I expect we'll all be neighbors, though I don't know how far Long Island is from Chicago. Surely not that far?"

"I have no idea," Anya said. "I was told the ship will pull into the harbor in New York City, then I'll have to take a train from there to Chicago."

They'd been talking about fifteen minutes when another of their friends approached their table. Anya couldn't help staring at the pretty blonde with big blue eyes beneath thick black lashes; her lips painted with bold red lipstick so many of the English girls wore.

"Just the girls I've been looking for!"

"Gigi, meet my friend Anya," Sybil said. "She's a war bride just like us."

"And fancy if you aren't a pretty little thing. Pleased to meet you, Anya."

"Nice to meet you, too."

"Well then, with that accent you're obviously not a Brit like us. Where do you call home?"

"I'm from The Netherlands. Utrecht."

Gigi grimaced as she pulled up a chair and joined them, asking about Anya and her American husband. Anya couldn't help envying Gigi's confidence and bubbly personality. Her natural beauty most likely made her quite popular with the Americans.

"And you're living here in London now?" she asked, snatching one of the fries.

"No, not yet. I'm staying in Framlingham with—"

"You don't want to be all the way up in Framlingham when the Yanks finally send us sailing, do you? Which brings me to the reason I was looking for your two friends here today. I've found us the *perfect* flat to rent while we wait. It's in Covent Garden, and it's available whenever we want it, for however long we need it, and with the four of us sharing the cost, it's a steal of a deal."

Kate patted her bulging tummy. "Just tell me the bedrooms are all downstairs. I can't keep lugging the two of us up and down the stairs, especially when I have to go to the privy in the middle of the night."

"All downstairs, and four bedrooms, so we'll each have our own privacy."

"What do you say, Anya?" Sybil asked. "Now will you come?"

"Yes, just think how much fun we'll have together!" Kate added.

Gigi grabbed Anya's hands. "That's three to one, so how

about it, love? Say you'll come too?"

Anya wasn't sure she'd ever get used to these English girls with their chummy ways and free spirits. And she wasn't sure she was ready to move just yet. Her heart ached at the thought of leaving Sophie and Charlie and dear Patrick. Even so, all she really wanted was to be with Danny. And if living in London would speed the process, then perhaps it was time to move here. Or at least think about it.

"Would you still have a room for me if I don't move quite yet?"

"What are you thinking?" Sybil asked.

"Perhaps a few weeks? A month at most?"

Gigi made eye contact with Sybil and Kate, placing her palms down on the table. "What do you say, girls? Shall we save her a room?"

Sybil then Kate slapped their hands on top of Gigi's.

"Then it's settled! We'll all be flatmates!"

24

27 September 1945

Framlingham, England

The pub was busier than usual on Thursday night. Week-ends were always crowded, but week nights could go either way. Right around dusk, a thunderstorm rumbled into Framlingham, and with it a truckload of British soldiers whose lorry had broken down on the outskirts of town. A rowdy bunch, Anya surmised from the kitchen, as their voices grew louder with each round of pints.

"And aren't we glad Charlie's here to lend Da a hand?" Sophie offered as she swung through the kitchen doors. "Reminds me of the good old days when the Americans from the 390th would stuff our little pub and fill it with laughter."

"That seems a lifetime ago, doesn't it? To think, it's only been a few months." Anya retied the kerchief wrapped around her head. "Shall I warm more bread? We've only a few loaves left."

"Yes, I suppose so. What about the pasties? How many are left?"

"One more tray about ready to come out of the oven."

"Coming through," Charlie called with the keg of beer hoisted on his shoulder. "And I thought we Yanks drank a lot. I'm pretty sure these guys could drink us all under the table, as they say."

"Ah, but think of the muscles you're building," Sophie teased. "You'll be a regular Johnny Weissmuller before you know it."

"Me Tarzan, you Jane?"

"Out you go, Tarzan. Thirsty patrons are waiting out front."

Charlie laughed as the swinging doors slapped behind him.

"I remember Danny talking about the Tarzan movies," Anya said, "but I never saw any of them. They sounded rather silly to me."

"Oh, that they are. Absolutely ridiculous. More of a fellow's cuppa, I suppose. Speaking of Danny, I forgot to ask. Any letters today?"

Anya gave the remaining stew a stir. "Yes, actually. The post was later than usual today, but there was a letter Danny had written way back on the fourteenth. I can't understand why it takes his letters so much longer to get to me than mine to him. It's really quite frustrating."

"Better late than never." Sophie stood at the sink beside her, plunging dishes and steins into the soapy water to wash before rinsing. "Any news? Is he still threatening to commandeer a plane and fly back here to get you?"

Anya kept her focus on the stew. "No, not really."

Sophie rinsed her hands and dried them on a dish towel. "Not to worry. I bet he thinks about it every day. Wouldn't be surprised if he showed up in one of those Forts and dipped his wing as he passed over us here." She tucked a strand of hair back in her snood and glanced over at her friend. "Anya?"

"Yes?" she answered without looking up.

"What is it? What's wrong?"

Anya bit the inside of her lip. "Nothing you haven't heard before. Honestly, Sophie, I'm so tired of waiting and whining about it. I can't help wishing it was all over so I could stop having these stupid thoughts."

Sophie nudged some wisps of hair off her forehead then folded her arms across her chest. "What is it? What's got you so upset? Did something in Danny's letter—"

"Yes, actually. Something he wrote." She set the wooden spoon down then stretched out the kinks in her neck. "It's absurd, of course. I'm just reacting like a silly schoolgirl, but—"

"Just tell me. What did he say?"

Anya pulled the letter from her trouser pocket and read aloud the section where Danny mentioned seeing his college sweetheart again. Hearing the words out loud made her feel even more childish. She stopped mid-sentence. "I'm sorry. I shouldn't have read this to you."

Sophie squeezed Anya's forearm. "Of course you should, and I can see why you might jump to conclusions, Anya. But you have nothing to worry about. Danny *loves* you! Anyone who's ever seen the two of you together knows that."

"But that's just it, don't you see? We're *not* together. I'm still here, and he's back there in Chicago, America with all his family and friends, and now this Beverly person. It's hard enough to be apart for so long. Now I have to worry about some stupid old girlfriend who's obviously turning to Danny in her grief. And you know as well as I do that Danny would never just turn his back on someone who's suffering. He has such a good heart, so who knows what he'll—"

"You and I both know what he'll do. He'll be a perfect gentleman because that's who he is. Anya, he's your husband now. He's off the market, and for the record, he has been for a long, long time. Look, I know how news like this can intensify the stress you're already feeling. All these months apart and the sheer distance between you? Why, it's positively brutal. But the one thing I do know—because Charlie talks about it all the time—is that Danny McClain is a good and decent man who is utterly *smitten* with you.

"Oh Anya, I know it's hard, but you have to trust Danny. So you must promise me you won't worry about this Beverly person anymore." She leaned over to look into Anya's face. "Say it."

"I'll try not—"

"No, *promise* me you won't worry."

Anya huffed and rolled her eyes. "Fine. I'll say it. I won't worry about this Beverly person."

"Good. Now that we settled that, we best fill some orders before all those boys come storming back here looking for their food."

As the evening wore on, they had little time for more conversation. Another lorry of soldiers squeezed into the pub, friends of the first bunch who were clearly more inebriated.

Anya worked in the kitchen, while Patrick stayed busy at the bar. Sophie and Charlie took orders and replenished pints.

Later, Patrick pushed his way into the kitchen. "Anya, have you seen my glasses anywhere? I must have laid them down somewhere, and I must confess, I can't see a thing without them." He turned to face her, patting his pockets with a sense of urgency.

Anya wiped her hands on a dish towel. "I think I might know where they are." She smiled as she approached him, then removed the glasses from their usual spot on the top of his head and handed them to him.

"Goodness me, that's a rummon. I must be losing my marbles!" He dug a handkerchief out of his pocket and started wiping the lenses. "Are you all right, Anya? You look a bit tired, if you don't mind my saying so."

"I'm fine, Patrick. It's about time to close, isn't it?"

"Yes, it is. Time for last call." He stuffed his handkerchief back in his pocket, put on his glasses, and headed back through the swinging door.

Anya was grateful for the solitude, preferring not to deal with customers, or even make small talk with Sophie, for that matter. Even though she promised she wouldn't worry, the familiar pressure on her chest registered another wave of concern.

Yes, she knew she could trust Danny.

Yes, she was glad he was safe, living at home with his family.

Yes, she would surely sail for America in a few weeks and never again be apart from him.

But that didn't stop the images traipsing through her

mind and hovering around her heart. Images of a beautiful college girl who'd once been the love of Danny's life. Images of that same girl, now a grieving young widow in search of solace, perhaps hoping to find it in the arms of her former sweetheart.

"STOP!" she growled. "Stop it! Stop it, stop it!"

Sophie walked in on Anya's outburst. "Stop what? Are you all right?"

Anya whipped around. "Yes, I'm fine. Really."

Sophie lowered a tray of dirty dishes. "You sure about that?"

"I'm just tired, that's all. Aren't you?" She grabbed the tray from Sophie and dumped the dishes into the sink of soapy water.

"Yes, terribly. And I've had a time of it with those fellas out there tonight. Da should have tossed them out hours ago. But it's last round now, and they'll all be gone soon. Let me collect the rest of the empty pints, and I'll help you with those."

Charlie came in and out, helping Patrick close the pub for the night. He sent the last of the drunken stragglers on their way, then started wiping down the tables. Sophie and Anya finished the dishes and tidied the kitchen.

"All right then," Sophie said. "I'll just take this rubbish out to the alley, then we'll be done. Go on up to bed, if you like. And thank you for your help tonight. We couldn't have managed without you."

"Of course you could." Anya lifted the apron over her head and hung it on the peg, then poured herself a glass of water to take upstairs. She pulled the scarf off her head and let her hair loose as she took a final look around the kitchen. Noticing the pile she'd left after sweeping the floor, she got the dustpan and brush out of the closet again to finish the task, wondering what her mother would think to see her now. Oh, how they'd fought whenever Mother asked for help cleaning the house. Yet here she was, compelled to leave the kitchen spotless.

As she swept the last specks of dust into the shallow pan, she heard voices coming from the front of the pub. Raised voices. Or were they from back in the alley? She took the loaded dustpan to the back door, thinking she'd dump it out in the alley. That's when she heard a scream.

Sophie!

Anya threw open the back door as a peal of thunder cracked overhead, and with it a sudden downpour. She cupped a hand over her eyes, trying to see through the rain and darkness.

Another scream. This one cut short by a loud smacking sound. A commotion in the far corner of the alley caught her eye. The dustpan clattered on the gravel as she rushed toward the two people fighting.

"ANYA!"

As she closed in on them, she could see the tall image bent over Sophie pinning her left arm to her body, the other dangling helplessly.

"HEY! Leave her alo—"

WHACK!

A fist smashed into Anya's jaw and sent her reeling. She landed hard, sprawled in a heap on the puddled gravel as white stars danced in her eyes.

"ANYA! HELP —"

WHACK!

Sophie's cry stopped.

"SHUT UP!" a man's voice shouted. "Both of you, just SHUT YOUR—"

Anya pounced on his back, locking her arm in a vise around his throat. He let go of Sophie, dropping her as he straightened. He grabbed at Anya's arm with both his hands. She clung tighter, but her rain-soaked arm kept sliding off his slippery neck.

"Get OFF ME!" he roared, spinning and bending over in an attempt to throw her off his back.

She held tight, both arms wrapped around his throat as she squeezed as hard as she could. He clawed at her, ripping her blouse, then yanking a handful of hair in a grip so hard, it sent her flying against the stone fence with a howl of pain.

"ANYA! LOOK OUT!" Sophie cried.

As she tried to stand, he was already rushing toward her headfirst. In a split second, she rolled out of his trajectory, causing him to lose his balance, unable to stop. His head smashed into the craggy stone fence. A flash of lightning showed his bloodied face as he spun around groping for her. He reached out just as she ran at him like a runaway locomotive, her head aimed right at his gut. She heard the whoosh of air leave his lungs as he fell to his knees, rocking and reeling as he fought to right himself.

She thought she heard voices calling her name, but she couldn't stop. Not until the beast was dead. Still rocking on his knees, he was more accessible, so she locked her arm around his neck again. With every ounce of her strength, she jerked it hard one way then the other, the snaps rendering his body limp. He fell forward, landing face first on the gravel.

Charlie reached her as she scrabbled backward away from the brute's body.

"Anya! Are you all right?" He reached out to steady her, but she jumped back, batting his hand away.

"Anya, honey, it's me—Charlie!" He raised his palms to reassure her. "I'm not going to hurt you."

She stared at him, then down at the man she'd just killed.

"Charlie!" Patrick said, his voice urgent. "Give me a hand here. It's Sophie!"

Charlie rushed to his side, bent over Sophie in the dark corner of the alley. Anya heard them talking but couldn't understand a word because of the pounding inside her head. She covered her ears, trying to stop it; her chest still heaving in search of a breath.

She squeezed her eyes shut, trying to blank the image of the body just inches from her. Opening them, she forced her eyes toward her friends.

Sophie cried out in pain as Charlie lifted her off the ground. "It's my arm." She tried to stand on her own, looking up as Anya approached her. "Oh, Anya! Are you all right?"

Anya stared at her friend, her right eye already swollen, her blouse ripped off one shoulder. She couldn't bear it, the thought of what might have happened. What if she hadn't stopped to sweep that last pile of dirt in the kitchen? Hadn't heard Sophie's cry for help? Hadn't stopped the beast from—

She bent over and vomited so hard, she nearly passed out.

A moment later, she did.

25

28 September 1945

Every inch of her body ached. Anya pried open her eyes, startled at her surroundings. Tiny slivers of morning light squeezed their way past boarded-up windows. That's when she remembered where she was. The control tower beside the perimeter track on the grounds of the 390th. She'd hidden beneath a built-in counter on the second floor after running there last night through driving sheets of rain.

Grateful to find an unlocked door at the back of the building, she'd felt her way blindly through the small rooms, then eased her way up the stairs to the second floor. There she found a couple of old farm jackets among the odds and ends left behind. She rolled one of them for a pillow, and used the other as a cover against the night chill. Each carried the lingering scent of pipe tobacco; strangely comforting as she tried to stop shivering and blot out what had happened.

Taking off from the pub in the middle of the night had

been rash. The memories fluttered through her mind now, leaving behind a wake of profound fear. She tried to get up, refusing to let it paralyze her for a single moment. But the effort proved excruciating, her head spinning as she lay back down, stuffing the jacket beneath her head again. Tears fell from her eyes, trickling down toward her ears as she tried to make herself relax.

Oh Danny. What have I done?

She reached for the charms of her bracelet—it wasn't there! *No, no, no!* She pulled herself up, crying out from the pain of her bruised ribs. She felt around the dirty floor, searching, patting, hoping to find it here somewhere. *Please be here. Please!* But she knew better. More than likely, she'd lost it during the scuffle in the alley behind the pub.

Its absence grieved her, stealing the last ounce of her strength. She lay back down and curled up on her side, consumed with sorrow. Would it never end? Was the rest of her life destined to be nothing more than a series of ugly messes and constant heartache?

She shook away the thoughts and the anger roiling in her gut, unwilling to give in to them. Unwilling to let them defeat her. Unwilling to let them paralyze her. She covered her face with her hands and forced them from her mind.

Sophie!

Was she all right? Had they kept her overnight at the hospital? Had she sustained other injuries, apart from her broken arm? When the ambulance rounded the corner and came to a stop in the alley, Anya had panicked and slipped away into the darkness.

Some friend you are.

Killing the soldier had come so naturally, it terrified her. She could still feel the snap of his neck and his body going limp. And with it, the immediate realization she might never see Danny again. The authorities would never allow her on one of those war bride ships after what she'd done. Never mind that she was trying to protect Sophie. All that would matter was the fact that a Dutch girl had killed a British soldier.

Downstairs, a door creaked open. Anya sat up, the room spinning around her. She clamped her hands on her head, willing the dizziness away. As she tried to get up, she heard a muffled voice. Her heart hammered hard against her chest as she searched for an escape. No way out except by the main stairway?

The rooftop!

She crawled out, then crouched down low as she tiptoed toward the door leading outside to the tower's rooftop observation deck. She carefully reached for the doorknob and turned, realizing her mistake a split second too late. A shaft of light blinded her as she pushed it open, her hands instinctively covering her eyes.

"Anya!"

She turned, her eyes narrowing as she tried to regain her focus.

The overhead lights flickered on. "Anya, it's me, Charlie."

"Charlie?"

Suddenly he was before her, reaching out to grasp her shoulders. "What are you doing here? We've been worried sick!"

"I didn't ... I was—"

He caught her as she swayed, wrapping his arm beneath

hers. She gasped as it pressed against her ribs.

"Whoa, take it easy. Come sit down. Are you hurt?"

He helped her over to the counter, then eased her up to sit on it. "Let me take a look at you."

"Sophie? Is she all right?"

"She's fine. She has a broken arm, but otherwise she's okay. The doctor insisted on keeping her overnight, but she'll be just fine. Mostly she's worried about you. One moment the ambulance was pulling up, and the next, you were gone. Why did you run?"

"Why do you think, Charlie? I killed a man! A British soldier! They'll put me in prison for the rest of my life—"

"But—"

"—or ship me back to Holland if I'm found. They'll *never* let me go to America, don't you see?"

"But you *didn't* kill him, Anya. He's alive."

She blinked. "What? Of course, I did. I felt him go limp when I snapped his neck! There's no way he could have survived that."

"Well sure, you temporarily paralyzed him, but you didn't kill him. The doctors seem to think he'll regain use of his legs at some point. And for the record, he's *not* a British soldier. Why did you think that?"

"Because he was wearing a uniform. And the pub was filled with soldiers last night. I assumed he was one of them."

"No, according to Patrick, he went AWOL over a year ago, which explains the uniform. He just showed up in town last week. He's one of the Roberts boys from the village. His name is Clay. Mean as a snake, from what I'm told."

"What does this mean—*a wall?*"

"A-W-O-L. Absent without leave. At least, that's what we call it in the American military."

"Is he in hospital?"

"Yes, and he'll be there a long time."

"But surely it's not the same hospital Sophie's in? Is someone guarding her? Is Patrick with her? Someone has to—"

"Anya, calm down. You need to take a deep breath and relax. Sophie's fine. Patrick is with her until I get back. We won't leave her alone. Roberts is on another floor, and there's a guard posted outside his room. And since he's unable to move, you don't need to worry about him right now. Why don't you come with me so we can let the doctor have a look at you?"

"No. I'm not going. I can't."

"But your face and arms are bruised, and more than likely your ribs are injured. You're white as a ghost, Anya. Just let the doctor check you over to make sure you don't have any serious internal injuries."

"I don't know, Charlie." She dropped her head in her hands. "I need to think. There's just too much at stake. Are the constables looking for me?"

When he didn't answer, she looked up and found his blue eyes searching hers.

"Yes, they are. But it's for your own protection."

"Somehow I doubt that. Don't you see? If I'm arrested or accused of assaulting that man, it could jeopardize my leaving. I could be stuck here forever." She stared at him, expecting an answer.

Then finally, "Look, you'll just have to trust me. You're not going to be arrested. We told the authorities exactly what happened, how you were trying to protect Sophie. When I tell you they want to protect you, it's with good reason. This Roberts family is apparently a rough bunch of good-for-nothing thugs who like to throw their weight around. They're bullies, always looking for a fight. Which is why the police sergeant wants to talk to you, and find somewhere safe where they can't find you."

Anya groaned. "I don't know, Charlie. I don't know. I can't think straight, I'm so tired."

He came alongside her and gently wrapped his arm around her shoulder. "Then let me do your thinking for you. Let me take you somewhere safe so you can rest."

After a long moment, she sighed. "I suppose I have no choice." She grimaced as she stood. "Wait—how did you know where to find me?"

His dimples deepened with his smile. "I'm smarter than I look."

"What's that supposed to mean?"

"I just figured you'd hide somewhere on the base, and where better than the control tower?"

She took a deep breath and tried to straighten her aching back. "I should have known you'd figure it out."

"Besides, I gave Danny my word that I'd take care of you in his absence. And that means I'll do everything in my power to get you on one of those boats sailing for America. Fair enough?"

She made no effort to smile, but appreciated his attempts to cheer her. "Fair enough."

As he helped her walk, she paused. "Wait—I've lost my bracelet. The one Danny gave me with the silver charms."

He looked around, the dim lighting not helping him search. "You mean here? You lost it here?"

"I don't know. Probably not. I tried to find it just a few minutes before you came, but I don't think it's here."

"When was the last time you remember seeing it?"

"I know I had it on while I was working at the pub last night. Do you suppose it might have come off when ... when I—"

He guided her toward the stairs. "When we get back to the pub, I'll take a look out back in the alley."

"But what if it's not there?"

"Don't worry about that right now. We'll find it. If I have to get down on my hands and knees, we'll find it."

Anya was surprised by the kind demeanor and concern of Framlingham's police sergeant. She wasn't sure what she'd expected, but the grandfatherly Sergeant William Ketner put her immediately at ease.

"As Lieutenant Janssen told you, we're always aware of the trouble that stirs up whenever these Roberts boys show up. We've had run-ins with the family for years. Their mother died when they were little tykes, and their father let them run wild. He's a drunk, and raised them to follow in his footsteps. Which is why we keep a close eye on them.

"I was told you gave Clayton Roberts quite a beating, young lady." A slight smile edged his lips. "I'm sure he had it coming. But I'm curious. Where did a young woman like you learn to fight off a big, nasty brute like Clay Roberts?"

Anya glanced over at Charlie. He nodded, encouraging her to answer.

"I served with the Dutch Resistance for many years."

He nodded. "I see."

"We were taught how to defend ourselves and how to ... eliminate hostiles."

He said nothing for a moment. Then, "Mrs. McClain, I'm sure you did what you had to do. Nothing to be ashamed about. It may be the ugly side of war, but you survived. And that is something to be thankful—"

"Yes, but you see, the war is over, and I tried to kill him," she blurted. "I *wanted* to kill him. It was as if I couldn't stop myself. I hadn't even thought it through. I just did it. As though I had no control whatsoever over my reaction, I just tried to kill him." She moved her gaze to her hands, trying to still them. "And it scares me ... to think I could do it without so much as a single thought."

Ketner came around his desk and pulled up a chair beside hers.

"Mrs. McClain—Anya. We have all done things these past few years that we never imagined ourselves doing. You must have been quite young when the Germans occupied your homeland. It is unspeakable, the atrocities they inflicted on your country and so many others. And just because the war is over and the skies are no longer filled with bombers, or the roads cluttered with armored tanks, no one expected the trauma to disappear overnight. It takes time. For some, lots of time. But one day you will realize that knee-jerk reaction to strike out has abated, and you will once again breathe a sigh of relief in knowing you've overcome the hurt and the heartache you've experienced. Not forgotten—just overcome. Does that make sense to you?"

Anya nodded as she looked up. The compassion in his eyes had an immediate calming effect on her.

He patted her hand then stood up and returned to his seat behind the desk. "But the immediate problem before us is this Roberts family. Once Clay is alert, we'll read him his rights and arrest him. Then once he's recovered sufficiently, he'll be moved to a cell here and prosecuted for assault. And much as I'd like to, I can't lock up his father and brothers, which means you are a potential target."

Ketner tented his fingers and turned his attention to Charlie. "As are you and your wife and Patrick, I'm afraid."

"I've had that same thought," Charlie said. "We'll be more vigilant, keep our eyes open for them."

"I'll have my men stop by more often, be more visible. Hopefully, that will keep them at bay."

"We'd appreciate that."

"But as for you, Mrs. McClain, I wonder if you might have somewhere else to go for a few weeks."

"What?"

"I'm concerned for your safety. While the rest of the town no doubt applauds your efforts to take down the likes of Clay Roberts, the fact remains that he comes from a large and violent family. Short of keeping you under lock and key, I'm not altogether certain we can protect you from them. They're a crafty bunch who've been able to dodge us on numerous occasions. I'd rather not risk you getting attacked, or worse. I understand you're awaiting passage to join your husband in the United States? Do you have any idea when that might happen?"

"No, none at all. I would have thought long before now. It seems everything we hear contradicts what we've been told previously."

"I'm not surprised. Quite a lot of you war brides, I'm told."

"Anya, what about your friend in London?" Charlie asked.

"Sybil?"

"Yes. Do you think you might be able to stay with her for a while? I'd rather you stay with us, but Sergeant Ketner is right. You're in danger here."

"Who is this Sybil?" Ketner asked.

"She's an English girl who also married an American," Charlie answered.

"I suppose I could," Anya said. "She and her friends have invited me to live with them until we sail for America."

"Well, then," Ketner said, on his feet again. "I suggest you talk with these young women and see what kind of arrangements you might make.

Both Anya and Charlie stood. "Yes, I'll call Sybil today," Anya said.

"Excellent." Ketner extended his hand first to Charlie, then to Anya. "And might I add, sooner rather than later?"

Charlie snapped his fingers as they turned to go. "I almost forgot. Anya, could you give us a moment? There's something I need to discuss with Sergeant Ketner."

"Of course," she said.

"Good. I'll join you shortly."

Anya walked gingerly, stiff after sitting so long. Ketner's assistant asked if she needed anything, but she declined. "I'd like to stretch my legs a bit. I'll be out in the hall."

She'd made three slow loops up and down the hall when Charlie reappeared, his face quite serious.

"Anya, there's someone who needs to speak to you."

"What? Who?" Her heart sputtered as she returned to Ketner's office.

The sergeant held the receiver out toward her with the slightest hint of a smile on his face. She was still puzzled by his expression when she held the phone to her ear.

"Hello?"

"Anya? Is that you?"

"Danny?"

"Yes, sweetheart! It's me! Oh honey, I miss you so much! How are you?"

"But how did—"

"Charlie put a call through with the help of someone named Ketner. He didn't tell me who that is, but I'm assuming he's a local friend there. Oh Anya, I can't believe we're finally talking!"

She stood speechless as Charlie and Ketner left the room, both wearing wide smiles.

"Anya, are you still there?"

"Yes, yes I'm here! I just can't believe it's you! Oh Danny, I'm so sorry ..." She held her hand over the receiver, not wanting him to hear the emotion in her voice.

"Sweetheart, there's nothing to be sorry for. If anyone should apologize, it's me. I should *never* have left you there. I should have stayed and figured out some way for both of us to travel back here together."

She took a calming breath and tried to steady her voice.

"No, it's not your fault. It isn't."

"I've even contacted some of our congressmen, trying to get assistance to speed up the process, but I've been told there's nothing they can do. Then I tried to get a visa to come back over—lots of GIs with wives over there have tried. But the Brits are adamantly against it, since they're still recovering from the war. I guess they're afraid we'll take up all the housing or be a burden. I don't know, but I wanted you to know I tried."

"But I just don't understand why it's all taking so long. No one tells us anything."

"I know, honey, and I'm frustrated just like you are. I've read some articles in *Stars and Stripes* about the plight of all you war brides. Basically, there's been an outcry from folks concerned that so many of our GIs in Europe and the Pacific are still waiting for transport back to the States. They don't think it's fair for any ships to be used to bring you brides over here until all the soldiers are home first. Quite a heated debate, apparently."

Anya sighed. "I suppose I understand their concerns. But that means it could be next year before they'll let us sail."

"I know, sweetheart, but we just have to be patient. Oh, I can't believe I'm *finally* hearing your voice! How are you? Charlie said you'd had a rough couple of days, but didn't say why. Is everything okay?"

She wouldn't worry him, and she wasn't about to spoil these precious few moments together. "Yes, I'm all right. I think I'm going to move to London and wait it out with Sybil. Since we still don't know when we might go, I'd hate to be up here in Framlingham and risk missing the call when the time comes. She's been offering for me to stay with her, so I believe I will."

"Really? I'm sure Sophie and Charlie will hate to see you go."

"I know, and I'll miss them too, but I think it's for the best. But enough of all that. How are you? How is your family?"

"We're all doing fine. Little Jimmy is growing like a weed. I can't wait for you to meet him. And everyone else, too. They all send their love."

"That's very kind. Please give them mine."

"Absolutely! Oh, honey, I could talk to you all day and it would never be enough."

"I would love that. More than you know. Sometimes I wonder if I haven't just imagined you. That we never actually met and certainly didn't marry."

"Well, be assured that we both met AND married! Mom is praying you'll be home in time for Christmas, and you know how dependable her prayers are."

"I hope she's right."

"Me, too. You're all I think about. All day, every day. I love you with all my heart. So come home to me. Actually, today would be good. Or tomorrow, if that's more convenient for—"

The line went dead.

"Danny?" Nothing. She pressed the button several times. "Danny, are you there? Danny? Can you hear me?"

Nothing.

She slowly placed the receiver back on its cradle and closed her eyes, cherishing the sound of his voice in her mind. Oh, how she'd missed it. She couldn't help the smile on her face as his words played over and over in her mind.

You're all I think about. All day, every day. I love you with all my heart. So come home to me.

"I love you too, Danny. With all my heart."

Diane Moody

Part III

26

3 October 1945
Chicago, Illinois

Dear Anya,

I didn't think to ask for your mailing address in London, so I'm sending this to the pub so Charlie and Sophie can forward it to you.

I still can't believe we got to talk on the telephone the other day! After so long, it almost felt like we were those kids again who used to write each other before the war, halfway around the world. The sound of your voice was the best possible medicine, because I've been lovesick for you ever since we parted. Boy, does that ever sound corny. But it's true, Anya. It's like I'm only half a person without you. Isn't that such a strange thought? To think that not so long ago, I had no idea how much another person could affect every single part of my life, and how your absence would leave such a gaping hole in my heart. I'm not making any sense, I suppose. Just know that I miss you more than I ever imagined possible, and hearing your voice the other day was the sweetest sound I've heard in all the time we've been apart.

Now, I know this isn't one of your favorite subjects, but you'll have to bear with me here and let me tell you anyway:

THE CUBS WON THE PENNANT!!!

WE'RE IN THE WORLD SERIES!!!

They played a three-game series in Pittsburg last week-end, and clinched the pennant after winning the first game 4-3! They won the other two games against Pittsburgh, and took an overnight train back here to Chicago. Joey and I joined a huge crowd of fans welcoming them home the next morning. You should have seen them, Anya. The team, manager Charley Grimm, the fans—everyone was shouting and singing and cheering! Wish you'd been with us!

We'll be playing the Detroit Tigers in the World Series, with the first game tonight in Detroit. Joey talked Dad into broadcasting the radio feed through the speakers at the theater, so we've been spreading the word. Free admission and we're offering half-off on all the concessions. We can't wait!

The only thing that would make it better? If YOU were here to join in the fun! I promise you would enjoy it!

Well, my train is about to reach the campus, so I'll

close. The game starts at 2:10 this afternoon, so I'm skipping my last class to help Joey and Dad at the theater. Thanks for letting me have a little fun sharing the excitement with you. I'm determined to make you a Cubs fan if it's the last thing I do!

All my love,

Danny

When his *European Civilization* class ended, Danny dashed from the classroom building and raced for the train station. He stretched his arm through the closing door of the Red Line and squeezed through just in time. As the car jolted its start down the track, he found himself packed like a sardine with other Northwestern students, all of them excited about the game with rowdy conversations and contagious camaraderie.

When the car took its usual curve around the first bend, Danny reached for one of the leather straps to steady his balance. Someone else grabbed it at the same moment.

"Sorry," he said, turning to make his apology. To his surprise, he found Beverly looking up at him.

"Hello, Danny."

"Sorry, I didn't—"

"Let me guess. You're rushing home to listen to the game?"

"You guessed right. Well, I mean, no, I'm not going *home*. I'm headed to the theater. We're hosting a radio broadcast of the game. How about you? I assume you're still a Cubs fan?"

She just smiled, staring at him with those familiar hazel eyes. He could feel his face warming, so ducked his eyes for a glimpse out the window.

"Once a Cubs fan, always a Cubs fan," she said. "Isn't that what you used to say?"

He chuckled. "Something like that."

"I'm meeting some friends for a party while the game's on. Snacks, drinks. The usual."

A couple of moments passed. Then a couple more. Odd, how uncomfortable a few minutes could be, even on a crowded train. Then again, they had history.

"Any news from your wife?"

"As a matter of fact, yes. We finally had a chance to talk by telephone last Friday."

"Was that the first time you've talked to her since you've been home?"

"Yes, I've tried several times but could never get through. It sure was nice to hear her voice again."

"Any idea when she'll be coming?"

He told her what little he knew, thankful to have a chance to talk about Anya. He wasn't sure if she had asked just to be polite, or if she was interested. Regardless, after a brief recap of the situation, he didn't know what else to say.

She looked away for a moment, then changed the subject again. "Well, we've got to be pretty darn proud of our Cubs. I still can't believe we're finally in the World Series again, can you?"

"No, it still feels too good to be true."

"Did you hear what happened to the players' wives when they arrived in Detroit Monday night?"

"No."

"It was on the radio this morning. It seems all the wives were to be lodged on a passenger ship called the *Greater Detroit* that was docked at the harbor. But when the wives checked in on Monday night, they were furious because the rooms were tiny and rather tacky, according to some. They suspected it was intentional on the part of the Tigers, so they staged some kind of revolt that lasted several hours. They even woke up Grimm and the league's travel secretary to sort it all out. At two in the morning yesterday, they were taken to one of the hotels where members of the team were staying."

"Somebody's head will roll for that snafu. Wouldn't want to be that guy."

They chatted about the team and the season as a whole, even shouting a few times to hear each other when the other riders grew boisterous. Arriving at his stop, he said goodbye and made his exit. As he walked several blocks to the theater, he went over their conversation, wishing he hadn't run into her again. He didn't like the uneasy feeling nibbling at his heart, and he wondered how long it would take before he could see her and not feel so awkward.

He also decided not to mention it to Anya.

The packed crowd at the Windsor Park Theater almost cheered the roof off as their beloved Cubs scored four runs in the first inning in the first game. Despite the raw, frigid weather hovering over Detroit's Briggs Stadium, the Cubs' bats were smoking hot. No one was more surprised than Detroit's ace pitcher Hal Newhouser, the leading hurler who'd dominated the American League during the war years. By halfway through the third inning, after giving up three more runs by the Cubs, he was done. Even over the airwaves, the silence of the stunned Detroit fans made for an eerie hush behind Bert Wilson's elated commentary.

The Cubs' new star pitcher Hank Borowy got off to a rough start as well, but soon found his rhythm. The recently acquired pitcher from the Yankees had joined the Cubs in late July, and already proved worthy of every penny spent on his contract, delivering eleven out of the last thirteen games of the regular season. And he certainly brought his game to the World Series, going the distance with a six-hit shutout. Outfielder Bill Nicholson's bat helped run up the score with a single and a triple, driving in three runs. Then in the seventh, first baseman Phil Cavarretta iced the cake with a sweet line shot deep into the right-field bleachers, the first home run of the series. The Cubs won 9-0, celebrating their win in the mostly hushed Detroit stadium.

The event at Windsor Park Theater was such a success, Joey and his father agreed to broadcast the two remaining games played in Detroit. Danny had never seen his father so relaxed, even showing a rare smile when the Cubs won so handily. The fans lingered longer than expected, ringing the cash register from start to finish and depleting the theater's supply of popcorn and sodas. That evening, at the showing of the feature film, *When Our Hearts Were Young & Gay,* patrons didn't even complain about the lack of concessions. They were too jubilant about their Cubs' win!

The following day, Detroit showed more of their true colors with the return of right-hander Virgil Trucks on the mound for Game 2. Trucks had been discharged from the navy just two weeks prior, missing the last two seasons while serving overseas. He silenced the Cubs' bats, giving up only seven hits. Unfortunately, Cubs pitcher Hank Wyse struggled through the first six innings, giving up four runs, including a three-run homer by Hammerin' Hank Greenberg in the fifth. Cubs relief pitcher Paul Erickson halted the Tigers scoring, but the damage was already done. Detroit won 4-1. The series was tied.

On Friday, Cubs right-hander Claude Passeau pitched the best game in the entire history of the World Series, allowing only one hit and no runs—a shutout, winning 3-0. The crowd at the Windsor Park Theater went berserk, still whooping and hollering when they left hours later, eager to welcome their Cubs home to Chicago for Game 4.

27

6 October 1945

Chicago, Illinois

On Saturday morning, Danny joined his parents in the kitchen. Dad sat hidden behind the *Chicago Times* as usual, while his mother stood at the stove preparing breakfast. As she scrambled eggs in the skillet, Danny said good morning, kissed her cheek, then poured himself a cup of coffee.

"Have I mentioned lately how nice it is to have real eggs again?"

She chuckled. "Only every morning."

"If there's one thing the war taught me, it's an appreciation for all the little things I used to take for granted. Like real eggs and good coffee. I sure missed your cooking, Mom."

"And I sure missed cooking for you." She scraped the eggs onto a serving platter alongside a stack of crisp bacon and set it on the table beside a basket of piping-hot biscuits. "What time are you and Joey leaving for the game?"

"Be sure to dress warm," mumbled the voice behind the *Times*. "Forecast is for cold and damp through most of the day. Chance of rain."

"Wouldn't you know it? First home game of the series, and the weather's gonna be nasty. To answer your question, Mom, I'm not sure yet when we'll leave. Probably a couple hours before the game starts."

Joey walked in with little Jimmy held snug against his chest. "Game? What game?"

"Good morning, honey," Betty said, reaching for Jimmy. "And how's my sweet grandson this morning?" Jimmy cooed as she kissed his rosy cheek then cradled him in her arms. She took her seat at the kitchen table beside Frank.

The wall of newspaper came down with the arrival of his grandson. "Well, hi there, little fella." He patted Jimmy gently on his head as grandfather and baby shared a sweet smile.

Joey shot Danny a wink, acknowledging this new softer side of their father.

"He's full of vim and vigor, that's for sure," Joey said. "I thought I'd let Millie sleep in. She was up with him around three this morning. It's the least I can do since I'll be gone all afternoon."

"What time do you want to leave?" Danny asked.

"Funny you should ask. I don't know if you heard the telephone ring earlier, but Marv Clancy called to make sure we're coming plenty early."

"I still can't believe he's *giving* us those tickets. He could make a fortune selling them."

"Not if Mr. Wrigley has anything to do with it," Betty said. She pointed to the *Times* headline, "We're Burned Up, Too."

"The paper says Mr. Wrigley didn't go to Detroit for the first three games just so he could stay here and answer all the letters complaining about the ticket situation. Can you imagine? The owner of the Cubs missed the first three games of the series! I still don't know why it's legal for folks to scalp tickets. Mr. Wrigley is furious about it."

"He may be," Frank said, "but there's not a lot he can do about it now. Another article stated that twenty-five IRS goons will be out and about today checking on scalpers to make sure they're paying taxes on their ticket sales. If not, they'll press charges."

"What a mess," Betty said.

"I'm just glad Marv has such a big heart," Joey said. "I didn't realize these were his season tickets."

Danny set his coffee cup back down. "I didn't either. Wonder why he keeps them since he's working the gates?"

Joey took a seat across from him. "I asked him that this morning. He said he's had those same seats for twenty years. He and his son never missed a game when the Cubs were in town."

"Same son he lost at Pearl?"

"Yes, and he said after that happened, he couldn't handle it emotionally. Too hard to sit there beside his son's empty seat. So he got a job taking tickets, but held onto his seats. Just couldn't part with them. Instead, he always finds someone to give the tickets to. Usually veterans like us, but sometimes fathers and sons, or school kids. Sometimes for just one game; sometimes a whole season. He said he can almost feel his son smiling down on him when he hands over the tickets."

"What a wonderful gesture," Betty said. "He must be a very

kind man."

"He is. After we got acquainted at the theater, he'd stop by my office to chat. He said I was the only one he felt he could talk to about his son. I guess because I was there at Pearl. I think maybe it's helped him heal, you know?"

"I would imagine so, honey."

"I hope so, but I never imagined all those long talks would land us in premium seats for a World Series game!" Joey shook his head and laughed. Jimmy held up his tiny fists and sputtered a happy squeal.

"That's right, Jimmy. Your daddy's going to see the Cubs play in the *World Series* today! Wish you were older so you could come along. It's never too early to catch Cubs fever, little buddy."

Jimmy giggled again, his bright eyes riveted on his father.

Danny smiled at his nephew's antics. "Lucky for me you're *not* old enough, or I wouldn't get to go." He turned to his father. "You're still welcome to go with Joey, Dad. It's been seven long years since the Cubs hosted a World Series at Wrigley. You'd be welcome to go in my place."

The newspaper went back up. "They didn't win in '38, and I'm not holding my breath this time either. You boys go ahead. I'll listen to the game here at home."

"I thought you were opening the theater for Joey today?"

Joey fielded the question instead. "Dad and I decided to keep the theater closed today. No sense opening with everyone glued to their radios or at the game. Besides, our concession sales during the away games were fantastic, so we can afford a day off."

"I still can't believe we've got such great seats for this

game." Danny stood and took his dishes to the sink. "All this time, I was thinking we'd be lucky to get some bleacher tickets or standing room only spots. Instead we're smack-dab in two of the best box seats in the stadium."

"I doubt we would've been able to get tickets," Joey said. "Marv was at Wrigley when he called this morning. He said the crowds started gathering yesterday afternoon shortly after the game ended in Detroit, and kept coming all night long. He figured there were maybe 5,000 or more waiting for the box office to open this morning. They kept a vigil all night. Talk about Cubs fever."

"Sounds like a bunch of crazies, if you ask me," Dad grumbled.

"No, they're just anxious like we are to be a part of history," Danny said. "I just wish Anya could be here for it."

"I thought you said she hated baseball," Betty said.

"Well, sure, but that's only because she's never been to a game. Imagine what a thrill it would be if her first game was the winning game of the 1945 World Series? She'd love it."

"Sure she would," Dad uttered with a hint of sarcasm. "You just keep telling yourself that, son."

"You'll see." Danny dried his hands on a dishtowel. "So when do you want to leave, Joey?"

"Let's head downtown around ten. I figure the El will be jammed today, so we want to allow plenty of extra time."

"Sounds good. I'll be upstairs studying until then."

"How can you study on a day like this?" Joey teased. "Take a break, Einstein. It's not every day you get to go to the World Series!"

Danny had never experienced anything quite like it. The minute he and Joey arrived at the corner of Clark and Addison, they could feel the excitement crackling through the crowds as they moved en masse into Wrigley.

Danny and Joey had just settled into their seats when a ruckus erupted just a few rows behind them.

"I can't believe it." Joey laughed. "Look, Danny. Old man Sianis brought his goat. How the heck did he get Murphy through the gates on a day like today?"

Everyone in Chicago knew the story of the Greek bartender who'd rescued the billy goat years ago after it fell off a passing truck. He took quite a liking to the goat he named Murphy who soon became a fixture at his tavern. Sianis even grew a goatee and started calling himself "Billy Goat Sianis" to drum up business for his bar which he'd renamed the Billy Goat Tavern.

Danny craned his neck to see. "What's it say on Murphy's blanket?"

"It says, 'We got Detroit's goat.' I never understood why they let him bring that dumb goat during the regular season, but I sure didn't expect to see him at a World Series game. Wait 'til Mr. Wrigley hears about this."

"Oh look—" Danny pointed toward the nearest stairs. "Here comes Andy Frain. This ought to be good."

They watched as the owner of the company that provided ushers and security at the ballpark, pushed his way through the crowd, his face tight and pinched.

"Now, see here, Mr. Sianis. You take your billy goat back outside. I don't know who let you in here today, but there's no way I'm letting you—"

"But he's got a ticket!" Billy yelled, waving two stubs at Frain. "We *both* have tickets for these reserved box seats. Besides, Murphy here always brings good luck! They let us in at the gate, so if you'll stand aside, Murphy and I would like to take our seats."

Frain's face reddened as he muttered, "If he eats the ticket —that would solve everything."

"No way he'd eat his ticket," Sianis crooned. "Murphy knows how historic this game is. He'll save his ticket stub just like me, and we'll pin them both on the wall at the tavern."

A mix of laughter and boos accompanied the scene, as Billy played to his audience. "Murphy's a die-hard fan of the Cubs just like the rest of us!"

More laughter, more cheers.

"Mr. Sianis! I will not allow you to keep your goat here in the park today. You must leave at once, or I shall call the authorities!"

"That suits me just fine, Mr. Frain. Why don't you ask Mr. Wrigley?"

"Oh, that's exactly what I'll do!"

Frain pulled a hand-held gadget from his jacket and spoke into it.

"What the heck is that?" Joey asked. "Looks like the HTs we had in the navy."

"We had those, too," Danny said. "Didn't know they were

available for civilians."

A fan behind them joined in. "They call them *Handy-Talkies*. Bert Wilson was talking about them on his radio show this morning. Supposedly, Galvin Manufacturing outfitted all the Andy Frain ushers with them. First time ever. If you ask me, it's just a big publicity stunt."

The crowd grew more vocal as they waited while Frain chatted with others on his device. A brusque breeze fluttered through the stadium, and with it, a definite smell that was anything but pleasing.

Joey covered his nose. "Oh man, that's disgusting."

Others downwind of Murphy echoed similar comments.

"Hey, get that goat outta here! He stinks!"

"Frain, make him leave!"

"Sianis, take your smelly goat and go back to your tavern where you belong!"

Finally, as Frain finished the conversation on his device, he raised his voice toward Sianis loud enough for all to hear. "Mr. Wrigley says the goat goes! He's already heard complaints from fans about the smell, so he is to leave at once. You can either tie the goat up outside and return to watch the game, or you and your goat can go home."

Sianis left kicking and shouting as they escorted him and his bewildered goat toward the exit. "Well, that's a fine way to treat two of your most loyal fans! You haven't heard the last of this! I HOPE THE CUBS LOSE!"

The crowd booed, shouting for him to get out of the ballpark, amid a litany of colorful language, then cheered when the two disappeared down one of the tunnels.

"Well, that's something you don't see every day," Danny

mused. "I sure wish Anya could've seen that. She would've loved it."

"Yeah? Well, let's just hope the Cubs get the deed done and walk out of here as champions."

A few minutes later, the crowd came alive as Roy Nelson's familiar organ tunes filled the ballpark. And as the clock moved in on 1:30, announcer Pat Pieper started the game the usual way.

"PLAAAAAAAAY BAAAAALLLL!"

The crowd cheered as pitcher Ray Prim took the mound for the Cubs. Nicknamed "Pop" by his teammates for his gray hair and upcoming thirty-ninth birthday, Prim was the oldest player on the roster. Recently acquired by the Cubs after playing a stellar 1944 season for Los Angeles, the southpaw started Game 4 strong, shutting out the first ten Tigers' batters in order. But Grimm didn't hesitate to pull him when the hits started flying in the top of the fourth.

Before it was over, Grimm would call in three more relief pitchers—Derringer, Vandenberg, and Erickson—but to no avail. They'd been no match for Dizzy Trout, Detroit's ace right-hander, who had come to the mound with a long list of accomplishments during the war years. A hearing impairment classified him as 4-F, but it clearly had no effect on his pitching ability. He'd broken a long string of league records in 1944, and never was his talent more evident than today's five-hitter against the Cubs. Second baseman Don Johnson scored the only Cubs run, but the team lost the game to the Tigers 4-1.

The subdued crowd slowly made their way out of the stadium. Hard to believe this was the same excited folks who had filed in these same gates only a few hours earlier, optimistic that they would leave as World Champions. Instead, the series was tied with two games each.

On the ride home, some rambunctious fans ranted over manager Charley Grimm's decision to pull pitcher Ray Prim after giving up those four runs in the fourth. But like most of the other passengers on the train, Danny and Joey sat in stunned silence.

On Sunday, Danny and Joey joined the hopeful throngs of fans once again heading back to Wrigley for Game 5. Cubs' pitcher Hank Borowy would be back on the mound pitted against the Tigers' Hal Newhouser, just like Game 1. The Cubs needed a win to stay in it.

After five innings, Chicago and Detroit were tied, 1-1. But when Borowy threw four straight hits at the top of the sixth, giving up four runs, Grimm yanked him. This time, he would call upon four relievers—Vandenberg, Chipman, Derringer, and Erickson—but the damage was already done. Detroit's slugger Hammerin' Hank Greenberg hit his third double of the day off Erickson to give the Tigers the victory, 8-4.

Detroit had taken the lead, winning three games to Chicago's two.

28

8 October 1945

By Monday, the brisk breeze blowing in off Lake Michigan did little to calm the nerves or counter the disappointment of Cubs fans as they returned to Wrigley Field for Game 6. The forecast predicting a cloudy, windy, and colder day with a high of only fifty-six degrees, didn't help much to lift their spirits. Their one ray of hope was the pitching arm of Claude Passeau.

"Good morning, fellas!" Marv slipped their tickets out of his pocket and tore off the stubs. "Today's gonna be a great day for the Cubs!"

"I sure hope so," Joey said. "An awful lot of jitters in this crowd if you ask me."

"Ah, Joey, what's a few jitters here and there when we've got Passeau back on the mound again? How can we lose?"

"Here's hoping, Marv." Danny patted his shoulder then moved along with the flow of fans. "Thanks again for the tickets."

"You're welcome. Have fun!"

"Sure wish I shared his optimism," Joey muttered.

As the game got underway, pitchers Virgil Trucks and Claude Passeau were neck and neck for the first four innings, with only one run scored by the Tigers in the second. But the Cubs exploded in the fifth, scoring four runs to the deafening roar of the hometown crowd. Doing his part, champion batter Phil Cavarretta slammed a solid single to center field, allowing Passeau and Hack to score with Lowery advancing to second. The Cubs now led 4-1. Detroit manager Steve O'Neill yanked Trucks and sent in right-hander George Caster, who put a quick stop to the bleeding.

In the top of the sixth, Tigers' third baseman Jimmy Outlaw smacked the ball right back to the mound where it deflected off Passeau's bare hand. Passeau picked it up, throwing the runner out at first, then immediately calling a time-out when he realized the nail on his middle finger had been partially torn off by the renegade ball. After an extended time-out to have his hand treated, Passeau insisted he could finish the inning.

Bad mistake. The next Detroit batter, pinch-hitter Bob Maier, smashed another hit right back at the mound. Once again, the ball deflected off Passeau's hand, but this time his throw to first was too late. Passeau insisted on staying in, though in tremendous pain. To everyone's amazement, he struck out the last batter.

In their half of the sixth, the Cubs stretched ahead 5-1. Then, to everyone's shock, Passeau took the mound *again* at the top of the seventh. But when the first three batters got on base, he knew he was done. The crowd cheered with appreciation as Passeau trotted to Chicago's dugout.

In his place, Grimm sent Hank Wyse to the mound.

"What in the world is Grimm doing?" Joey cried. "If Wyse plays now, who'll start Game 7 if there is one?"

"But it won't matter if we don't win today's game," Danny said.

Wyse allowed another run before retiring the Tigers. The game stood at 5-3.

By the end of the seventh inning, Chicago still led at 7-3.

When the Tigers scored two more runs early in the eighth, Grimm took Wyse out and called up southpaw starter Ray Prim. But it didn't seem to matter which Cubs pitcher was on the mound when Tigers' powerhouse Hammerin' Hank Greenberg stepped into the batter's box. He promptly drove in two more runs, making it a tie ballgame. Detroit's dugout exploded as the Tigers began to taste blood.

Joey slid his cap down over his face. "I can't watch."

Danny elbowed him. "Where's your faith?"

"In the pit of my stomach."

Tigers manager Steve "Skip" O'Neill pulled out all the stops and called his fifth pitcher to the mound, starter Dizzy Trout. His gamble paid off as the seasoned veteran again shut down the Cubs. With his back against the proverbial wall, Cubs manager Charlie Grimm called up his ace Hank Borowy to pitch.

"You have GOT to be kidding me!" Joey yelled jumping out of his seat. "Borowy?!"

"He pitched six innings yesterday!" Danny added. "There's no way he's got anything left to pull this one out!"

The crowd echoed similar thoughts, much of it using more

colorful adjectives. Still, the anxious fans held a collective breath as Borowy threw several warm-up pitches to catcher Mickey Livingston. In short order, Borowy alleviated their fears and closed the inning with no more damage. Chicago's batters tried hard in the bottom of the ninth but failed to add any runs.

With the score still tied 7-7, Game 6 of the World Series went into extra innings.

For the first time all day, the sun finally broke through the clouds and drew its signature rays on the field; the pitching mound bathed in sunlight with the batter's box deeply shaded, giving pitchers the worst possible visual. The tenth and eleventh innings crawled by with no runs by either team; the crowd quiet and tense.

But the twelfth and final inning would more than make up for their malaise.

Borowy quickly put away Tigers' catcher Bob Swift and pitcher Dizzy Trout, but allowed shortstop Jim Hoover to get to first on a single to left field. Anxious to stoke the Tigers' fire, Hoover tried to steal second. But when he saw Chicago's shortstop Lennie Merullo catch the ball for the tag, Hoover slid into second, spikes up, intentionally slicing Merullo's forearm. The crowd booed and hissed as the Cubs on the field protested.

When the Cubs came to bat, they wasted no time. Williams grounded out to second. Grimm sent in Frank Secory to pinch-hit for the injured Merullo. Secory hit a line drive to center field, and was immediately replaced by pinch runner Billy Schuster. Then pitcher Hank Borowy struck out. With two outs and Schuster on first, crowd favorite Stan

Hack strode to the plate. He waited for Trout's fastball and swung, sending the ball sailing over Hoover's head. Greenberg raced in from left field, but the ball took a wild bounce over his head. Schuster rounded second, streaked past third, and headed home for the winning run.

The final score: Cubs beat the Tigers 8-7.

The wild roar of the crowd filled the chilly night air as the team raced out of the dugout to pile on Hack and Schuster.

"WE WON!" Danny shouted. "WE WON!"

Joey shook his head with a laugh. "I don't believe it! I saw it, but I don't believe it!"

"What did I tell you?" Danny yelled. "We're only one game away from winning the championship! We can do this! Nothing can stop us now!"

At three hours and twenty-eight minutes, the game set a new record for the longest World Series game ever played. They'd gone twelve innings, with twenty-eight hits, and a total of nine different pitchers between the two teams. As the sun began to set, the stands still rocked with jubilant fans, thrilled to have another chance. Joey and Danny eventually joined the others filing out of Wrigley. Already, a long queue of eager fans snaked through the corridor, lined up for tickets to Wednesday's Game 7.

But the million-dollar question remained. Who would pitch the final game of the series for the Cubs?

With the help of the Andy Frain ushers and police officers from the nearest precinct, Monday's overnight vigil by those lined up for tickets at Wrigley had remained calm and orderly despite the cold temperature dipping into the low 40s. The *Chicago Tribune's* Edward Prell described the scene of excited fans wrapped in blankets, some playing rummy, some warming their hands by fires lit in garbage cans. Mr. Frain and his men kept a close watch, and Frain quickly found himself the source of constant attention from folks trying to gain favor. A fan from nearby Waukegan even offered him a six-pound fish in exchange for good seats. Frain was amused but declined the offer.

When the twenty-eight ticket windows opened at 8:00 a.m. on Tuesday morning, owner Philip Wrigley was there to help supervise the distribution of tickets for Wednesday's Game 7. Wrigley was particularly interested in helping the loyal fans who had attended games throughout the war years who'd been unable to attend any of the previous series games because they couldn't get tickets. By 11:30 that morning, all reserve seats were sold out.

On Wednesday morning, the 5,000 bleacher seats went on sale, and when those were gone, the 2,500 standing room admissions were up for grabs.

If the Cubs fans were a bit tentative when they arrived for Game 6 two days prior, they were almost breathless with anxiety when they gathered at the corner of Clark and Addison. Like most others lined up, Danny and Joey kept their thoughts to themselves, just anxious to get the game started. When they reached Marv at the gate, he gave both of them a hearty handshake.

"Hi, boys! Today's the day!"

"I sure hope so," Joey said. "Regardless, there's no way we'll ever be able to thank you enough for these tickets. And just so you know, you'll never pay for another movie ticket at the Windsor. Understood?"

"Really? That's great. Thanks, Joey!"

Danny gave him a pat on the back. "It's been unforgettable, Marv. I can't tell you what a thrill it's been. Thanks so much, pal."

"Boys, it's been my pleasure. Now go cheer our Cubs to the final victory. I'm counting on you!"

Just before Roy Nelson's organ tunes filled the stadium, a collective groan rippled through the crowd as Hank Borowy left the bullpen and headed to the mound. No one would argue that Borowy was their best pitcher and had what it took to be a world-class champion. But with only one day off since pitching four innings in relief on Monday—and that, after pitching six innings on Sunday—most everyone questioned Grimm's decision to send Borowy in to start Game 7.

As Borowy and Nicholson warmed up with a few more tosses, the stands began to thunder with cheers so loud, Danny wondered if they weren't trying to infuse the Cubs pitcher with all their hopes and dreams for the championship.

"We can do this, Joey. We can!"

Joey said nothing, his eyes glued to number 26 as he wound up his first pitch.

The first inning did not go well. Borowy gave up singles to the first three Detroit batters. The stunned Chicago fans watched in disbelief as Charley Grimm marched out to the mound and held out his hand for the ball. Even from where Danny sat, he could see the surprise on the pitcher's face. They exchanged some heated words as reliever Paul Derringer arrived to replace him. In protest, Borowy waited until Grimm was back in the dugout before he made his own final walk off the mound.

Danny, Joey, and the rest of the fans stood and gave Hank Borowy a loud shout of thanks. Without him, they knew they would never have made it to the World Series.

Unfortunately, Derringer didn't fare much better. By the end of the first inning, Detroit had already racked up five runs. The Cubs answered with only one run on Detroit's well-rested pitcher, Hal Newhouser. The tone of the final game was set as Newhouser went the distance for Detroit, striking out ten batters and allowing only ten hits through nine innings. Grimm, on the other hand, blew through a total of six pitchers and still came up short.

The Cubs lost the game 9-3, giving the World Series championship to the Detroit Tigers.

"I should've stayed home," Joey moaned as they slowly made their way through the disheartened crowd. "I had a gut feeling this would happen. I just never thought it would all be over in the first inning."

"I'm guessing Grimm will be raked over the coals," Danny added. "He'll have to answer for a lot of poor choices."

"Just do me a favor," Joey said, rounding the final exit onto Addison. "If by some bizarre chance we make it back to the World Series next year, remind me not to go. It's too painful."

Danny hooked his elbow around Joey's neck. "Ah, c'mon,

Joey. They played great ball! They may have lost the last game, but they clearly out-hit, out-fielded, and out-pitched the Tigers. Think about it. If you took Newhouser and Greenberg off their roster, who would have won the series?"

Joey pulled away with a chuckle. "Yeah, yeah, but none of that matters. It's who comes up on top at the end, and apparently we're destined to come up short no matter how hard we play. This makes *seven times* the Cubs have been to the World Series. And how many times have we won?"

"Only two, but lest we forget, both those wins back in '07 and '08 were against the Tigers. This was only their second series crown."

"Yes, brother dearest, and lest we forget, who did they beat on their first visit to the series?"

"Okay, it was us, but—"

"Oh, give it a rest. It's over. I'm over it."

"Yeah, I can tell."

"But you've got to wonder if that stupid goat is to blame."

"Oh, c'mon, Joey, you don't really believe in curses, do you?"

"I didn't use to, but think about it, Danny. When old man Sianis and his goat got kicked out just before Game 4, he went back to his bar and started ranting about the Cubs and saying they'd never win another World Series as long as they didn't allow goats to attend. You yourself said we out-hit, out-fielded, and out-pitched the Tigers, yet we lost the series. It's got to make you wonder, right?"

"Nope. Just a silly rumor and nothing more. You mark my words. The Cubs will be back next year!"

29

25 October 1945

London, England

"Oh no, here comes another one—ahhh!"

If Kate's pinched and flushed face were any indication, Anya couldn't imagine the pain her flatmate was experiencing with each new contraction. They'd begun two hours earlier, just before four that afternoon, with long sporadic gaps in between. They'd rung the doctor who gave Anya some simple instructions, and told her to telephone again when the contractions were five to seven minutes apart for at least an hour. Anya had also telephoned Sybil at the Rainbow. She promised to be home as soon as she could find someone to take her shift.

None of them knew where Gigi was, but that wasn't unusual.

Anya noted the time then patted Kate's brow with the cool, damp cloth until the contraction passed. She fell back against the pillows stuffed behind her and blew out a long sigh.

"That one wasn't as bad, was it?"

"No, not really." Kate raked her fingers through her long dark hair and smiled mischievously at Anya. "Do you realize you're tensing when I do?"

"Am I? Really?"

"Yes, and every time you start breathing like I do." She feigned the short, puffy breaths.

Anya shielded her face behind her hands and laughed.

Kate rested her head back against the pillows. "Don't be embarrassed. Just think of all the practice you're getting for when you have babies of your own."

Anya felt her face warm. "Not if we never get on those blasted ships to America."

"True. Will we *ever* see our husbands again? Sometimes I wonder."

"Oh Kate—it just occurred to me that we haven't placed a call to let Joe know you're in labor. Shall I go back across the street to ring him?"

Kate's eyes drifted shut. "No, not yet. I'd rather wait until the baby is born. And at the rate I'm going, that could be next week. Maybe next month."

"Not a chance. He'll be here before the day ends."

"He? So you think it's a boy?"

"No. I'm not sure why I said that. Are you hoping for a boy?"

She opened her eyes again briefly. "Honestly, at this point, it doesn't matter. Either will suit me fine." She gently patted her enormous belly. "I just want this little one to pop out."

She winked then closed her eyes again with another weary sigh. "I think I'd like to rest now."

"Good. I'll be right here if you need me."

Anya moved to the overstuffed chair in the corner of the room and relaxed a moment before picking up her pen and paper. With a large book beneath, she tried again to start her letter.

Dear Danny,

First, before I forget, I was sorry to read in your last letter that your Cubs lost the World Series. It's a game I don't understand, but since I know how much you love baseball and especially your Cubs, I know it must have been very hard for you and Joey to watch them lose. Maybe they'll do better next year. I laughed out loud about the man who brought his goat to the first game. Do Americans often take their animals to baseball games? You don't really believe he cursed the Cubs, do you? Perhaps I'll bring them good luck when I move to Chicago, America.

You will not believe what I am doing right now. I'm sitting here with Kate, one of my flatmates, whose baby is on the way. She's resting now between contractions, so I shall write during these intervals until her little one decides to cause another stir. Sybil should be home soon, and the doctor has been notified.

It's a bit daunting, experiencing this birthing process. I witnessed lots of animal births when I used to help the Boormans on their farm back home. But this is so very different. Kate doesn't seem nervous at all, which is fine since I'm nervous enough for both of us.

I'm still not quite used to living here in London, and I miss Sophie and Charlie terribly. Patrick, too. They were beginning to feel like family to me, Danny, and I would gladly have stayed with them longer. But it makes more sense to be here, close by should I finally get my turn to board a ship to America. Sometimes I wonder if it will ever happen.

Anya stopped, her pen poised over the letter. Guilt heated the vicinity of her heart as she knowingly omitted the truth behind her move. Charlie and Sophie promised they would not tell Danny about the attack in the pub's alley and Anya's part in it. Sergeant Ketner's kind face flashed through her mind along with his warning: *You're in danger here.* She would not tell Danny yet because there was nothing he could do. She would tell him someday.

Still, the guilt had its way, haunting her. She shook off the dark thoughts with a shudder and continued.

It's quite different, living with three other girls. Sybil is so kind and has made me feel at home here. She's excited about her baby too, and ever so relieved that she'll be in America with Jack when hers arrives next February. I've been teaching her to cook some of the recipes I learned from Sophie at the pub. I had not known that Sybil lost both her parents in the Blitz. I couldn't imagine that anyone so cheerful and outgoing could have suffered such loss. But it has given us a bit of a bond, and I want to learn from her how to leave the wounds of war behind.

I think you will find Kate's story quite interesting. Her husband Joe lives in Long Island, New York. She met him at a dance club in Winchester. She said army lorries would stop by the Spitfire factory where she worked as a secretary and give the girls a ride to the dance club after hours. Joe was a musician who played in the Glenn Miller Band. I remember how much you liked Glenn Miller's music. Such a small world, isn't it? One night the band had taken a break, and Joe was standing off to the side of the stage. She thought him quite handsome, so walked right up to him and introduced herself. Just like that. They fell in love and married in May of last year. She was only seventeen—

Much later. I had to help Kate through several more contractions. I realize I've been rambling on about her, someone you've never met. Perhaps you'll meet her once we all sail to America—

It's happening—the baby's coming—off we go to hospital! More later.

Love,

Anya

Sybil rushed into the bedroom just as Anya was helping Kate to her feet. "Kate, darling! Look at you! You're about to have a—"

"Hurry, hurry! Get me to the lav! I can't hold it—"

A gush of water puddled the floor beneath her.

Anya's eyes went wide at the sight. "Wha—"

"Your waters broke!" Sybil squealed, her hands grabbing her own swollen abdomen. "Oh, Kate! I can't believe it—my baby just kicked! It's the first time!" She giggled as she yanked a coverlet off the bed and dropped it over the watered floor. "It's like Elizabeth's baby John who leapt in her womb when she saw Mary—"

Kate cried out with another contraction, losing her balance. Anya caught her just in time and lowered her to sit back on the bed.

"How can I help?"

All three turned to find a tall American in uniform standing at the door.

"You all remember Lieutenant Powell? From the American Embassy?" Sybil said. "He was at the Rainbow when you telephoned and offered to drive me home then take us to hospital."

Anya suddenly remembered why he looked so familiar. "You're—"

"MUST HURRY ..." Kate growled. "NOW!"

Powell rushed to her side. "Yes, ma'am. Let's get you to that hospital."

They all talked at once as the lieutenant wrapped Kate's arm over his shoulder and took as much of her weight as he could.

"Sybil, open the door then help me ease her down the steps to my car."

"I'm here, right behind you," she said. "Anya, find her wrap and handbag. Oh, and grab that quilt and a few towels out of the lav, will you?"

"Yes, and I'll be right there. Don't leave without me!"

Just as she hurried down the hall to the bathroom, the back door swung open. Gigi walked in, stopping when she saw Anya staring at her.

"Gigi! Where have you been? Kate's in labor and we're—"

"What? Now?" She hurried by Anya and poked her head into Kate's bedroom.

Anya turned to follow her. "Are you *drunk?*"

"Don't be daft. Where is Kate and—what *happened* in here?" She looked from the floor up to the ceiling. "Is that another leak from the roof?"

Anya shook her head. "No, Kate's waters broke. They're helping Kate into the automobile out front."

"Who's they?"

"Sybil and Lieutenant Powell. Now make yourself useful and find Kate's handbag for me."

"Well, you don't have to be so nasty about it."

"Just do it, Gigi."

A few minutes later, they all piled into Powell's automobile, with Sybil and Anya on either side of Kate in the backseat and Gigi in front with Powell.

He glanced in his rearview mirror. "I'll have you there as quick as I can, ma'am."

"Yes, please, thank you," she groaned.

"I didn't know hospitals were open again for delivering babies. Last I heard they were still evacuating all the prospective mums to the emergency maternity homes out in the country. Are you even sure they'll take you, Kate?"

"Why would you ask a question like that now?" Sybil snapped.

"Because it's a valid question! All the maternity wards were closed down when the Blitz started. And last I heard, they were still closed. Why are you snapping at me like—"

"I talked to her doctor earlier today," Anya interrupted. "He told us to bring Kate to St. Thomas's."

Kate groaned louder, clawing her fingers into Anya's arm and Sybil's knee. "Ohhhh hurry!"

Sybil winced silently, pulling Kate's hand off her leg. "You go right ahead and scream, love. We're just a few blocks away from hospital now."

Anya bit back a chuckle at the expression on Sybil's face. By the looks of it, Kate's manicured nails might have drawn blood on Sybil's knee.

"Hold on!" Powell warned, taking a corner faster than expected.

"Ow-ow-ow-OW!"

In a flash, he stopped the car at the emergency entrance, and Kate was whisked inside by an attendant with Sybil close behind. A few minutes later, the lieutenant joined them just as Sybil found them in the waiting room.

"Oh, Phillip, you don't have to stay with us. It was kind of you to drive us, but please don't feel obligated to stay."

"Unless you object, I'd prefer to stay. That way, whenever you three need a ride home, I can give you a lift." He motioned for Sybil to take a seat across from Anya and Gigi, then sat beside her.

"But it could be hours yet, according to the doctor. We wouldn't want to impose on you."

"You're not imposing at all. I had no plans for tonight, so I'm free to stick around. Unless you would rather I go?"

Gigi lit up a cigarette. "You might as well stay. If it's going to take all night, at least you can entertain us."

Sybil waved the cloud of smoke away from her. "Do you have

to smoke that in here? You know how queasy cigarette smoke makes me."

Gigi took another puff and blew it the other direction. "The way I see it, that's your problem. Not mine. Besides, it relaxes me."

"As if you needed anything else to relax you. You smell like a distillery. Where were you all afternoon?"

A naughty smile tugged at her red lips. "Just having a few drinks with a friend."

"Oh? What friend?" Sybil shifted in her chair to get more comfortable and glanced at Gigi's legs. "Are those new nylons you're wearing?"

"Yes, aren't they lovely?" Gigi stood, striking various poses.

Sybil tsked. "Good heavens, Gigi. Have you no shame?"

"*Another* bee in your bonnet? At least I'm not bare-legged like you and Anya." She turned to Phillip, placing a hand on his shoulder. "Tell us, lieutenant. Do Yanks look at a woman's bare legs and assume she's 'available'?"

Phillip blanched, sitting up straighter. "I'm, uh ... I'm sure I don't know what you mean."

"Oh, don't play coy with me, Lieutenant." She gave his shoulder a pinch then twirled around again."

Sybil dropped her head in her hands. "Gigi, will you just sit down and stop embarrassing yourself."

"Who says I'm embarrassed?" Gigi knelt before Sybil, lifting her skirt as she did so, just enough to show off her nylons as she tossed a flirty wink to Powell. "Syb, honey, you need to relax. No sense getting your knickers all in a twist. We're not living in the Victorian age anymore." She leaned in and placed a loud kiss on Sybil's cheek then took her seat again. "Well, Lieutenant?"

He hesitated a moment then shrugged. "Yes. I have heard some of our men on occasion say something along those lines. It's just that we're all used to women wearing nylons back home, and I suppose that's why so many of us—them—keep a supply handy. Girls like nylons, Yanks like seeing them in nylons. I suppose it's just one of those wartime customs." He paused for a moment then chuckled.

Gigi smirked. "What?"

"No, it's nothing—"

"Yes, it is. What's so funny?"

The lieutenant's face tinged with a blush as he tried again to brush it off.

"Out with it!" Gigi insisted.

"Okay, fine. I just remembered the first time I heard a buddy of mine complain about the gravy stains on his uniform. He'd been dancing the jitterbug all evening with an English girl." He tried not to laugh but couldn't seem to help himself.

Gigi giggled, and Sybil joined her.

Anya didn't have a clue. "Gravy stains? Will someone please tell me what's so funny?"

When their laughter ebbed, Sybil explained. "A proper English girl does *not* go out with a young man without wearing her nylons. But they became so scarce during the war that some girls took to more ... *creative* methods to fake the appearance of nylons."

Gigi stamped out her cigarette in an ashtray. "I found their methods ridiculous, but some girls would literally paint their legs with a tinted tanning cream. Or even worse, they'd actually smear their legs with gravy, then have a friend draw a black line down the back of their legs."

Anya scoffed. "You're not serious, are you?"

"I'm afraid she's right." Phillip laughed again and raised his arms to stretch. "My friend was a terrific dancer, and boy was he furious when he saw all those stains all over his uniform."

Sybil leaned her head back. "Oh, the things we do for love."

When the laughter waned, Gigi glanced back at Phillip and pointed a long, manicured finger at him. "We haven't been properly introduced. I'm Gigi. Phillip, is it?"

Anya glanced at the large diamond on Gigi's left hand which apparently meant nothing to her. She wondered if Jack had any idea of his wife's proclivity to "go off the rails," as they called it here.

Sybil elbowed the lieutenant. "Phillip, forgive me for not introducing my other flatmate, Anya McClain."

"Oh, yes, of course. I knew I recognized you, Mrs. McClain. I processed your file the day you first visited the embassy, as I recall. It's nice to see you again."

"I remember you too, Lieutenant."

"Please, just call me Phillip."

Gigi wasted no time. "So, Phillip, how is it that all our husbands are back in America, and yet *you* are still here?"

"Because it's my job to make sure all you war brides get transported across the Atlantic to join your husbands." He glanced back at Sybil. "We still have a lot of work to do before they send the rest of us home."

Gigi straightened. "We all attended the protest at your

embassy last week, though a lot of good it did. If you ask me, no one seems to have a clue what they're doing."

"Yes, I was watching from my office window," he said. "You all had a huge turnout, several hundred of you, and even more that evening at Caxton Hall. They estimated several thousand came that night to hear Lieutenant Commander Agar address the problem." Powell leaned forward, resting his elbows on his knees. "Actually, I thought it shed some light on the problems we're facing, primarily the question of transportation to the U.S. We're doing our best to work with the British, but it's going to take at least another month or more to commission the ships we need."

"We keep hearing there's a breakdown in communication between the American commission sent over to sort it all out and their British counterparts," Sybil said. "It seems to me everyone's talking, but nothing's happening."

"I'm sure it seems that way, and to be honest, that's the nature of diplomacy. Lots of talk and not much action. But in fairness, the end of the war requires a massive amount of government interaction, and unfortunately, war brides aren't the priority. I wish I could offer some hope to you, but it's a colossal undertaking, as I'm sure you know."

Anya pressed on. "We keep hearing that all the Americans back in the States think every single American serviceman should be returned home before they'll start transporting us. I understand why they feel that way, but I was appalled to read that many American women think of us as tramps who've stolen their men. Is that true, Lieutenant?"

He smiled. "It's Phillip, remember? But no, I don't think that kind of rhetoric is widespread. That said, there is quite a resentment among the British men here that American servicemen have somehow snatched all the eligible British women, so I guess it goes both ways. But that's the nature of war and its aftermath. A lot of misperceptions."

Gigi waved her hand, dismissing the conversation. "Enough of all that. Phillip, tell us how you know our Sybil?"

Phillip blinked and leaned back in his chair. "We met a few weeks ago at Rainbow Corner. Obviously, I've seen her working there before, but we'd never talked. Until recently, anyway."

Sybil shook her head with a smile. "He's quite the gentleman by not telling you *how* we met. I spilled a full tray of Cokes, and Phillip was kind enough to come to my rescue."

Gigi smiled. "Ah, fancy that. Such a kind fellow helping a damsel in distress."

A matronly nurse approached them. "Friends of Kate Miller?"

Sybil stood. "Yes, we are. How's she doing?"

"Quite well, as a matter of fact. She just gave birth to a little girl and asked me to let you know."

Anya joined them. "Already?"

"But she only just arrived!" Gigi said, snuffing out her cigarette.

"Yes, and if you've done this as long as I have, you learn that babies come when they're ready. I'll be returning to Mrs. Miller now. I'll let you know when she's moved to the maternity ward." She turned and padded quietly down the hall.

Anya stared after her. "I can't believe it." She looked up at the clock on the wall. "Kate's first contraction started less than four hours ago. I thought it usually took hours and hours to deliver."

Powell shook his head with a smile. "I guess there's no rhyme or reason why one takes a day or two while others just pop right out."

"Is that so?" Gigi's brow creased. "Are we to assume you have children, Phillip?"

"No, ma'am, but I'm the oldest in a family with six kids, so I know a thing or two about babies."

"A baby girl." Sybil sighed happily, resting her hands on her abdomen again. "Is there anything sweeter? Isn't it wonderful? After all these years of war, we're finally learning how to be happy again."

Anya couldn't help sharing the joy of the moment, wishing with all her heart that Sybil was right.

30

November 1945

With Kate and her baby's return home, a renewed spirit of hope seemed to flourish in the London flat. Sybil and Anya took turns tending to little Jocelyn, eager to rock or feed or bathe her whenever Kate needed rest.

Gigi kept her distance, always offering clever excuses for her lack of attention to the baby. Anya suspected it wasn't a dislike of babies per se, but rather a simple case of not knowing anything about them or even how to hold them. They tried to teach her, but she always pressed a quick kiss on Jocelyn's cheek, murmured a fond goodbye, then left the house again.

By contrast, Anya loved cradling the baby in her arms and marveling at her ten perfect fingers tipped with ten tiny nails. She loved the baby's scent fresh from a bath, the innocent curiosity in her little eyes, and the way her small oval mouth made sucking motions as she slept.

It was only these times, when everyone else slept, and she had little Jocelyn all to herself, that Anya allowed herself to dream of one day holding her own baby.

Will she have Danny's easy smile? Will she have my eyes? My hair? Will she love to laugh like her father? Or have a more serious nature like mine? Or if we have a son, will he have Danny's strong jawline? Or a complexion like mine?

These stolen moments always made her miss Danny, more than she thought humanly possible. From the beginning, their relationship had never been easy. She wondered again if they were destined to be apart forever, never having more than a few weeks or months together. It's why she rarely allowed herself to dream, because the pattern of their life together was no pattern at all. And yet, with her eyes still fixed on the precious baby sleeping in her arms, Anya recognized the smallest glimmer of hope the little one had given her.

It was a start.

In early December, Sybil arranged for one of the photographers at the Rainbow to come to the flat and take pictures of Kate and little Joss, as they now called her, to send Joe. The talented photographer was a delight to work with; easygoing and quite gifted at staging more natural poses of the new mother and her daughter. Sybil decided they should all have individual pictures made to send their husbands in America, as well as a group photograph. They scurried around helping each other pick out their most flattering attire. Gigi insisted Sybil and Anya shake their hair free from the snoods they'd all grown so accustomed to wearing.

Gigi snapped her fingers at Sybil and motioned for her to sit, then proceeded to use her arsenal of soot and charcoal to highlight Sybil's facial features.

"I will never get used to wearing make-up," Sybil complained. "Jack was always buying it for me, but I don't like the feel of it against my skin. We never wore it before the war, then the Yanks came, expecting all of us to look like their Hollywood stars back home. And here we are, still painting our faces to keep them happy."

"You just don't know how to wear it." Gigi dusted Sybil's face with powder. "You need the touch of an expert like me. There." She handed Sybil a mirror. "Take a look, but first get up so Anya can have a seat."

Anya stiffened. "No, I'm not wearing any of that on my face."

Gigi parked a fist on her hip. "Trust me. You need it. You look positively ashen. You don't want Danny to see your photograph and think you're all washed out like an old dish rag. Sit."

Anya folded her arms across her chest. "No."

The blonde narrowed her eyes for a moment, then shrugged. "Fine. But don't blame me if he starts to wander. Didn't you tell me he's back in university? Why, he's probably surrounded by pretty young girls every—"

"Gigi, leave her alone." Sybil set the hand mirror on the dresser then hooked her arm through Anya's. "Ignore her. Otherwise, she'll have all of us looking like a bunch of strumpets."

The photographs were ready a few days later, all of them fabulous. Those of Kate and Joss would surely warm Joe's heart, and the ones of the baby with her chubby cheeks and sweet smile were truly angelic. Gazing at the pictures, Anya thought Kate was prettier than any of those Hollywood stars on the big screen. And yet, there was also something so beautifully wholesome about her.

Though Sybil's abdomen was discreetly hidden from the camera's eye, she seemed to glow in her photograph. Anya could easily imagine her as royalty; a princess living at Buckingham Palace waiting to give birth to an heir to the throne. Jack would be thrilled to receive the picture, such a lovely likeness of his English bride.

Anya had never liked having her picture taken, but she was pleasantly surprised by the genuine happiness on her face in her photograph. Neither stilted nor somber in some awkward pose, she marveled at the smile on her face, almost unfamiliar with it. She had obviously gained some weight since Danny left, most of it while working at the pub. She hoped he would be pleased to see her looking healthier.

And while she had refused Gigi's lavish help with make-up, Anya liked the subtle dash of red lipstick Sybil had suggested. She often wondered why all the English girls wore such bright-red lipstick until Sybil explained it as a sign of British patriotism, often called "the red badge of courage." That made sense. And even though the photographs were black and white, she had to admit the darkened tint on her lips helped her smile stand out.

As for the group picture, Sybil said it best. "We look like the four-and-a-half musketeers," even though Joss had slept through most of the session. Anya loved the picture and wanted to keep a framed copy on her nightstand.

She and Sybil found some pretty frames at a small shop around the corner. While there, Anya discovered a Christmas ornament with a tintype image of London's Big Ben on one side, and the dome of St. Paul's on the other. She thought it the perfect gift for Danny's family, and carefully wrapped it before tucking it inside the box with her framed photograph to post to America.

As the brisk winter days passed, they settled into an easy schedule, always making sure at least one of them was home to help Kate. Sybil cut back on her hours at the Rainbow; a timely decision since fewer Americans remained in London. Anya thought her friend looked quite fatigued of late and tried to convince her to quit working altogether. Sybil remained adamant, saying the job helped pass the time.

Thankfully, Gigi seemed to have an endless flow of cash from her husband Paul in California. She insisted on paying the rent in full each month and kept the pantry well stocked, explaining Paul's insistence that she take care of them all. Anya couldn't help wondering if Paul suspected his wife might be cheating on him, thinking he could buy her faithfulness. Or perhaps it was Gigi's way of buying their discretion since all of them knew how often she'd been unfaithful?

Anya couldn't imagine living such a lie.

Or maybe she could. Wasn't she living one herself? Nothing as scandalous as adultery, but hadn't her father always taught that a lie was a lie, whether committed or omitted? Hadn't he often preached about "the slippery slope" of mistruths? Had Gigi's deceitful habits begun with a series of little white lies in order to save face?

Anya shook off the thoughts. She would tell Danny the real reason she had to leave Framlingham. She would. Someday.

By mid-December, the wait for news about the war bride ships had become excruciating. Anya received another letter from Danny's mother. Betty had been so faithful to write, three or four letters a month, though Anya found it increasingly difficult to respond to her ever-cheerful notes. The latest letter, dated earlier in November, told of the family's upcoming plans for Thanksgiving and how much they had hoped she could have celebrated the traditional American holiday with them. Instead, they would look forward to Christmas, confident Anya would surely be there to open gifts around the tree with them. She asked if Anya had any favorite Dutch Christmas cookies she might teach her to make, and expressed how much she was looking forward to sharing many happy hours in the kitchen baking with her two daughters-in-law.

And, as she always did, Betty mentioned her constant prayers for God to "open the way to bring you home to us, however He might do so."

Anya read the letter three times the day it arrived, wishing the words on the page would lift her spirits. Not a single war bride ship had sailed, nor had she or any of her flatmates been notified about a pending date. The disappointment grew with each passing day.

Danny's letters came less often. She wasn't worried or surprised since he'd taken a part-time job working at the campus library. Between that, his classes and studies, and occasional shifts at the theater, he stayed busy. In his last letter, he mentioned meeting a fellow veteran who also worked at the library and attended classes. Danny wrote how sorry he felt for the guy who'd been in a Japanese prisoner of war camp for more than two years before the war ended.

As I've gotten to know Lee, I was reminded how blessed I was to make it home with a sound mind. He battles depression and has horrific nightmares. His injuries may not be physical, but the emotional damage is severe. I'm actually surprised he's able to work and study at all. Poor guy. I'm trying to be a friend to him. I'm not sure what else I can do to help.

Anya understood the emotional scars all too well, which is why she worked so hard to suppress them. She remembered Danny's letter about his father's war experience and how it had molded him into the gruff man he is today, still haunted by those memories all these years later. She would not let this war dominate her life. Not now, and certainly not when she arrived in America to begin her life with Danny. She paid careful attention to the words she wrote him, careful to sanitize any trace of fear or angst she might be experiencing. Hadn't she vowed to stop all the self-pity? She remembered the day she walked back to the pub in Framlingham when she promised herself to master her emotions before crossing the ocean.

No more tears. No more gloomy thoughts. No more sadness.

But with all that transpired, she'd nearly forgotten that vow. She closed her eyes and remembered how good the optimism had felt that day, and promised herself once more to live in a realm of hope and not despair.

Still, the weeks dragged on. Helping out at Rainbow Corner

had helped, though the number of American servicemen seemed to dwindle more each day. There was talk of closing London's most famous Red Cross club, most likely sometime after the first of the year. But Anya needed to work to keep her spirits up and found that even the most menial tasks helped pass the time. Just a week before Christmas, Anya was downstairs working behind the counter at Dunker's Den when she heard a familiar voice.

"Hello, Mrs. McClain."

She turned to find Lieutenant Powell taking a seat on one of the vinyl stools at the counter.

"Hello, Lieutenant. I haven't seen you in a while. Sybil and I wondered if perhaps you'd been transferred back to America."

"No, I'm still here. I've been working a lot of overtime, as you can imagine."

Anya finished drying some glasses and put them away. "I hope that means you've come to tell me to pack my bags."

He made a clever face, then turned to glance over his shoulder for a moment. He crooked a finger, motioning her to lean in, then whispered, "Can you keep a secret?"

"Of course I can."

He looked around again as if spies might be listening in on their conversation. "Because this is strictly off the record, okay?"

Anya rolled her eyes playfully. "Yes, all right. What is this 'strictly off the record' secret?"

He leaned in closer. "I saw the list today. You're on it. You and all three of your flatmates will be sailing for America shortly after Christmas."

"WE'RE GOING?!" Anya cried and rushed around the counter to hug him as he stood. "Are you SURE, Lieutenant? Are you ABSOLUTELY SURE?! We're GOING TO AMERICA?!"

He laughed hard, placing a finger over his lips. "What happened to keeping this a secret?"

"I can't help it!" She dug a handkerchief out of her pocket to stem the sudden flow of tears. "I was beginning to think this day would never come!" She finally stilled, trying to catch her breath. "Oh, you're not just teasing, are you? You wouldn't do that, would you?"

He touched her elbow and steered her to the nearest table. "Please sit. You're making me dizzy. And let's dispense with the formalities. It's Phillip, remember?"

She took a seat but could hardly contain herself. "Yes, then, Phillip. And you must call me Anya. She grasped both his hands in hers. "Tell me you're not making any of this up. Promise me. You *actually* saw a list with our names on it? All four of us?"

"Yes, I *actually* saw a list with all four of your names on it. No, wait. Make that five names. Mustn't forget little Jocelyn."

Anya suddenly realized she was still holding his hands and pulled hers back. "Sorry, oh I'm just so ... I can't seem to ... is it ..." Then, without a moment's hesitation, she squeezed her eyes shut and whispered another squeal.

Phillip laughed again, shaking his head. "It's a good thing it's just the two of us down here right now. I'd be in all kinds of trouble for letting the cat out of the bag."

Still grinning, she slowed her laughter for a moment. "I'm sorry, did you say you had a cat?"

Phillip laughed, shaking his head. "No! I hate cats. It's an expression. And by the look on your face, it must be an American expression. It means telling a secret, like I just told you. My commanding officer insisted we sit on it until after the holidays."

"Sit on what?"

He smiled again. "Sorry. Again. Sit on it—don't do anything or say anything about it yet."

"But why? If we're on the list, why not tell us so we can get ready?"

"With all the protests and complaints over the past few months, he's afraid those not yet on the list will cause more problems. Obviously, we can't put every war bride on the first ships to sail. We hope to avoid any more incidents with all you ladies shouting at us from the street."

Anya leaned back in her chair, unable to stop her smile. "Then why have you told me? Why risk it?"

Phillip laced his fingers behind his neck and stretched. When he faced her again, he looked up with a sheepish expression. "I shouldn't tell you why."

"No, you must." She sat up, resting her elbows on the table. "Either tell me, or I shall march right over to that microphone and announce it throughout the entire building."

"Okay, okay! I'll tell you." He rubbed his hand across his chin and scratched the day's whiskers on his neck. "The thing is, this morning I was told I won't be able to go home for Christmas. I haven't had a leave since the war ended, and I was supposed to have two full weeks off to go home."

"But that's not fair. Why can't you go?"

"My CO had a family emergency back home, so he goes, and I stay. Simple as that."

"I hope it was something truly serious."

A slight grimace waved over his face. "Well, yes, it was. His father was killed in a hunting accident yesterday."

Anya mirrored his grimace. "Sorry. That was horrible of me to say."

"It's all right. I had the same thought myself before he told me."

"So your Christmas leave was cancelled? That's why you told me we're on the list? I don't understand."

"No, it's more selfish than that, if you must know. I was hoping..." He lifted his shoulders then shrugged. "I was thinking I might share this good news with the four of you in exchange for an invitation for Christmas dinner." Another shrug. "There. Now you know."

Anya laughed softly. Until that moment, she'd never noticed his good looks before. To her, he was just the man at the American embassy who'd been kind to her that first day, promising to put her name on the all-important list for transport—

Something fluttered through her heart as a thought suddenly occurred to her. Was Lieutenant Powell another answer to Betty's prayers? Had God orchestrated for Anya to be in his queue that first day at the embassy? Had He used Phillip to "open the doors" to bring Anya home to America? Was that possible? Had God also placed him here that night Sybil was working when Anya called to tell her Kate was in labor? Had it been more than a mere coincidence that he had a vehicle and offered to help take Kate to hospital in time to have her baby?

Another strange flutter played with her heart as she

realized *none* of that could have been pure coincidence.

As her heart accepted the truth, she found herself still staring at him. She'd never noticed the kindness in his blue eyes, or the laugh lines gathered beside them. Never noticed a smile so genuine, its mere curve put her at ease.

"Well?"

She blinked. "Well what?"

"I told you my dirty little secret. Anything you'd like to say in return?"

"Oh, yes. Sorry, Phillip. I don't know what I was thinking." *Liar.* "Yes, of course, you can come. We would love to have you join us on Christmas. It would be such an honor, especially now that you've given us something to celebrate."

He chuckled. "You mean besides the birth of Christ?"

"Well, yes, besides the birth of Christ. To finally know we're going to America soon? I cannot think of anything that would make us all happier."

31

Christmas Eve, 1945

Anya placed another unlit candle on an upper bough of the spruce fir, then stood back for a better view of their decorated tree. Satisfied, she glanced over her shoulder as Joss cooed happily in her mother's arms.

Kate smiled. "Well then, Auntie Anya, Joss just told me you've done a masterful job decorating our lovely tree."

"Did she?" Anya knelt beside the rocker and gently tickled the baby under her chin, eliciting a perfect giggle. "Kate, have you ever wondered how a child learns to laugh?"

"No, I suppose I haven't. You?"

Joss curled her fingers around one of Anya's and pulled it toward her mouth.

"Not until now. I'm fascinated how quickly she's learning everything. Even this—how did she know to reach out for my finger like that?"

"I have no idea. As for pulling it toward her mouth? I'm

fairly confident this little one has a bottomless pit in that adorable tummy of hers. She'd chomp down on your finger if she had so much as a single tooth."

Anya stood, her finger still the object of the baby's attention. "There now, Joss. I must insist you give me back my finger so that I can finish decorating our tree."

"It's beautiful, Anya. Who could have known we'd have such a pretty tree with all the rationing still trying to spoil our fun?"

"We must thank Gigi for that, I suppose." Anya adjusted one of the paper snowflakes she'd made then adjusted it again. "I'm beginning to think her Paul is made of money."

"Let's just *hope* it's from him," Kate murmured.

Sybil waddled into the drawing room. "Hope what's from whom?"

"Never mind," Kate said. "I was being unkind, and here it is on Christmas Eve."

"You? Unkind?" Sybil lowered herself onto the sofa then used her apron to fan herself. "Don't be ridiculous."

Anya took a seat beside her. "How are you feeling? You look a bit flushed."

"I'm fine, but it's terribly warm in here, don't you think?"

"Not really," Kate said. "But when I was expecting, I always felt like a furnace was roaring inside me."

"Dreadful," Sybil groaned, then leaned back and closed her eyes. "If this keeps up, I may walk outside and lie face-down in the snow."

"Why don't you rest awhile?" Anya said.

"That's exactly what I'm doing. I just don't want to miss anything."

Kate closed her eyes and inhaled deeply. "Isn't it wonderful, the aroma of a turkey roasting in the oven? We must remember to thank Phillip for providing it. Especially since rationing is so much worse now that the war is over. "Without it, we might have been stuck with Lord Woolton's Pie or a plateful of floddies."

"Floddies?" Anya asked.

"You know, those shredded potatoes we fry like little pancakes."

"Oh, yes. Now I remember."

"And don't forget the extra sugar Phillip gave us," Sybil continued. "How else would we have made a proper pudding?"

When the doorbell rang, Anya headed for the entry hall. "That must be Phillip. He's early, but we can put him to work in the kitchen." When she opened the door, she found their landlord stomping snow off his boots and carrying a stack of boxes.

"Hello, Mr. Grafton."

"Hello, hello, Mrs. McClain. We must have had a substitute postman on the route yesterday. He left these parcels on my porch next door, but they belong to you ladies. Didn't discover them until late last night, if you must know."

"Please, come in. And thank you for bringing them by."

"No problem, but I can't stay. Grandchildren are on their way over. Just dropping these off." He set them on the table next to the door. "Oh, and a few letters here on top." He removed his cap and leaned into the drawing room. "Right, then. Merry Christmas, ladies."

"Merry Christmas to you as well."

"Thank you for bringing the parcels, Mr. Grafton," Kate added.

Anya started to close the door after he left when she saw Phillip stepping out of his auto with an armload of gifts.

"Hello, Phillip. Do you need some help?"

"No, they're lighter than they look."

As he walked up the steps, Anya asked, "What's all this?"

A mischievous smile warmed his face. "I ran into St. Nicholas, and he asked if I'd drop these by."

"Did he, now?"

"Yes. I'm simply doing the old coot a favor."

"I'm sure you are. Come in where it's warm."

The girls made a fuss over the lieutenant as he joined them, welcoming him to their home. After setting his packages under the tree, he pulled off his gloves and overcoat.

"Let me take those for you," Anya said. "I'll hang them on the hall tree. Would you like something to drink?"

"Not just yet, thank you."

"How are you, Phillip?" Sybil asked.

"I'm fine, thanks. I can't tell you how much I appreciate you all allowing me to come over today. Especially since I invited myself."

"We're pleased to have you," Kate said. "Nice to have a man in the house for a change."

"Not to mention that heavenly turkey roasting in the oven," Sybil added. "We'll never be able to thank you enough."

"The pleasure is all mine, I assure you." He leaned over the baby, gently tapping her button nose. "Just look at you, Miss

Jocelyn. Why, you're as beautiful as your mother."

"Don't you be flirting with her, Lieutenant," Kate teased. "Not for another eighteen years or so."

"Point taken." He turned and took a seat beside Sybil. "And how's our next expectant mother feeling today?"

"Quite fat and terribly hot, if you must know," she said, still fanning herself.

"Nonsense. You look lovelier than ever. When is your baby due?"

She patted her rounded stomach. "Early February, and I'll thank you to make absolutely sure I'm in New York by then."

"I'll do my best."

"Oh Phillip, we're so grateful for the news you shared with Anya about our names being on that list," Kate said. "Any dates set for our departure?"

"Nothing yet, but if I had to guess, I'd say sometime around the last week in January."

Kate beamed. "That's wonderful! We'll start a countdown as of today, won't we girls?"

Phillip raised his palms. "Now, I said it was just a guess, so don't come hunting me down if it's a week or two later."

"Oh, but we will." Sybil patted her stomach again. "I've got a countdown of my own here, remember?"

Just then, Joss cackled a bit of a laugh that ended in a prolonged coo.

"That's right, Joss, you tell him," Sybil teased.

"Listen to that, will you?" he said. "She's not only beautiful, but quite the entertainer as well."

"Would you like to hold her?" Kate asked.

"I thought you'd never ask." Phillip stood and pulled off his uniform jacket.

Kate placed Joss in his arms.

"Now, if you ladies will excuse me, Miss Jocelyn and I need to have a little chat." He slowly made his way over to the Christmas tree and chatted quietly with her.

Just then, the front door flew open. "I'm home! I'm home!"

Gigi rounded the corner, holding up two bulging cloth bags. "And I've got mistletoe and lots and lots of wine, so let the Christmas cheer commence!"

Anya glanced at Sybil, who rolled her eyes. They hadn't seen her since the day before, and wondered where she'd been.

The afternoon passed with a curious mix of conversation, laughter, and carols playing on the phonograph. With rationing tighter than ever, theirs was not as festive a table as hoped, but with the turkey Phillip provided and some scrimping and saving of ration coupons, they were able to make do. They served the roasted turkey with a tasty stuffing, roasted potatoes and carrots, and for dessert, a savory plum pudding.

After dinner, they settled back in the drawing room with hot cups of tea. Gigi uncorked another bottle of wine, pouring one for herself and another for Phillip. Joss slept peacefully in the cradle beside her mother. They lit the candles on the tree and put another Christmas record on the phonograph.

"Our first Christmas after the war." Sybil sighed. "Isn't it wonderful?"

"After the Blitz, I wondered if we'd ever live to see another one," Kate said. "And yet, here we are."

"Thank God for that," Gigi added. "No more blackout

curtains, no more nights crammed in the shelters."

"No more bombs whizzing overhead," Kate said.

Gigi shivered. "No more of those creepy barrage balloons bouncing around us."

"Remember how awful Christmas was last year?" Sybil said. "We were so sure the war would have ended after D-Day, and when it still wasn't by Christmas, we were all so depressed."

"Yes, well, enough of all that." Gigi raised her glass. "It's over, and now we can all look forward to happier days ahead in America!"

"Here here!" they cheered as Gigi tapped her glass against Phillip's.

"Anya, I've been meaning to ask you," Kate said. "What is Christmas like in Holland?"

"We actually celebrate Sinterklaas on the fifth of December."

"You should have told us," Gigi teased. "We could have celebrated all month long."

"How do you celebrate this Sinter—"

"Sinterklaas," Anya said. "We always made gifts for each other. Sometimes thoughtful gifts, but most often something silly. You have to write a poem for each person, and they have to read it aloud before opening their gift."

"What a delightful tradition," Sybil said. "What was the funniest gift you remember receiving?"

"That's an easy one. I used to be such a pest to my brother Hans. Whenever he would ask a favor of me, I would say, 'When pigs fly!' and of course, never do what he asked. So the last time ... the last time we celebrated Sinterklaas as a family, Hans wrote a clever poem about me flying away on a pig with wings."

As her friends chuckled, Anya used the moment to steady her emotions.

"So he gave you a *pig?*" Gigi asked, rendering more laughter.

"Yes, but not a live one. He carved a little pig with wings." She cleared her throat, trying so hard to keep smiling. "I felt awful, of course, because I'd always been such a terrible nuisance to him, and here was his gift, so kind and thoughtful."

Another deep breath. "And when I returned to my home after the war ended, I found that little carved pig with wings amidst the debris. I couldn't believe it, because our home had been ransacked by the Germans. One of its wings was broken, but I was so happy to find it. In fact, that was the same day Danny came back for me. It's strange how often I think of that little pig."

"Oh Anya, that's such a sweet memory," Sybil said.

Gigi huffed as she poured herself another glass of wine. "Oh, now, let's not all sit around getting weepy and sad. What about you, Phillip?

What is Christmas like in America?"

"Similar to yours, I think. We decorate trees in our homes. We exchange gifts and—"

"The gifts!" Gigi jumped up, set her glass on the table, then knelt before the tree aglow with candles. "Enough of all these melancholy strolls down memory lane. Let's open our gifts!"

32

"Shh! Gigi, you're worse than a little child," Kate said, tapping the foot of the cradle to set it gently rocking. "Keep it down, will you?"

Jocelyn stirred but never opened her eyes.

"See? Nothing to worry about."

Gigi danced around the room as she distributed the gifts, including a couple for Phillip, and the parcels that just arrived from America. "I can't wait to see what Paul sent me!"

Sybil suggested they take turns opening their gifts so they could all enjoy each other's surprises. "As for me, I'm saving the best for last." She clutched the small package from Jack.

"Not me!" Gigi tried to open the box from Paul, but couldn't. "Phillip, you wouldn't have one of those pocket-knives you Yanks love so much, would you?"

He stood, plunging his hand in his trouser pocket. "Here you go. Don't cut yourself."

"Not a chance." She ran the knife carefully along the taped edge and pried it open. Inside were several wrapped boxes of different shapes and sizes. "How sweet is my husband? Look at all these!"

"Just open one for now, so the rest of us have a chance to open ours," Kate said.

"What, and spoil all my fun? Oh well, fine. Let's see what might be in this little box." A moment later, she stretch a lacy pink lace garter between her fingers. "Oh Paul, you naughty, naughty boy!"

Phillip uttered a fake groan. "Somehow I doubt I'll find one of those here for me."

"You never know," Sybil teased.

They continued opening their gifts with smiles and laughter bubbling with Christmas cheer. The girls unwrapped an assortment of scarves and jewelry, perfume, and hosiery from their husbands, and thoughtful keepsakes from their husbands' families. From her in-laws, Kate received a pale pink dress for Jocelyn. Its delicate smocking and tiny hand-embroidered roses elicited a sweet round of oohs and aahs from all of them. They all agreed Joss should wear it the day they arrived in America.

The girls had chipped in to buy Phillip several tins of biscuits and some proper English tea, along with a handsome teacup boasting the Union Jack.

In return, Phillip gave them tins of chocolate, bags of pear drop candies, and handkerchiefs embroidered with both the Union Jack and the American Stars and Stripes. Anya was delighted that hers also included the flag of The Netherlands.

"Phillip, where did you find one with a Dutch flag on it?"

"I didn't. I had them made for you. For all of you."

"It's just ..."

"Perfect, Phillip," Sybil added. "They're absolutely perfect. What thoughtful gifts."

"I figured this was quite a momentous Christmas for you, and what better way to remember the occasion?"

When Anya opened her final gift, she found a miniature jewelry box from Danny. Inside, she found another charm for her bracelet, this one an American flag. She quickly feigned a smile and teased about the recurring flag theme of their gifts and held it up for them to see. Tonight was not the time to once again open a door to her loss and grief. She carefully detached herself from the night she lost her bracelet. She would tell her friends someday. And someday she would find the courage to tell Danny. Someday.

Only one more gift remained. Sybil's box from Jack. "Isn't it fun to think we'll all be in America next Christmas?" She tore open the brown paper.

"We're counting on you, Phillip," Kate added. "If we're all still here next year, we'll want all our gifts back. Just so you know."

He hung his head in mock frustration. "And don't I know it."

Sybil opened the box and froze.

"Syb, what is it?" Kate asked.

She didn't answer, but lifted a leather wallet from the box.

"Good heavens, why would Jack send you a man's wallet?" Gigi asked.

"Wait, it looks just like the one you sent Jack, doesn't it?" Kate asked.

"That's because it is," Sybil whispered. She set it aside and reached for something else in the box.

"I don't understand," Anya said. "Why would—"

"And aren't those the handkerchiefs you bought him at the shop around the corner?" Kate asked, her voice quieting to little more than a whisper. "Syb, what's going on?"

Anya felt a slow rising panic as she watched Sybil's face go ashen. She moved to kneel before her. "Is there a note?"

Sybil's stare at Anya was blank, as if she'd somehow drifted away.

"Sybil?" Anya pressed, reaching for her hand. "Are you all right?"

She blinked, her eyes moist as she gazed back into the box and lifted an envelope from it. She stared at it a moment, then handed it to Anya. "You read it."

"No, Syb, I don't think I should—"

She closed her eyes, a single tear rolling down her cheek. "Just read it, Anya."

Anya's hands trembled as she opened the envelope and quickly scanned the contents. Her heart ached at the words she'd feared she might find there. She closed it and turned to Kate, then Gigi, then Phillip.

Gigi waved her hand in Anya's direction. "Anya, just read it, will you?"

She turned back to Sybil who took a long, unsteady breath, then placed a hand over hers. "If it's bad news, I'd rather have it here and now with all of you than alone in my room. Please, Anya."

"If you're sure?" Anya looked around at the others, wishing for help.

"I am."

Anya's heart ached as she read the letter aloud.

"Dear Sybil,

I'm sorry to send this to you at Christmas, but it's important that you know before getting on one of those war bride ships. When I returned home, I met someone. Actually, I've known her for years. We grew up together in Long Island. Rita wrote me often during all the years I served in the war. I suppose I never thought of her as anything but a good friend. Until I got home, that is. She was waiting with my family when I got off the subway, and we've been inseparable ever since. I know I should have told you sooner, and for that I am truly sorry—"

"Stop, Anya," Kate insisted, her voice hushed and sad. "I think we've heard enough."

Sybil shook her head, her eyes filled with dread. "No. I need to hear the rest of it. Just read it, Anya. Please."

Anya looked at Phillip whose jaw was clenched as he shook his head slowly, then back at Sybil. She watched her, wishing this awful moment wasn't happening. Sybil motioned for her to continue.

"I told Rita from the start that I was married. Told her all about you and showed her the picture taken right after we were married. But as time passed those first few weeks I was home, I couldn't deny my feelings for her. We have so many memories from our childhood. And Sybil, God forgive me, but I knew in my heart it was right between us. Then a couple of weeks ago, she found out she was pregnant—"

"No more—" Sybil gasped for breath as she tried to stand. "I need air. Please—"

She tried to step over Anya's feet, but her feet got tangled causing her to fall face-first into the Christmas tree—

It all happened so fast, all of them jumping up. The tree was already burning as Phillip reached for Sybil. "Put out these candles!" he shouted as he lifted Sybil in his arms and rushed her out of the room. "Get Jocelyn away from the tree!"

They sprang into action. Kate whisked Joss out of the cradle then kicked it away from the tree as Gigi tried to blow all the candles out. Anya pulled all the wrapping paper and boxes away from the tree, then tried to help Gigi. The tree blazed in a matter of seconds.

"Anya, run next door and tell Mr. Grafton to call the fire department!"

She collided with Phillip. "Anya, go stay with Sybil!"

"But I have to go next door and—"

"I'll send Gigi, now GO!"

As she turned, she glanced over her shoulder, stunned to see the entire tree already engulfed, its flames licking the ceiling.

"ANYA, GO!"

Jocelyn's startled cries matched the panic beating in Anya's heart as she rushed down the hall. Kate and Anya hurried to Sybil's bedside.

"Sybil, can you hear me?" Kate cried.

She groaned and thrashed about, pulling her hand from a bloody gash across her forehead. Anya took hold of her hand, hoping to calm her. Instead, Sybil screamed out, pulling her arm back in obvious pain.

"I'm sorry! Is it your wrist? Your arm?"

Sybil didn't answer, but held her hand up, fingers splayed, signaling Anya not to touch her.

"Oh Sybil, what hurts? Tell us!"

Sybil's eyes flashed open as her face contorted. She gasped as she clutched her belly. She tried to speak, then sat up halfway before turning her head aside and vomiting.

Anya grabbed a folded quilt off the bed and placed it beneath Sybil's chin. "Just take it easy, Sybil. We're here for you. Just try to relax."

Even over Jocelyn's wailing, they could hear sirens grow louder then come to an abrupt stop. A rush of panicked voices filled the hallway. Anya looked back, frightened at Sybil's ashen face.

"Sybil? Sybil, can you hear me?" She patted her cheeks. "SYBIL!"

Suddenly, Phillip was at her side. "We have to get out! I'll get Sybil—"

"I think she might have stopped breathing!" Anya cried. "Shouldn't we do something?"

"Kate, get Jocelyn out of here NOW. Anya, go! WE HAVE TO GET OUT!"

In one motion, Sybil was back in Phillip's arms as he rushed toward the back door. Anya was right behind Kate, who held Joss pressed tight against her shoulder.

Frantic voices and breaking glass filled the house.

"OUT! GET EVERYONE OUT!"

"But I have to go back! I have to get my gifts!" Gigi shouted.

As Anya rounded the corner, a fireman threw Gigi over his

shoulder in one smooth move.

She pounded on his back. "PUT ME DOWN! I HAVE TO GET MY PRESENTS! PUT ME DOWN THIS INSTANT!"

Seconds later, Anya joined the others in the street out front. Gigi continued berating the fireman who'd finally set her down. Phillip helped the medics place Sybil on a stretcher then watched as they lifted her into the ambulance.

"I'm going with you!" he shouted.

The medic held up his hand "No, sir! We can't let you do that. You can follow us to St. Thomas's."

Anya joined Phillip, watching as they attended to Sybil.

"You need to know that she's pregnant!" Phillip shouted.

The medic was about to close the doors. "Yes, sir, I can see that."

"Wait!" Phillip shouted. "You don't understand! She's due in just a couple of months, and she just took a serious fall—"

"Yes, sir. Thank you. We'll take care of her." The doors slammed in his face just as the ambulance took off.

Phillip turned to Anya. "Did everyone get out? Kate? The baby? Gigi?"

"Yes, we're all here."

"Thank God." Phillip leaned over, clutching his hands on his knees, then turned to look up at her. "Are you all right?"

"Yes. Are you?"

He nodded. "I think so. I'm just glad everyone got out alive."

As she turned to face the house, smoke still billowing out the front windows, Anya felt her knees go weak. Phillip caught her, wrapping his arm around her waist.

"Take it easy. We're all safe, and that's what matters most."

Something niggled at Anya's heart. Something she'd missed. Something important. She shook her head, trying to gather her senses. Something wasn't right.

But what?

33

Two hours later, Anya remembered.

They'd huddled in a corner of the busy waiting area nearest the emergency room. Joss had finally cried herself to sleep in Kate's arms. Phillip insisted on staying with them, pacing in the cramped quarters while the girls sat anxiously awaiting news of Sybil's condition. At a few minutes after midnight, a doctor approached them. They stood in unison.

"Family of Sybil Townsend?"

"Yes. Well, no, not actually family," Kate stammered. "We're her friends. Flatmates."

"No family?"

"None here," Phillip said. "How is she, Doctor?"

"She's sedated now. A few broken ribs, some cuts and abrasions. She'll be quite bruised for the next couple of weeks, but otherwise I expect she'll recover."

"So she's all right?" Anya asked.

"Yes, and from what I'm told, you're all lucky to be alive."

"What about her baby?"

Anya knew the second she saw the doctor's jaw clench. "I'm sorry to say she lost her baby."

Kate gulped a sob. "No, no, please. Don't let it ..."

Phillip reached for Joss, lifting her from Kate's arms. She dropped her face in her hands as Anya and Gigi came to her side.

"Poor Sybil," Gigi muttered. "It was just too much. Too much."

"It's not fair." Kate dashed away her tears. "She was so excited about going to America and having her baby there."

The doctor patted Phillip on the shoulder. "As I said, I'm very sorry. We'll keep Mrs. Townsend for a few nights, maybe more. The nurse will let you know when she's moved to a room upstairs."

He patted Phillip's back once more, then left.

Blood on Sybil's bed. Lots of blood.

That's what Anya hadn't remembered! The scene replayed in her mind. In the rush to get out of the house, Phillip had lifted Sybil as if she were light as a feather and not seven months pregnant. And in that moment, Anya had glanced back at the bed for a split second and noticed a crimson stain where Sybil had lain.

She tried to swallow past the knot in her throat. She braced her hand against the wall, then fell onto the nearest empty chair.

Kate fell into the chair beside her. "Oh Anya, please tell me this is all just a bad dream." She leaned her head on Anya's shoulder. "This can't be happening."

She couldn't speak. She watched as Phillip walked the

crowded room with Joss sound asleep against his shoulder, giving them a moment of privacy. She glanced over at Gigi, who'd begged a cigarette off someone in the waiting room. She stopped briefly to say something to Phillip, then kissed Jocelyn's head and left.

Just as well.

As Anya watched her leave, an unbidden thought crossed her mind. It occurred to her that Gigi's infidelities were no different from Jack's. And none of this would have happened if Jack had stayed true to Sybil. No returned wallet and handkerchiefs. No farewell letter. No word of his pregnant girlfriend. A girlfriend who probably looked and acted like Gigi Williams; at least in Anya's mind. With Gigi gone now, she dismissed the troubling thought and leaned her head against Kate's.

"You're right. It *isn't* fair. None of it is fair. I've only known Sybil for a few months, but I've been so grateful for her friendship and the home we share with you and Gigi. With the war over, I suppose we've all been learning to hope again and dream about our lives in America. And now this."

"And now this." Kate sat up and wiped the tears from her eyes. "What will happen to Sybil? She has no family, and we'll all be leaving soon. I can't bear the thought of leaving her behind and all alone. Think what that would feel like, watching all of us board a ship bound for America and knowing she can't come too?"

"I don't know. I suppose we'll sort it all out. But for now, we need to stay as close to her as we can in the time we have left. We'll have to find a place to stay, won't we?"

"For now, yes. I don't think the fire spread much beyond the drawing room, but I can't imagine living there until it's all cleaned up."

"But where will we stay?" Anya asked.

"I was just thinking about that." Phillip took a seat next to Kate, with little Joss still sound asleep on his shoulder. "I think I might have just the place."

Kate gently cupped her hand over Joss's soft curls. "Where?"

"My CO is out of the country, as you know. He has a suite of rooms at the Savoy, and obviously won't be needing them for the next couple of weeks."

"Are you sure he'd allow us to stay there?" Anya asked.

"I'll ask, of course, but not for a few days. He's home to bury his father, and there's no reason to disturb him just yet. In the meantime, I'll talk to the Savoy's manager and sort it out."

Kate looked at Anya. "What do you think?"

"I think we have no choice."

They left a message with the nurse in the emergency room, giving her the Savoy's telephone number, should they need to reach them. They found Gigi outside smoking, shivering in the bitter cold night air. Moments later, they were in Phillip's auto and on their way to the Savoy.

The opulent hotel, situated on the north bank of the Thames, had a long history of lavish hospitality for those whose pockets ran deep. During the war, many of the wealthiest Londoners lived here after their personal servants left to work more profitable jobs in the wartime factories. Here, they were pampered by chefs unfettered by rationing, and barely inconvenienced by the pesky bombing since the most luxurious of all air raid shelters in London was just below them. The Savoy's refuge attracted the rich, the powerful, the famous ... and the Americans.

Anya was shocked by the posh suite of rooms with its view overlooking the Waterloo Bridge. To think that American leaders had lived in such comfort during the war while the rest of them barely scraped by. Still, she was grateful they had a place to stay. Gigi wasted no time, pouring herself a drink from the CO's bar cabinet while Anya and Kate checked out the other bedroom. Kate grabbed the blanket off the bed and used it to line an empty dresser drawer for Joss until a crib was brought up. She gently placed the sleeping baby in the drawer, then left the door ajar before they joined the others.

Phillip stood. "I'm just down the hall in room 235, though I assure you my room is nothing like this. I'm going back over to your flat to make sure Mr. Grafton keeps an eye on it until daylight."

"Do you need us to come with you?" Anya asked.

"Not me, I'm knackered." Gigi fell onto the long sofa and propped her feet on the coffee table, careful not to spill her drink. "You can go, Anya."

"There's no need," Phillip said. "I won't be long. Oh, and I'll stop by the desk downstairs and alert them to ring you should someone from the hospital call."

"Phillip, how can we ever thank you for taking such good care of us?" Kate tried to stifle a yawn. "I don't know what we would have done without you."

"It's my pleasure. You all get some rest. I'll stop by first thing in the morning."

At half past eight the next morning, Phillip knocked on their door. He gave them time to freshen up and said he'd see them downstairs for breakfast in the hotel dining room. After they arrived and placed their orders, he told them he'd gone by the hospital to see Sybil.

Kate adjusted Joss on her lap. "How is she?"

"Despondent. The nurse told me she was still somewhat sedated, so I didn't stay but a few minutes."

Gigi set her teacup back on its saucer. "Does she know about the baby?"

"Yes, I'm afraid so. She started to say something then broke down, so I just sat with her a while and let her cry."

"She must be devastated," Kate said. "It's not just the loss of her child, but the horrible news from Jack."

"It would have been easier if he'd died in the war." Anya stiffened when she realized she'd spoken her thoughts out loud.

"You're right," Kate said. "Death is much easier to accept than outright rejection. Especially the way it all happened."

"I know, but I shouldn't have said it."

"You only said what the rest of us were thinking," Phillip added.

"Did they say when they'll release her?" Gigi asked, waving for their waiter's attention.

"The doctor wants to keep her for at least another night."

"How did the house look?" Kate asked.

"There's a lot more damage than I expected, to be honest.

It's mostly smoke and water damage, which means the place will smell pretty bad for quite some time. Mr. Grafton plans to hire a crew to clean it up and salvage what they can, but with the holidays, it might be a while before they begin. I told him you all are welcome to stay here until it's ready."

"Phillip, we couldn't possibly stay here that long," Kate said.

"Are you daft?" Gigi balked. "This is the lap of luxury compared to that smelly old flat. So yes, Phillip, we'll stay as long as we can. In fact, when your boss comes back, he can just bunk down the hall with you." She tossed him a wink and flashed him her brightest smile.

Anya shook her head, too tired to argue. The waiter returned to refill their drinks. He assured them their food would be out straight away.

"I have to ask," Phillip began, "and I apologize because it's an awkward question any way you look at it. Do you think it will be difficult for Sybil to stay here in the same suite with you?" He nodded at Joss who was still sound asleep.

"Oh," Anya said. "I see your point."

"Maybe Joss and I should stay somewhere else." Kate cupped her hand over the baby's curls. "I could probably get a private room set up at the Rainbow—the Rainbow!" She stood abruptly waking Joss. "I completely forgot! I'm on the schedule to work this morning!"

Phillip stood with his hand raised. "No, you aren't. I stopped by there after I visited Sybil and let them know you and Anya would need a few days off. Your manager understood completely. He was sorry to hear about the fire. I didn't think it was my place to tell him about Sybil, so I'll leave that up to you. But he sure thinks the world of you girls for all your help, especially these last few months."

"Oh, thank you, Phillip," Kate said, settling back on her chair. "That's such a relief. How thoughtful of you to think ahead like that. Burt is a treasure, isn't he? He treats us all like daughters."

Their food was served, and they ate with little conversation. When Phillip finished ahead of them, he insisted on holding Joss so Kate could finish eating.

"Careful, Phillip," Gigi warned.

"About what?"

"Kate might get used to having you around as her personal nursemaid. Best not to spoil her."

Anya shook her head as she smeared jam on her toast.

"Good heavens," Gigi scoffed. "As if I'm the only one who thinks a man who's good with babies is a splendid catch?"

Phillip laughed it off. "You think I'm good with babies? Just wait until Joss fills her diaper—or *nappy* as you call it— and see how fast I'm out of here."

Gigi chuckled with Anya and Kate, then folded her arms across her chest. "You're forgetting you told us you were the oldest in a family with six kids. I'm sure you've changed your share of soiled nappies."

"Might we change the subject?" Kate chimed in. "I'm still eating, thank you. But back to your question, Phillip. I think you're right. I'll ask Burt if Joss and I can stay there at the Rainbow for a while."

"No, I didn't mean you should leave the hotel," he said. "I was just suggesting we put you in another room. The hotel will have more rooms available now that Christmas is over, so there shouldn't be a problem."

"How much are the rooms here?" Gigi asked as she pushed her plate aside. "A fellow told me a while back the rates here are ridiculous. Unless you're an American officer, of course."

"Oh, I didn't mean to imply you'd have to pay for another room," he said to Kate. "I've already got that covered."

"But I couldn't let you," she argued. "You don't have to do that."

"You're exactly right. I don't have to, but I'd like to. It's the least I can do for you all."

"There." Gigi patted Phillip's forearm then stood. "All settled."

"Where are you off to?" Kate asked.

"I have some errands to run, then I plan to go by the house and see if we can gather some of our things. They'll reek of smoke, so we'll have to have them washed, I suppose." She pulled out a mirror and dashed her mouth with a fresh coat of lipstick, then dropped both back in her purse. "I assume they have a washing service here, don't they?"

"Yes, of course."

"Well, there you go."

"Gigi, how are you—"

"See you later, girls." Off she went.

Anya and Kate shared a glance.

"I don't even want to know," Kate murmured.

"Neither do I."

"And I'm not even going to ask, so there we are," Phillip added, getting to his feet. "Joss, how about you and I take a walk over to the front desk and see if we've had any calls."

Half an hour later, they picked their way through the smoky remains of their flat. Mrs. Grafton insisted on keeping Jocelyn so Kate could do what she needed. Phillip helped, carting several armloads of clothes to his car.

Anya was relieved that her bedroom at the flat had been spared. She collected her treasures, thankful the American flag charm Danny had sent her had survived the damage. She gathered her clothes and a few other belongings and placed them in her suitcase. Phillip was right; the stench of smoke permeated everything.

Kate's room had substantial water damage from the fire hoses that doused the adjacent drawing room. A large section of the wall had been hacked down by the firemen's axes.

"What a mess," Anya said as she helped Kate gather her clothes and some of Joss's things.

"I refuse to look at this with negativity," Kate said. "We're all alive, and that's all that matters, right?"

"Yes, all of us, except for Sybil's baby."

Kate straightened. "Yes. Except for Sybil's baby. We'll just have to pray for her. I doubt there's anything any of us can do or say that will lessen her grief, but I believe God can."

Anya busied herself with more of Joss's clothes. "I didn't know you prayed."

"Well, of course I pray. Don't you?"

She pulled a blanket from Joss's crib and folded it. "No, not really."

"Why, Anya? You do believe in God, don't you?"

"Yes, I believe in God. I'm just not sure He has anything to do with our lives here on Earth. How else can you explain the war and everything we've all been through?"

"But that's just it. We don't *have* to explain the war, or anything else for that matter. We just have to trust Him to see us through all of it."

"Is that what you'll say to Sybil? Would you pat her on the arm and quote some scripture to her? 'The Lord giveth and the Lord taketh away; blessed be the name of the Lord'?"

Anya took a sudden breath. "I'm sorry, Kate. That was unkind. I'm not arguing with you, but try to see it from Sybil's point of view. Or mine, for that matter. It's much harder to trust God when you've lost everything and everyone you ever loved. Where was He when all that happened?"

Kate was quiet as she finished packing her clothes. "I can't say, Anya. I didn't lose those dearest to me. My family is safe and sound in Winchester. I haven't walked in your shoes." She reached for Anya's hand. "I know I must sound like such a simpleton, spouting beliefs I was taught in church as a child. I can't begin to imagine the grief and heartache both you and Sybil have endured. We live in a world saturated with sin and evil and horrible people like Hitler and his followers. But God allowed us to survive for some reason, and I still trust in Him, because the alternative is just too frightening."

Anya didn't say anything. The same battle trampled her heart and mind every single day, but it wasn't something she liked to talk about.

"I don't pretend to have the answers, but I know God does. So for now, I'll pray for Sybil. And for you, too. I care so deeply about both of you." She closed the suitcase. "But enough of all that. Let's get out of here before our pores soak up this wretched stench of smoke."

34

Danny had read Anya's letter three times that day and couldn't get her off his mind. Another glance at the large clock gave him a few more minutes to kill before the library closed. He reached for the envelope and unfolded it one more time. It was dated 29 December 1945.

Dear Danny,

I've so much to tell you, I don't know where to begin. Before I forget, I want you to know how much I love the American flag charm you sent me for Christmas. It's such a perfect reminder of you and the life we have before us. Thank you for such a thoughtful gift.

But our Christmas was one of sorrow, Danny. It's a long story, which I'll try to keep as brief as possible here. As we took turns opening our presents on Christmas evening, Sybil had saved her parcel from Jack for last. In it, she found the gifts she recently sent him for Christmas and a letter saying he'd fallen in love with his childhood sweetheart who was now expecting his child, so he wanted an annulment. Sybil went into shock, and when she tried to leave the room, she tripped over my feet and fell into our Christmas tree. A fire broke out from the lighted candles on the tree. Most of the house was salvaged, though the smoke and water damage was extensive.

But far worse, Sybil lost her baby. Even now I can't believe it. All of us are still grieving, though we've tried to lift her spirits now that she's out of hospital. We're staying at the Savoy Hotel thanks to Lieutenant Powell, the man from the American Embassy. Phillip was the one I wrote to you about who drove us to hospital when Kate had her baby back in October. We had invited him over for Christmas, so thankfully, he was there when it happened. He's been a tremendous help to us, especially to Sybil. I honestly don't know what we would have done without him.

With all that's happened, we haven't properly celebrated the good news, which is our notification to register at a place called Camp Tidworth in Salisbury Plain by Monday, 14 January. I'm told it's not far from Southampton, which is where we will board our ship for America. I'm sure you heard about the War Brides Act that was just passed by your Congress yesterday, giving us non-quota immigration status. We've been told we don't even need visas to enter the U.S. Imagine that, after all these months of standing in queues for days on end to get all our papers in order.

By the time you get this letter, we may already be at Camp Tidworth. I have no idea when we might sail, but they've told us we'll be able to telegram you once the date is set. I'm not sure what to expect. To be honest, I feel quite numb about it. I want desperately to be with you, Danny. For months, I've dreamed of the moment I'll see you at the pier in New York. But I'm so heartbroken for Sybil, and feel so wretched that the three of us will be leaving her behind. My only consolation is that Phillip will still be here. He spends whatever time he can spare at her side, and for that we are all grateful.

Our landlord Mr. Grafton has been wonderful, making sure we all get our letters. I had a letter from Sophie, and I'm so pleased for her and Charlie as she told me they're expecting a baby next July. I can't believe all these babies being born or on the way. It seems the world is trying to forget the long years of war and start over. A fresh start, it would seem. I had hoped to take the train to Framlingham for a visit before I leave, but time won't allow.

I can hardly wait to see you, Danny. It won't be long now.

Love,

Anya

Danny tucked the letter back in the envelope. He still couldn't believe he would be seeing her in just a few weeks. Finally! But the news concerning Sybil had diminished the joy. To lose a baby seemed unthinkable, especially on the heels of such awful news from her husband.

He'd heard similar stories, of course. Lots of them. With thousands of veterans returning to civilian life, the inevitable adjustments after so many years away at war created a built-in tension on the home front. Newspapers and magazines addressed a number of these problems. For some, the mere fact they'd come home when so many of their fellow soldiers or sailors hadn't, evoked a peculiar and unexpected sorrow that loomed over them. Just as bad, the smoldering resentment many of the veterans felt toward those who hadn't "done their part," no matter the cause for their deferment, leaving them behind to advance their careers instead.

Other veterans experienced a tremendous "let down" as they tried to retrain themselves for a mundane existence after years of constant adrenaline flowing through their veins. The unexpected flare of temper when things don't go their way. The frustrating search for jobs with precious few available. The lack of housing and clothing and other necessities resulting from years of industries transitioned to provide resources for the war.

And on the actual home front, an even tougher adjustment unfolded as veterans often came home ... different. Changed. Their personalities radically altered, dusting up unbearable showdowns with family and friends alike. Millie had told him many of the popular ladies' magazines were featuring articles for wives and children, cautioning them about sporadic outbursts, inexplicable anxiety, horrific nightmares, and severe depression. They stressed the importance of "keeping an orderly house and serving delicious meals" as they got reacquainted.

But only a few of these articles addressed the exploding divorce rate among those who had returned from the war. Danny wasn't surprised. He'd known plenty of guys like Sybil's husband Jack. It was a game to them, sweeping English girls off their feet and dazzling them with hopes and dreams of living in a country unscathed by war. What he didn't understand was why guys like Jack even bothered marrying the English girls in the first place. What was the point when they had no intention of staying faithful to their brides? How could guys like Jack turn their backs on their wives so soon after they got home?

Danny shook his head as he glanced at the clock again. He didn't have to close the library tonight, so he gathered his things and headed for the door. He pulled on his gloves then wrapped the wool scarf around his neck and descended the library steps. He lowered his head against the cold blast of air and dashed across campus.

"Danny!"

He turned to find Beverly waving at him from the parking lot across the snow-covered lawn, then realized she was waving him toward her.

"I can't! I've got a train to catch!"

She started toward him, her face serious. "I can take you home. Danny, I need to talk to you."

He held up his gloved hand. "Sorry, but I've got to run."

"Please, Danny? It's important ..." She stopped in her tracks and dropped her head in her hands.

He paused, knowing he should wave again and keep going. She was crying, which meant a lengthy encounter. He weighed the pros and cons in his mind, wishing he could just walk away. But regardless of their history, he couldn't just leave her like this. He started toward her with a stern reminder to keep his guard up.

He closed the gap between them, stopping a few feet from her. "What is it, Beverly? What's wrong?"

She looked up, her eyes red and her face streaked with tears. "I just need to ... I don't have anyone to ... I'm sorry but I ..." She closed her eyes and sobbed.

He stepped closer. "Beverly, what is it? What's wrong?"

She gave her head a toss as though trying to shake it off. "Danny, I'm sorry. I'm such a mess, and I know I shouldn't bother you, but—"

"No, it's okay."

She pulled off her gloves and wiped beneath her eyes. "I just can't seem to pull myself together, and then I saw you, and I know I shouldn't bother you, but I felt like if I didn't, I'd just ..." She stopped blubbering and shook her head, wrapping her arms around herself as she shivered.

"Look, it's freezing out here. How about we go get some coffee at the diner?"

What? Did I just say that out loud? All he wanted to do was go home. He prayed she'd take a pass.

"No, I don't think I should."

Whew. "That's okay." He looked at his wristwatch. "It's pretty late. Maybe you should just go home and get some rest. Whatever's upset you will probably be okay by tomorrow."

"No, I just meant I shouldn't go anywhere looking like this."

"Oh ... okay."

She sighed. "Just let me take you home, Danny, and we

can talk on the way. You need a ride home, and I need someone to talk to." She turned halfway, her eyes pleading.

He swallowed hard. It wasn't that he didn't trust himself with her. He didn't know if he could trust *her*. He saw her often on campus and usually just waved and kept walking. A few times they'd actually talked; all superficial, though she always asked about Anya and if she'd come yet.

He looked at her, his mind still in debate. Even with bloodshot eyes and a flushed face, she was still beautiful. He wasn't blind, but neither was he attracted to her anymore. At all. With that settled in his mind, he agreed. He followed her to her Packard, the motor still running.

He opened the driver's door for her, then made his way to the passenger side and climbed in. She pulled a handkerchief from her purse and dabbed at her eyes, turning the rearview mirror toward her. "You must think I'm such a wreck. I'm dreadfully sorry, Danny. I just can't stop crying."

A trace of alcohol wafted between them. He'd never known Beverly to drink, but wasn't entirely surprised either. It also dawned on him it was long after her office closed. Had she waited and come looking for him?

This was a mistake.

"Danny?"

He startled. "No, it's okay. I'm just sorry you're upset."

She turned toward him, leaning her back against the car door.

He looked around then back at her. "I thought you were going to drive me home." He wondered if she should be driving. How much had she had to drink?

"I will, I just need a moment." She touched the edge of

both eyes with her handkerchief then folded it on her lap. When she finally looked up at him, she apologized again. "Really, Danny, I'm sorry about this."

"Why don't you just tell me what's wrong?"

"Do you remember that time we talked after we first ran into each other on campus here? When we met for coffee?"

"Sure. That's when you told me Ronnie had been killed in action."

"Yes, and do you remember what else I told you? About the girl who came to see me and said she was pregnant with Ronnie's baby?"

"Uh, yes, now that you mention it."

"Her name is Margaret, and I ran into her at the grocery store this afternoon. And there in her arms was a little boy who looked so much like Ronnie ... and I couldn't talk or do anything ... I couldn't even breathe. I just kept staring into his face and seeing Ronnie ..."

She broke down, sobbing so hard and trying to talk that he couldn't understand half of what she said. She trembled and looked back up at him, her face flushed, her eyes wild and searching. Then suddenly, she slid across the seat and wrapped her arms around his waist, pressing her head against his shoulder and clinging as hard as she could.

"Oh Danny, just hold me. Please just hold me."

He freed his arm and put it around her shoulders, understanding her grief but wishing again that he'd never climbed in her car, never responded when she'd called his name.

"That should have been *my* son. I should have had Ronnie's baby, not her."

"I know," he said. "I know."

353

"I wanted a baby so badly. I begged Ronnie before he left. Why wouldn't he want me to have his child? Why?"

"Shhh. I don't know. Don't think about that right now."

She sat up and looked at him with such pain in her eyes, it actually alarmed him. "No, I'm asking. I need to know! Why didn't he want me? Why wouldn't he let me have his baby? Why did *she* get to have the child who should have been mine?"

He tried to untangle himself from her. "Beverly, look. I'm really sorry. I know it must have been awful to see her kid, but—"

She kissed him. Without warning, she kissed him hard as she wept, her hands locking around the back of his head. She groaned with such hunger, it made him dizzy. The wine on her lips tasted sweet, the warmth of her breath sending uninvited shivers down his spine—

"NO!" He pushed her away. "Stop. Just stop."

"No, Danny, please. I need—"

He pushed the door handle and propelled himself out of the car, grabbing his satchel from the floorboard on the way out.

She lunged for him, still clinging to his arm. "Danny, PLEASE. Don't leave me! I'm afraid! I'm so afraid I might do something desperate. You can't leave me like this!"

He stood straight and shook off a quaking shiver.

"Go HOME, Beverly."

He slammed the door and never looked back.

35

By the time Danny got home that night, it was almost ten. He tried to calm his nerves while on the train, but the thought that kept hammering at his heart, the image he kept seeing in his mind, was that of Anya's face if she'd happened upon the Packard with the windows steamed and Beverly in his arms.

No, it would never happen, of course. Anya was still in England, thousands of miles away.

No. She's right here in my heart.

He refused to feel guilty for Beverly's behavior, but was furious with himself for getting into her car in the first place. He knew better. He may have felt sorry for her, but he was the *last* person to console her.

He would tell Anya. Not now, and certainly not the moment she stepped off the ship. But he would tell her. They would have no secrets. They wouldn't play the games other couples played. They would always be transparent with each other. He was sick and tired of unfaithful spouses and all the heartache and destruction—and illegitimate babies—left in their wake. He wanted nothing more to do with anyone else, only the wife he loved.

He wanted Anya home. Now.

He uttered a muffled growl to shake it off as he hurried up the porch steps of his home. He wouldn't talk about it, not even with Joey. All he wanted to do was grab something to eat then go to bed. Just as he reached for the doorknob, the door opened. Joey stood there with an awkward smile on his face.

"It's about time you got home," he said, the smile still plastered on his face. "Someone's here to see you."

"Yeah? Who?" Danny stepped inside and closed the door, pulling off his coat and scarf. Sophie danced at his feet, waiting for her nightly greeting. He rubbed behind her ears sending her tail in a blur of wags.

"A friend of yours from England." Joey's smile didn't change, he just blinked a couple of times.

"Anya?" Danny's heart soared as he rounded the corner into the living room. "Is it An—"

"My friend! My friend!"

His heart dropped like a cinder block. "Cosmos?"

He threw a salute. "Sergeant Cosmos Benedetto, reporting for duty, SIR!"

Danny stared at the goofy kid. Why on earth was he here in their living room? Two separate universes collided, leaving him utterly baffled. He returned a less passionate salute just before the Italian gave him a hearty bear hug.

"Lieutenant, I'm so thrilled to see you again!"

Danny looked over at his family who offered an odd assortment of reactions. Joey was still fighting the urge to laugh. Millie pressed her lips together as she rocked little Jimmy. His mother leaned her head to one side with her *isn't-that-sweet* smile. His father rolled his eyes and shook his head as he got up from his chair.

Even Sophie got in on the act, her tail wagging as she wandered around their feet.

"At ease, there, Sergeant," Danny said, pulling out of Cosmos's embrace. "What in the world are you doing here?"

"I'm out of here," Dad groaned. "It's long past my bedtime."

"Mr. McClain, wait!" Cosmos reached for a camera. "If I might, before you bid us goodnight, could I have one quick picture with you and Lieutenant McClain?"

Frank turned around and started to say something when Betty caught his arm. "I think that's a lovely idea, Frank. Come along. It will only take a moment."

"Betty, I want—"

"—to smile big for the camera, don't you, dear?"

Joey patted his father on the back. "Come on, Dad. One quick mug shot for the funny papers, and Cosmos will let you call it a night. Isn't that right, Cosmos?"

"Yes, yes, of course! Now, look at the camera, and I'll count to three. One, two, three!"

"Dad, you weren't smiling," Joey teased. "Be a good boy and smile for the camera this time."

"That's right, Mr. McClain. I've got plenty of film so—"

"Yeah, yeah, just take the picture already."

"One, two, three!"

Joey sighed. "Well, not your best smile, but I guess it will do."

Frank turned his back and headed for the stairs. "Keep it

quiet down here."

Millie stood, lifting her sleepy son to her shoulder. "That's it for us as well. It was so nice to meet you, Cosmos."

He tiptoed to her side and patted Jimmy's back ever so softly. "Good night, Mrs. Millie. Good night, little Jimmy."

Millie tossed Danny a wink and tiptoed up the stairs.

"Danny, I saved you a plate from supper," his mother said. "Have a seat in the dining room, and I'll bring it to you."

Cosmos patted his stomach. "Your mother is a fabulous cook, Lieutenant. I was delighted to be included as a guest with your family for the evening repast."

Danny took his usual seat at the table. "Yes, she's a good cook. But do you mind if I ask you what you're doing here?"

"Don't be rude, Danny." His mother set a glass of tea and a plate of food in front of him. "Cosmos, how about another piece of pecan pie?"

"That would be delightful, Mrs. McClain."

"I'll have one too, Mom." Joey took a seat across from his brother. Cosmos sat on the end between them.

Cosmos clasped his hands together. "To answer your question, Lieutenant—"

"We're civilians now. Just call me Danny."

Cosmos leaned back, beaming. "Oh, I was hoping you'd say that. I didn't want to presume, of course, since you outrank me, but I had so hoped we might be friends. Just a couple of chaps getting along, as our English friends back in Framlingham used to say."

Danny ate a bite of meatloaf and stared at him.

"Cosmos, tell Danny how you knew where to find us." To Danny, "You're gonna love this."

"I bet."

"Oh, Lieu—I mean, *Mr. Danny*," Cosmos began, his face aglow. "Your brother Joey is right. I guarantee this will touch your heart. It all goes back to the day you left the 390th to fly home. On that very day, I took it upon myself to personally see to the welfare of the lovely Mrs. Lieutenant—or Anya, as your family reminded me. In respect, I shall call her Mrs. Anya."

Danny took a sip of tea. "Yes, go on."

"Each evening, after completion of my work on base, I ventured over to Quincy's Pub to check in on Mrs. Anya. Over the course of several months, it was my immense pleasure to become friends with her."

"Yes, she wrote me that you often visited the pub."

"She did?" His eyes brightened. "To think that I was mentioned in her letters to you ... it almost takes my breath away." He paused abruptly, raising a palm. "But lest you worry, you have my word. We were *just* friends. Nothing sordid or inappropriate, I assure you."

Joey clapped him on the back. "There, now. See, Danny? Nothing to worry about. Cosmos here was just keeping Anya safe for you. All on the up and up, right, Cosmos?"

"Oh yes, all on the up and up. You have my word."

Danny ignored his brother's sarcasm, focusing instead on his next bite.

"I would always inquire as to how she was doing; ask if she'd heard from you, if she'd heard from the American Embassy in regard to her passage here to these United States. She is such a delight, your wife. Always kind and friendly."

"Yes, that's our Anya," Joey added. "Always kind and friendly."

"Go on, Cosmos."

"Yes, well, this is the good part. On my last night there in England, my friends and I gathered one final time at the pub. As you might not know, I play a mean fiddle. Unusual, you might say, since I hail from New Jersey, but nonetheless an instrument I have loved playing since I was a little boy. My mother tried to interest me in the accordion, but the fiddle was my true passion. And your Mrs. Anya always loved to hear me play. So on that last night, in her honor, I rendered an exceptionally poignant version of the beloved Irish song, "Danny Boy." He paused, pressing his fist against his mouth. "Dare I say, not a dry eye in the house, as it happened ..."

He dug a wrinkled handkerchief from his pocket and blew a loud honk. Below the table, Sophie barked.

Joey sighed. "Ah, I would've paid a million bucks to hear that. Wouldn't you, Danny?"

Danny nodded appreciatively, still avoiding his brother's eyes. "That's nice, Cosmos. I'm sure that meant a lot to Anya."

"Oh, Mr. Danny, you have no idea. The hug she gave me, I shall remember to the day I die."

Joey couldn't seem to help himself. "Isn't that the sweetest thing you ever—"

"I appreciate your regard for my wife, Cosmos. That was very kind of you."

Cosmos nodded, still wiping his eyes and nose. He cleared his throat and continued. "Then, on the day we left from Wickham Market Station, many of the locals came to see us off. Among them your lovely wife. That's when I asked if she would be so kind as to give me your home address, rightly asserting my despair at the thought of never seeing the two of you again. Naturally, kind soul that she is, she jotted down your address for me." He pulled a tattered index card from his shirt pocket and showed him. "There. You see?"

"Yes, that's her handwriting, all right."

Joey patted Cosmos on the back again. "What a gal, that Anya. Wasn't that nice of her, Danny? Giving Cosmos our address?"

He kept his eyes glued to the tea in his glass as he drank before answering. "Yes, it sure was."

"I shall never forget her kindness." Cosmos honked in his handkerchief again. Sophie barked again.

Betty rounded the table, picking up their empty dishes. "Cosmos, do you have a place to stay for the night? If not, you'd be welcome to sleep on our couch."

Danny pinned her with a glare.

"How gracious of you to offer; however, I would never dream of imposing. When I arrived in Chicago this morning, I got a room at a nice motor lodge not far from here. But thank you for your exceptional hospitality, Mrs. McClain."

Danny stood. "Well, then. It's been a long day, and I'm sure we're all tired, so—"

"Not me!" Joey sprang from his chair. "I could stay up all night. How about you, Cosmos? How about another rendition on your fiddle? I hate that Danny missed all the fun today. What do you say?"

Danny shot a stern glare at his brother.

"I appreciate your request, Mr. Joey, but I shall be off. I've got a long walk ahead of me, so—"

"Nonsense. Danny will give you a ride. Won't you, Danny?"

"Oh no, that isn't necessary." Cosmos made his way to the

living room and snapped the locks on his fiddle case.

"We won't take no for an answer. Besides, it's frosty out there. Probably twenty below."

Cosmos joined them in the front hallway where Joey helped him into his overcoat. "Oh, we survived much colder temperatures in England, didn't we, Mr. Danny?"

"Well, then. There you have it." Joey dug in his pocket and produced his keys. "A drive will give the two of you a chance to reminisce. Put your coat back on, Danny. Like I said, it's probably twenty below out there."

Danny narrowed his eyes at his brother and reached for his coat. "Don't wait up."

"Oh, I won't. I'll be snug as a bug in a rug by the time you come home." He stuck his hand out for a shake. "Cosmos, if you ever decide to come back and live in Chicago, you come see me at the theater. I'd be honored to have you work for me."

Cosmos's eyes shone as he collected himself again. He hugged Joey, then grabbed both his hands for a final shake before turning to go.

But by the time they'd climbed in Joey's car, Cosmos found his voice again and didn't stop talking until they parted at the motor lodge.

The house was quiet when Danny got home. As he plodded up the stairs with Sophie at his heels, he chided himself for his attitude toward Cosmos. After all, he'd been kind enough to look in on Anya after Danny left. And he'd gone out of his way to come to Chicago for a visit, thanking him again and again for the 'unforgettable journey" they'd shared on the Chowhound mission over Utrecht.

Face it, Danny reasoned as he brushed his teeth, *the guy's a harmless teddy bear.* It also occurred to him that in all likelihood, for guys like Cosmos, the war was much more than an obligation to serve his country; it might well be the high point of his entire life to come.

He chuckled, remembering the Italian's parting words.

"I shall never forget your kindness, Mr. Danny, and that of your family who so warmly welcomed me into your home."

"It was our pleasure, Cosmos."

"And I shall continue to pray for Mrs. McClain and her trip across the sea. Who knows, maybe someday I shall return and take up Joey's offer to work for him at the family theater. I've always wanted to pursue a movie career. Perhaps this would be a good place to start."

Danny laughed. "Well, there you go. Have a safe trip, Cosmos."

Cosmos straightened and threw a final salute. "Sir, yes, sir! I shall indeed. God speed, Mr. Danny."

36

26 January 1946

Camp Tidworth on Salisbury Plain, England

Dear Danny,

I'm writing to you from Camp Tidworth, not far from Southampton. It's what they call an "embarkation station," where we are to await passage for America. Kate, little Joss, Gigi and I left London yesterday morning after a tearful departure at Waterloo Station. I'm not sure we could have left Sybil had it not been for Phillip standing there beside her. He's been so kind to her the past couple of weeks and promised to take good care of her. I must admit I hope that in time, Sybil might look upon him as more than just a friend. She deserves some happiness after all that's happened.

After all these months of waiting, suddenly things were quite chaotic. We received a flurry of letters from the embassy with all manner of forms and instructions, all of them requiring immediate attention. Where to go, how much luggage we're allowed with notation that it will be weighed and inspected, how to tag our luggage ("cabin baggage" which will stay with us; "hold" for baggage that would be stowed in the ship's cargo hold). What to do about money, what kind of jewelry and toiletries and other kinds of personal effects are permitted, certification about inoculations, and on and on. And always, the ongoing confusion about all the documentation required since the War Bride Act was just enacted. Such a mess. Even though all of these requirements came through the U.S. Army Transport Corps, Phillip was able to help us make sense of it all, taking every opportunity to joke about their endless streams of paperwork.

Afterward, on three separate occasions, we were notified that our departure dates were delayed. We all began to think we would never see the shores of America. Then all at once we received our "movement" notices with warnings of how vitally important it was to follow the instructions IMPLICITLY—or else! We were told to complete a questionnaire and return it within 48 hours. Frustrating in that we've answered all the same questions a thousand times before. We were also advised to be ready to travel on short notice.

When the day finally came, after we said our goodbyes to Sylvia and Phillip, we joined the others inside at a lovely reception with music and refreshments hosted for us by the British Women's Voluntary Service.

We left London on a train filled with hundreds of other war brides, many with babies and young children. Quite a party atmosphere, with everyone excited to finally be on our way. A few couldn't stop crying, some as young as sixteen or seventeen, having never left home before. Of course, we heard all kinds of rumors. Someone said Camp Tidworth was a "luxury retreat" much like the fancy country clubs in America. They said we'd be treated like royalty.

Once we arrived here by bus, we realized those were <u>huge</u> exaggerations. Perhaps it's because we're among the first war brides to be processed here. But it is a ghastly place with no heat to speak of, and run by American soldiers who have an obvious disdain for us. Someone said it's because they're all angry about having to take care of us when they'd rather be home in America by now. The rest of the workers are stewards and groundskeepers, all of them German and Italian prisoners of war who've not yet been deported. I'm keeping my distance from them.

Those with children were separated from the rest of us, which meant Kate and Joss are in other barracks. Gigi and I are managing. There are sixteen of us in our barracks, a far cry from a "luxury retreat." Most of us have never dressed and undressed in front of so many others, and we find it very unsettling.

Dinner was so strange, Danny. None of us had any idea what they served us. I heard one of the wives say it looked like corned beef and hash, but it was disgusting. I poked around at it, but mostly nibbled on a bread roll. Some of the girls ate like they hadn't eaten in years, which might actually be the case. Many of them threw up on the grounds outside the mess hall when they left. Too much, too soon.

After dinner, we enjoyed a movie in the camp's theater, but for the life of me I can't remember what it was about. I could hardly stay awake. I'm told we'll have entertainment every night we're here.

Our orientation began this morning and will continue until we leave to board our ship. The fingerprinting left dark stains of ink on the pads of my fingers. No one seems to know how to get the ink off. We exchanged our sterling for American dollars. More confusion about tagging our luggage. I cannot understand why that seems to be such a constant problem. Thankfully, the Red Cross is helping with some of the processing. We're told they'll be available for counseling and guidance, as well as teaching classes to help us assimilate into the American culture.

I hesitate to tell you what happened next. We'd all heard rumors about the physicals, but nothing could have prepared us for it. I've never been so humiliated in all my life. They put a group of us in a room, and told us to take off all our clothes then put on the army robes they provided. They lined us up in the hall outside the theater, then called a few of us at a time to stand on the stage before two doctors in white lab coats who were seated at a desk. One by one, we had to open our robes so they could shine a flashlight under our arms and between our legs! Danny, I was so

367

angry, I had to clench my fists and lock my jaw to avoid punching those doctors who were obviously getting their jollies. I doubt they were even doctors. We were told they were checking for lice, but I assure you it was nothing more than a legitimized peep show. How could they do that to us? And how could those in charge condone this kind of behavior? Yet, had I refused, it would've meant certain expulsion from the camp and no passage to America.

Many of the girls cried throughout the ordeal, but I just glared at those horrible men. Once we were excused, we dressed again and returned to our barracks. You've never heard so many angry women crying and carrying on. I told Gigi I was going to place a telephone call to Phillip at the embassy and report this atrocity. It's a disgrace. No one should be treated like that.

I should not have told you, but I'm still too angry and too tired to pretend otherwise. Please don't think I'm ungrateful for this journey, Danny. I'm so anxious to see you, and I know I can survive almost anything as long as it takes me to you.

It's late, and I must get some sleep. But would you do me a favor? Would you ask your mother to pray that I can keep my mouth shut and not get kicked out before our ship sails?

Love always,

Anya

The next morning, Anya dropped off her letter to Danny in the camp's post office on her way to the mess hall. She pulled up the collar of her coat against the chill of the blustery wind. Though she'd slept both nights in a surprisingly comfortable bed, she was fairly certain she had shivered all night beneath the thin wool blanket. With only a small stove in the center of the room, she wondered if they would all get sick before leaving the camp.

"Anya!"

She turned at the sound of Kate's voice and joined her at the end of the queue outside the mess hall. Joss was sound asleep on her mother's shoulder, bundled up with only her little face showing.

"I was hoping to find you this morning," Anya said. "Just because we aren't staying in the same barracks doesn't mean we can't eat our meals together. How are the mummy accommodations?"

"Dreadful. I'm absolutely exhausted and so is poor little Joss. She hardly slept at all, for all the other crying babies who couldn't sleep because they were so cold." Kate shook her head. "I just hope and pray the ship has better accommodations. And heat."

"Does Joss have her own crib?"

"They ran out of cribs, so she's sleeping in a footlocker. I would put her in bed with me, but the bed is so narrow, I worried she might take a tumble onto the floor." Kate shook her head. "There was a young girl in the bed next to mine. She just turned sixteen a week ago, and her baby boy is four months old. I heard her whimpering most of the night. I can't imagine how frightening it must be for one so young."

"I'll put your food on my tray. Just tell me what you'd like."

They made their selections, thankful the breakfast items looked more familiar than last night's dinner. Anya avoided making eye contact with the German prisoners of war working the food line. Others talked of their brusque behavior and leering looks. With a guard close by to keep watch over the Germans, Anya chose to spare herself from any unwanted confrontation.

They found some open seats at a table and settled in to eat.

"Maybe I can take care of Joss for a while after we eat so you can get some sleep."

"That's not likely to happen. Have you seen the list of classes we're required to attend today?"

Anya took a sip of coffee. "Yes, all of them quite riveting, don't you think?"

Kate yawned as she held Joss against her chest then munched on a piece of toast.

"That was a joke, by the way."

"Sorry. I'm too tired to care one way or the other at the moment." She offered a weary smile then gazed down at her sleeping daughter. "It isn't at all what we'd been told, is it? But I keep reminding myself we'll only be here another day or two, then off we'll sail for America and finally reunited with our husbands."

"I wish we could sneak you into our barracks. Other than

a few who snore like a freight train, it's been relatively quiet."

"That's kind of you, but we'll be fine."

"There you are." Gigi slid her tray onto the table and took a seat beside Kate. "Why did you go off and leave me, Anya? I thought you were going to wait."

"I told you, Gigi. I had to drop my letter by the postbox, remember? You hadn't even showered yet, so there was no point in waiting."

"Oh, and wasn't it lovely, having such a long hot shower?" She raised her hands to the heavens. "Thank you for all that hot water, American Red Cross! I feel positively revived!"

A spattering of applause and cheers passed through the mess hall. "I can't even remember the last time I took a shower. All these years having to wash in a bathtub with water limited to five inches and not a drop more? Heaven. Pure heaven. I could have stayed in that shower for an hour. Oh, and isn't this lovely?" She held a piece of bacon over her plate and closed her eyes. "Oh, little piggy, how I've missed you. You're a smidge too crisp for my liking, but I shall eat you anyway. Mmm."

Anya stood. "I'm finished. Kate, let me hold Joss so you can eat."

"Thank you, love." She handed the baby over and took her seat again.

Gigi pointed her fork at Kate. "You know they have a nursery available. You could drop Joss off and pick her up at the end of the day. Or even leave her there overnight so you can get some rest. You'd save yourself a world of trouble."

Kate glanced in her direction with a tired stare. "No, I would never do that."

"Why not? That's what it's there for. I heard they have plenty of childminders. Might be nice to have a little time to yourself."

"I stopped by there for a peek on the way to dinner last night. You've never seen so many babies in all your life, and most of them screaming. I wouldn't leave Joss with those strangers and all that chaos."

Gigi took a sip of coffee. "I say you should live a little while you can, Kate. Did you hear there's going to be a follies show? We should put together an act. Maybe a song and dance number?" She looked back and forth between them, her face bright with optimism. "Time to have a little fun! What do you say?"

Kate leveled her eyes at Anya. "Do I look like I want to sing and dance in front of all these people?"

Anya chuckled, gently rocking Joss back and forth. "Judging by your expression, I would have to say no."

Kate's eyes fluttered then closed. "And you would be correct."

Gigi lit a cigarette and took a drag. "Fine, then. Anya, what about you?" Gigi tipped her head back and blew a long stream of smoke. "Do you dance?"

Anya scoffed. "No, Gigi, I don't dance, and before you ask, I'm told I sing like a frog."

"Oh, stop. You're just saying that."

"No, it's true. When I was young and sang in the children's choir at our church, the lady in charge told me to mouth the words but not actually sing."

Gigi clowned a grimace. "That's so sad! Poor little Anya. I bet the other children teased you terribly."

"They did, but I didn't care."

"Yes, I would imagine you didn't." Gigi set her cigarette on the edge of her plate and took another bite of bacon. "Well then, I shall be on my own. I'll think of something."

The rest of the day brought a flurry of classes, long queues for checking and rechecking to make sure all the necessary forms were completed. More interviews. More inoculations. Anya wondered if any of it was necessary, or if perhaps those in charge merely shuffled them all around like a merry-go-round that wouldn't stop until they departed.

Anya fought an ongoing undercurrent of angst while at Camp Tidworth, but said nothing about it. While most of the war brides appeared excited and anxious to make the journey across the Atlantic, she wondered how many of them like her might be worrying about the drastic changes their lives were taking. As eager as she was to begin her life with Danny, she tried to tamp down the constant prickly sensation in her stomach that riddled her with worries and fears. It would all be over soon. Surely?

"I'm so glad I kept Joss with me," Kate said when they gathered again for the evening meal. "Have you heard all the rumors about the strange sickness spreading through the nursery?"

"No. What kind of sickness?"

"Massive problems with diarrhea. They said the stench is unbearable. We were told to bring a twenty-one-day supply of nappies before we came, but the babies in the nursery are going through them much too fast. Plus, there's nowhere to wash or dry the nappies. It's ridiculous."

"Do they know what's causing the diarrhea?" Anya asked.

"Someone said the women in the Formula Room are mixing the formula incorrectly, doubling the strength instead of the normal amount. But I can't help thinking some of the children were already sick when they arrived."

"But I thought all the children were given physicals." Anya leaned back in her chair with Joss sound asleep on her shoulder.

Kate shook her head. "What a joke. When we arrived, the doctor barely glanced at Joss. For all they knew, she could have had the plague."

"All right, all right," Gigi groaned, stubbing her cigarette in the ashtray. "Enough of this gloom and doom! We won't be here forever, ladies, so why can't we ignore all the negative chatter and just keep cheerful thoughts?" She picked up her tray and turned to go.

"Where are you going?" Kate asked.

"I don't know. I need some fresh air. I'll see you all later."

37

30 January 1946

Two days later, Anya, Kate, and Gigi and hundreds of other brides received the notice they'd all been waiting for. They were to report to Pier 54 in Southampton at ten the next morning where they would board the SS *Wisteria*, an American cruise ship.

As soon as the notices were distributed, Anya and her friends joined the long queue waiting to wire telegrams to their husbands with the name of their ship, and the date and time scheduled for its arrival in New York. The Army Transport Company would further update the families after departure should the arrival date and time change. Afterward, the girls hurried back to their barracks to pack their belongings.

They were awakened at quarter past four the next morning and instructed to have their bags ready before their five-thirty breakfast. By half past six, they waited in another queue to have their luggage weighed once again, and all their forms checked one final time. At eight, they boarded one of the many buses for Southampton, some sixty miles away.

Once they arrived, they gathered their carry-on bags and followed the mass of women and children all heading toward the port's main entrance. A ripple of barely-contained excitement surrounded them with smiles all around. Even the bitter cold temperature couldn't dampen their spirits. Only a few of the youngest brides sobbed as they said their goodbyes to family members who'd come to see them off. Emotions ran deep in both directions.

"ANYA!"

She turned, scanning the crowd. "Did you hear someone call out my name?"

"Yes! Over there, Anya," Gigi said pointing across the crowd. "That couple running there. Do you see them? She's wearing a red beret."

"Where? Oh ... oh my goodness! I can't believe it!" She dashed away from the queue, pushing her way through the crowd.

"We'll hold your place in line, but hurry, Anya!" Gigi cried.

"Sophie! Charlie? I can't believe you're here!" She flew into their open arms, colliding in hugs and kisses, their laughter puffing bursts of clouds in the chilly sea air.

Sophie hugged her again, squeezing her tight. "Oh Anya, I'm so glad we caught you before it was too late! We would have been here earlier but the traffic came to a stall the closer we got to the pier. We finally parked the automobile and made a run for it."

Frosty tears of joy blurred her vision. "But how did you know I'd be here? We only found out yesterday that we'd be sailing today."

"Never underestimate the American spirit," Charlie teased. "We had already told Danny we wanted to come see you off and made him promise not to tell you. He wired us as soon as he got your telegram yesterday. We made a few quick calls, jumped the automobile, and here we are."

"Yes, and Da sends his love. He's fighting the tiniest bit of a cold, so I insisted he mind the pub while we're away."

"Please give him my love and tell him I hope he feels better soon."

Sophie grabbed Anya's gloved hands with both of hers. "We know you can't stay, but we had to at least try to see you off. We've missed you *so* much, Anya. Are you well? Are you terribly excited?"

"Yes, yes, but let me look at you!" Anya stepped back for a better look at the expectant mother. "Open your coat so I can see."

Sophie quickly unbuttoned her coat and displayed her rounded belly.

"Oh Sophie, look at you!" She patted her friend's tummy. "I'm so happy for you. You must promise you'll come to Chicago, America once your little one is born."

"ANYA!" Gigi yelled. "We're about to go through. Hurry!"

"Yes, yes! We promise. We would love to come see you and Danny in America." Sophie hugged her again and kissed her cheek. "Now go so you don't miss your ship!"

Charlie hugged her, planting a loud kiss on her other cheek. "Safe travels, Anya. You tell that husband of yours to—"

"Oh, Anya, I almost forgot!" Sophie dug in her pocketbook and pulled out a small velvet pouch which she handed her.

"Oh, you shouldn't have, Sophie."

"Open it. Hurry!"

Anya pulled open the drawstring and looked inside. "Oh ... I can't believe it!" she cried, lifting out the sterling silver charm bracelet.

"I found it in the alley when I was making room by the fence to stock more firewood. The sunlight happened to hit it just right, and I knew exactly what it was."

"ANYA! Hurry!" Gigi yelled.

"I can't believe it! Oh, thank you, thank you!"

"You're welcome!" Sophie said. "Isn't it the most perfect send-off? Now, off you go. We'll stay to see you sail away so watch for us! We love you!"

Anya turned to go, looked back one more time to wave, then rushed to catch up with Kate and Gigi.

"Friends of yours?" Kate asked.

She turned for a final look, but the gate blocked her view. "Yes, the dearest of friends. They're the ones I stayed with in Framlingham—"

"Charlie and Sophie? I remember! You told me about them. They were in your wedding, right?"

"Yes. Oh, I just can't believe they came all the way from Framlingham to see me off. And look—" She held up the bracelet. "They found my bracelet!"

"Danny's bracelet? I mean, the one Danny gave you on your honeymoon?"

"Yes, I just can't believe he found it!"

"Oh Anya, how wonderful!" Kate said.

"Come on, girls. You're holding up the queue!" Gigi shouted.

As they made their way closer to their pier, Anya shivered in the brisk morning air and took a deep breath. "It's really happening, isn't it? We're not just dreaming, are we?"

"I just had the same thought," Kate said, tugging the knitted cap on Joss's head to cover her ears. "We're standing here, but for the life of me, I still can't believe it. We're *finally* going. We're going! After everything we've been through, I just can't believe it's happening."

"Isn't it wonderful?!" Gigi squealed, huddling them in a group hug.

Jocelyn giggled with a toothless smile.

"Did you hear what they're calling these sailings?" Gigi asked. "They've dubbed them *Operation War Bride.* Fancy that, we have our very own operation."

"I heard someone else call it *Operation Diaper Run,*" Anya added.

"I've never seen so many women and children in my whole life," Kate marveled. "Good thing it's a big ship."

All three tilted their heads back as they looked up at the bow of the SS *Wisteria.* The ship was quite beautiful and majestic, despite its gray wartime exterior. Anya tried to imagine it in its previous glory as a luxury cruise liner.

"You think this is big?" Gigi said. "I'm still upset we don't get to sail on the *Queen Mary* or the *Queen Elizabeth* over there. Just look at them! This old tub looks like a shabby baby compared to those grand ladies."

"That's a bit harsh, don't you think?" Anya challenged. The *Wisteria* may not be as big, but she's still beautiful. Like a smaller version of the *Titanic.*"

"Anya, take that back!" Gigi snapped. "You take that back this instant! You mustn't banter about such a thing when we're about to board. It's bad luck."

"Don't be so superstitious. It's been more than thirty years since the *Titanic* sunk—"

Gigi gave her a loud *shush.* "Don't be daft. Don't even *say* the name of that ship. Don't even *think* it!"

Kate hugged Joss closer. "I have to agree with Gigi, Anya. People at sea are quite superstitious, so be careful what you say about such things."

As they neared the gangway, a magpie suddenly flew down from the ship's railing and landed only a short distance from them.

Gigi shrieked as she backed away from the bird. "NOW see what you've done?" She blew a kiss toward the bird then saluted it.

Kate turned her back and moved away, holding Joss even closer. "Oh no, this can't be good."

Anya looked at them, bewildered. "What's wrong with you two? It's just a silly black bird."

Gigi shook her head. "No, it's not! How can you *not* know that magpies are bad luck? Especially if you see only one. 'One for sorrow,' as the saying goes."

"If that's the case, why did you blow it a kiss and salute it?"

"Honestly, Anya, you can't seriously tell me you don't know? To ward off the risk of bad luck, of course. Now, thanks to you, we'll probably all die at sea."

"Gigi, I think you're overreacting—"

"Ladies, if I may have your attention."

The crowd slowly quieted to hear the voice over the

loudspeaker.

"This is Captain Neville Masterson. Welcome to this historic voyage of the SS *Wisteria*. As you board, please mind that the identity cards you were given are displayed in plain sight. This will help our stewards move you along to your assigned cabins. If you have any questions pertaining to our ship, please address them to the stewards. All other questions regarding your journey across the Atlantic to your new homes may be addressed to the American Red Cross representatives at a later time. With your help, we can all accomplish this vast undertaking with efficiency in order that we may depart on time this evening. Thank you for your cooperation and welcome aboard."

Anya lost track of time as they moved along at a snail's pace. Once they climbed the steps up to the gangway, a swell of fear surged through her, nearly taking her breath away. She gripped the side rail to steady herself, careful not to look down at the water below. When she left Holland, she'd ridden the ferry across the choppy English Channel without so much as a single moment of seasickness. The *Wisteria* was still anchored at the dock. It wasn't moving. So what triggered the sudden strange feelings?

"Are you all right?"

She looked up to find Kate turned toward her, one hand on the rail, the other cradling Joss. "Yes, I'm fine. I think."

"Move along, ladies," Gigi prodded. "You heard the man."

Once aboard the ship, they were attended by American soldiers who helped carry their luggage and led them to their assigned cabin. All three girls were awestruck by the grand staircase taking them down a flight of stairs.

"Have you ever seen anything so beautiful?" Kate crooned as she ascended the crowded stairs. "I had no idea these ocean liners were so elegant."

They turned down one hall, then another and another. Next, a long stretch of hallway where they passed clusters of excited brides all chatting and carrying on about their good fortune. Another turn, then another. Then another long stretch of hallway gave way to another crowded flight of stairs.

"I'm so very glad you know where you're going, soldier," Gigi said. "If I didn't know better, I'd think you were purposefully trying to confuse us."

"Or taking us in circles," Kate teased.

The young soldier turned to look over his shoulder. "Don't you worry your pretty little heads. It just takes time to get your bearings. You'll find your way soon enough."

"Will I?" Gigi asked. "And if I don't will you show me the way?"

"At your service, ma'am. We're here to help." He offered a ready smile as he turned a final corner. "Here you go. Cabin 245. Mind your step."

They followed him into a large stateroom paneled in rich polished cherry with brass wall fixtures giving off a soft glow to the room. But those were the only luxuries. The rest of the room had been stripped bare of furnishings and replaced with several double bunks lining all four walls. Some of the girls were already stowing their bags and claiming their bunks. The soldiers set their bags beside three open bunks.

"There now. Take your time settling in. The captain will make another announcement later with further instructions.

Any questions?"

"Might there be a crib for my little one?" Kate asked.

"Oh." The soldier blinked as if he hadn't noticed the child. "My mistake, ma'am. Those with little ones are in another section of the ship." He reached for her bags. "I'll be happy to take you there."

"But please, can't I stay here with my friends? It's such a long journey, and I can't imagine being separated from them."

Gigi slipped between them and worked her magic. "Come on, love, have a heart. We're meant to stay together, the three of us." She busied herself straightening his tie. "If I ventured a guess, I bet you could sneak one of those cute little hammocks in here so Kate and her sweet baby can stay with us." She patted his tie and let her hands linger on his chest. "You would do that for us, wouldn't you?"

A warm flush spread across the soldier's face. Anya and Kate shared a look, each suppressing a smile.

"I'm not entirely sure I—"

"Oh, but *I'm* sure. And I would be most appreciative of such a kindness on your part." She glanced over her shoulder at Kate and Anya. "We would *all* be most appreciative, wouldn't we, girls?"

"Oh yes, absolutely," Kate answered.

"Positively," Anya added.

Gigi turned back to him. "Well, then. There you go."

"Uh ..." He scratched the back of his neck. "Well, then. I suppose I could—"

"Splendid!" Gigi stood on her tiptoes to give him a quick kiss on the cheek. "I knew you were a kind and considerate fellow the minute I laid eyes on you."

"Yes. Well, then. Right. I'll just be ... on my way." He offered a quick, nervous smile then left.

"Well done!" Kate cried. "That was brilliant. Oh, *thank* you, Gigi. I promise I'll never again tease you about your flirting."

"Of course you will, but you're welcome anyway."

One of the other brides in the room applauded. "My, and aren't *you* quite the clever one? Well done! Quite masterful, if you ask me."

"Did you see him?" another added. "Putty in your hands, he was. She's right, you know. That was brilliant. Quite brilliant indeed."

"Why, thank you, ladies." Gigi took a deep theater bow then twirled to give another to the other side of the stateroom.

They introduced themselves to their new roommates and got acquainted. Helen—a tall beauty with a head of copper curls and a splash of freckles across her nose. Agatha—short and round and full of giggles. Ruth—a quiet girl with traces of tears on her pale cheeks. Four others stayed to themselves; all of them wrapped in long fur coats. The remaining bunks showed evidence of others who had stashed their bags and left the cabin.

"I do hope it's all right with all of you that I keep my little one here," Kate said. "I promise she won't be a bother."

"No bother at all, and we're pleased to have her," Helen said, moving her hand to her flat stomach. "I've only just found out I'm in the family way myself, so I'll enjoy having a little one about."

"Congratulations," Kate said. "Then your husband is still

here in England?"

"No, he left a month ago. He worked at the American Embassy in London."

"Really? We have a friend there who's been so helpful to us through all this waiting. Lieutenant Phillip Powell. Do you know him?"

"The name is familiar, but I only met my husband a few months ago. He quite literally swept me off my feet and proposed two weeks later. We were married only a month before he left. It was all rather sudden."

"The Yanks are rather spectacular at that, sweeping us off our feet," Gigi added as she pulled a cigarette from her silver case. "Makes you wonder if they come out of the womb that way—"

"Gigi, don't be vulgar—"

"—or if they're taught in school to have all that charm. Either way, we love them, don't we?" She struck a match.

"Oh, please don't think I'm a bother, but would you mind not smoking in here?" Helen's face tinted with her apology. "I'm so terribly sorry, but lately I find I'm quite queasy with even the slightest hint of smoke."

Gigi's brows arched as she waved the match out. "You poor dear. Not to worry. Plenty of deck up top where I can puff away."

"Forgive me for asking, Helen, but how in the world did you process all your papers in such a short amount of time?" Kate implored. "It seems like we've been filling out papers and standing in queues for the better part of six months."

"I suppose it's because my husband worked at the embassy. Inside shortcuts and all that."

A few moments later, the young soldier returned with the small hammock and showed Kate how to hang it from the bunk above her. The lad was quite nervous, voicing concern he might incur the wrath of his superiors if they learned of his unsanctioned accommodation.

Gigi escorted him to the door. "We'll never tell a soul. You can count on that, soldier." She stood on tiptoe and kissed his other cheek. "You have our word."

His handkerchief was already out of his pocket as he turned to go. "I should have mentioned we're not supposed to fraternize with the passengers, so I would appreciate it greatly if you pay me no mind from here on."

Gigi tossed him a wink. "My lips are sealed."

He stared at her a second longer then turned and disappeared down the hall.

Agatha's merry laughter filled the room. "Honestly, it's like having our very own cinema, watching you work your magic on the boy! I do believe Vivian Leigh may have met her match."

Half an hour later, a loud chime sounded over the intercom before an announcement was made that the ship would sail in one hour. Passengers were encouraged to line the decks to wave goodbye to friends and family.

Anya was relieved to find a map of the ship's layout in the packets provided on each bed. She studied it before they left, circling their cabin then looking for the simplest passage to the deck. There they joined hundreds of brides and children, each claiming a section of the rail to wave to those below.

"Can you see them?" Anya asked Kate, scanning the crowd below for Sophie's red beret.

"I'm looking. Can you believe all those people are here to

see us off?"

Gigi waved both arms then blew loud, exaggerated kisses. "Goodbye, England! We're off to America! We'll miss you!"

"Oh, there!" Kate cried, pointing to their far left. "Down there toward the end of the dock. See her? She's waving her cap!"

"Oh yes! There! Goodbye, Sophie! Goodbye, Charlie!"

They couldn't possibly hear them amidst the shouts and laughter, but they all waved nonetheless. Anya loved the festive spirit and feeling a part of something so wonderful and exciting. She waved and waved even as tears stung her eyes at the sight of Charlie and Sophie waving back at her.

They covered their ears when the long horn blasted from the ship's smokestacks signaling their departure. Kate covered Joss's ears and held her close as all of them laughed and shouted with joy. When the horn finally silenced, the passengers and crowd below continued their jubilant farewells.

"Goodbye, England!"

"Wish us luck!"

"Mummy, I'll miss you!"

"Write me! Every day!"

"I love you, Mummy! I love you, Daddy!"

With a bit of a jolt, the great ocean liner slowly, slowly began to move, as the tugboat towed it out to sea.

"I can't believe it! We're on our way!" Gigi squealed long and loud, hooking her arms through Kate and Anya's. "America here we come!"

As the ship distanced itself from the pier, the women and children scurried back inside, out of the frigid air. But just as

Anya turned to go inside, she noticed the shy girl from their cabin, huddled on a deck chair and sobbing.

"Girls, wait," she said, touching Kate's arm. "Let me see what's wrong with our cabinmate."

"Don't worry," Kate said. "We haven't a clue how to find our stateroom without you. We'll wait inside where it's warm."

Anya took a seat on the deck chair beside the crying girl. "Ruth, isn't it?"

The girl looked up, startled, then nodded as her face crumbled again.

Anya placed her gloved hand over the girl's trembling bare hand. "Is there anything I can do to help?"

Ruth shook her head, then paused for a moment and nodded. She dropped her head in her hands again. "I've made such a terrible mistake. I should never have come here. Never got on this boat."

"I know it's hard to say goodbye, but it will get better. And you've got all of us making the trip with you. We've all had to leave loved ones behind to make this journey."

Ruth cried more softly, her head still shaking back and forth. "I'm only sixteen. Mum told me I was a fool to marry so young, and to a Yank at that. And Father wouldn't even come to see me off, he's so upset. Told me he didn't raise his little girl to go off with some fast-talking Yank. But my Eddie, he's not like that."

"What's he like? Tell me."

She wiped her face with a crumpled handkerchief then attempted to square her shoulders and sit straighter. "Eddie's such a nice wonderful boy. Just a farmer's son from somewhere called Iowa." A wavering smile lightened her face. "He's just eighteen. He lied about his age when he enlisted a couple years ago so he could do his part to help win the war."

"Where did you meet him?"

She dipped her eyes with a shy smile. "I grew up in Thorpe Abbotts in Norfolk. My father has a pub there, and I worked there after school. Then when the war started, the Americans built an airfield there for the 100th Bomb Group. That was Eddie's group. One night he came into the pub with his friends, and they were all teasing him because he didn't like the pints much. He came up to the bar and started talking to me." Her trembling smile widened. "It was love at first sight. For both of us."

"Then that's what you must focus on while we cross the sea. That love that drew you to each other, and the new life you'll make together. And remember that just because you're moving to America now doesn't mean you'll never see your parents again. These big boats travel both ways, you know."

Ruth took a shuddering breath and slowly let it go. "Yes, that's true. I hadn't thought about that before." She straightened a little more. "Thank you ... Anna, is it?"

"Anya. And you're welcome." Anya stood. "Why don't you and I go join our friends inside where it's warm."

Ruth stood and immediately embraced Anya, clinging to her. "Thank you. Thank you ever so much. I don't feel quite so afraid now."

"My pleasure, Ruth."

38

By the time the *Wisteria's* passengers were seated for dinner, any who might have braved the cold wind on deck would no longer be able to see the shores of England. Some experienced a mild wave of seasickness, but most were able to enjoy the bounty of food offered in the ship's dining area. Unlike the peculiar dishes served at Camp Tidworth, the *Wisteria* presented more traditional English cooking which the girls welcomed eagerly.

"Quite a sight for sore eyes, it is," Helen said, appraising the steaming cottage pie before taking a bite. "No more ration coupons or Lord Woolton pies for us, and aren't we glad?"

"I have to say, I rather like a good Lord Woolton pie," Agatha added. "My mum's recipe was fabulous. We always fought over it, my brothers and sisters."

Gigi's lip curled as she feigned a shiver. "Not me. I couldn't stand the stuff. I can't wait to get to America and eat their juicy cheeseburgers and salty French fries and thick, rich milkshakes like we served at the Rainbow."

With Joss sleeping in one arm, Kate closed her eyes and savored a bite. "Mmm. I had forgotten what really good food tastes like."

"And a nice cup of tea, finally," Helen said. "The kitchen staff at Tidworth hadn't a clue how to brew a proper cuppa. I'd wager a guess some Brits are staffing the *Wisteria's* kitchen."

Gigi reached for her cup. "Rather a delightful trip ahead, all things consi—"

"Whoa." Helen braced her hands on the edge of the table. "Did anyone else feel that?"

The salt and pepper shakers slid a couple of inches.

"Feel what?" Gigi asked.

"That," Helen said. "The ship tilting."

"Only a little," Kate said. "Are you all right?"

"I don't know. I feel a bit off balance."

Gigi buttered a dinner roll. "You'll get used to it. They say it sometimes takes a while to find your sea legs."

They continued their conversations, much of it centered on food and all the other things they'd missed out on during the war. Anya noticed that Helen wasn't eating, just pushing food around on her plate. Moments later, the salt and pepper shakers slid back the other direction.

Ruth set down her fork. "Yes, I felt that one. I think I—"

Helen turned just in time to spill the contents of her stomach on the floor. Ruth immediately did the same. Moments later, their actions spawned a chain effect of lost meals throughout the noisy dining room.

When Anya noticed Kate looking a bit green in the gills,

she grabbed Joss and helped her stand. "You and Joss need to get out of here. Can you find your way back to the cabin?"

"I don't think so."

"Then wait for me at the first staircase. I'll see if I can help Ruth and Helen."

A quarter hour later, the girls straggled back to their cabin. Only Anya and Gigi had been spared the miserable effects, despite the sickening stench which had quickly overtaken the ship's corridors. They helped the others to their bunks, then one by one assisted their cabinmates as they changed from soiled clothing to nightgowns. By the time everyone was settled—at least for the time being—they fell into their beds exhausted.

"Why didn't anyone tell us we'd be so sick?" Agatha groaned from her top bunk.

"If they had, would you have stayed home?" someone asked.

"No. I suppose not."

"I'd have thought about it, that's for sure," Helen added.

"The motion sickness will pass, won't it?" another asked. "We're not meant to be sick all the way to America, are we?"

The quiet chatter continued, though Anya tried her best to tune them out, needing a break from the subject.

"Anya, why do you think you didn't get sick like everyone else?" Gigi rolled over on her stomach and propped herself up on her elbows. With Anya on the adjacent upper bunk, their pillows were just inches apart. "I had years of practice with my younger brothers and sisters. Someone was always tossing their biscuits at home. Since I was the eldest, Mum expected me to help care for the little ones. She said I had a stomach made of cast iron. I suppose she was right. How about you? How'd you keep your biscuits down today?"

"I'm not sure." A dark cloud of memories troubled her mind. Instinctively her stomach clenched. "I suppose I saw too much during the war. Things I wish I'd never seen. Maybe I learned to push through it because there wasn't time to be sick or weak."

Gigi twirled a curl with her fingers. "That makes sense. I'd forgotten you were in the Dutch Resistance. So tell me. What's the worst thing you ever saw?"

Anya winced as the scene flashed on the screen of her mind's eye. She and her friend Wim, hiding in the woods alongside his family's farm, knowing something was terribly wrong when they found little Inge crawling in a cultivated field. The little one was the youngest sister of Anya's best friend Lieke. Like so many other Dutch Jews, they'd come to the Boorman's farm to hide during the Occupation. Moments later, Wim had grabbed the child and rushed her back to Anya before inching his way to the barn to find out what was going on.

Before he returned, a German soldier had pressed a gun to the back of Anya's skull. Moments later, he shot little Inge with a single bullet to her forehead. Anya had screamed, wailing at the heartless German as blood poured from the baby's head. A second later, she set Inge's body down just before throwing up.

Despite her protests, the German had forced her to her feet, shoving her forward with his gun to her back. She'd begged him to let her take the baby's body. "Leave her," he'd barked. "Let her body rot and serve as fertilizer for the crops.

Perhaps she'll be worth something after all."

Her eyes stung with the memory, and she could do nothing to stop them. Wim had snuck back, smashing the German's head with a large stone, thinking he'd killed the soldier. Wim held her in his arms, heartbroken to tell her what he'd discovered at the farmhouse. His entire family had been killed—lined up and executed. All of them, including all the Jews they'd sheltered in the hideout beneath their barn. Even her dear friend Lieke. All of them dead.

Then, as she and Wim comforted each other in that ghastly moment, another shot rang out. Wim slumped against her. Only then did she see the smoke of the dying German's pistol now aimed at her. A second later, he crumbled to the ground and died. As Wim's life was slipping away, he told her to run as fast as she could, but she refused, pleading for him to hold on. His hand trembled as he placed his palm against her cheek, his eyes struggling to focus.

I love you, Anya. I have always—"

"Anya?" Gigi asked, tapping her hand and interrupting the haunting memory. "Sweetie, are you all right?"

Anya swallowed hard, thankful to blink away the horrible memories. "No. I was just remembering ..."

Gigi reached for Anya's hands and squeezed them. "I'm so sorry. It was a stupid thing to ask. Please forgive me."

Anya took in a deep breath and tried to relax. "No forgiveness needed."

"Sometimes I think I haven't an iota of sense left in my ridiculous head. It's bad enough we've had to wade through all the muck and sop up all their sick. The last thing we needed was to scrape off the scab of some ghastly memory. Oh Anya, I'm so sorry."

She was surprised at the glistening in Gigi's eyes and the honesty of her apology. The bubbly blonde was never one to let down her guard, always careful to maintain a mask of confidence and control.

Anya squeezed back. "It's all right. But thank you."

"Thank *me*? For what?"

"For caring enough to apologize, even if it wasn't necessary."

Gigi gave a shrug. "Oh, you know me ... just one big walking, talking apology."

No sooner had their conversation ended than the ship took a hard roll one way, then back the other. The room filled with moans and the gross and disgusting sound of stomachs heaving whatever was left in them.

Gigi groaned as she jumped down from her bunk. "Here we go again."

39

THE WISTERIA WAVE
The Ship's Daily Newspaper
Saturday, 2 February 1946
Ship's position as of noon today:
49° 40' N. Latitude; 20° 30' W

A Word from our Captain
By now, as we continue steaming along these waters to the shores of America, I hope those of you who have suffered from seasickness have at last found relief. We have made every effort to make you as comfortable as possible, thanking Mother Nature for doing her part to smooth the waves upon which we now travel. A tremendous thanks to the medical staff and the Red Cross personnel on board who have worked diligently to aid those affected. Please do not hesitate to ask for help if you are still under the weather.

We look forward to seeing more of you at our evening events. The onboard staff have worked tirelessly to provide nightly entertainment for your journey. You will find a list of those activities on the reverse page.

In addition, the Red Cross continues to offer a wide range of classes to help you adapt to your new life in America. You will find them listed on the reverse page as well. I hope you will avail yourselves of these many opportunities.

If we may be of further assistance, please let us know by contacting any of the stewards on board.

May God grant us smooth sailing ahead,

Captain Neville Masterson

* * * * *

And Now a Word from our Chaplain

What a grand privilege and honor it is to sail with all of you on your inaugural voyage to America! Please join us for daily services at half past ten each morning in the ship's chapel, B Deck, Aft, Portside, next to the ship's Library. We sing hymns, pray, and read a brief passage of Scripture. All faiths are welcome.

Vespers over the ship's public address system are offered each evening at half past seven.

As we sail ever closer to America's shores, many of you may find yourselves second-guessing your decision. Perhaps your seasickness is accompanied by an over-whelming wave of homesickness. For those with children, you may worry for your little one's health and happiness as he or she is carried to a strange land amongst a new family of strangers.

Whatever your lot, I am available to help, and I welcome you to stop by for a visit. My office is located on B Deck, next to the Chapel in Cabin 236. My office hours are 8:00 a.m. to 7:30 p.m. daily.

Wishing you God's richest blessings,
Chaplain William Traverse

* * * * *

From the Editor

As we continue our historic adventure across the high seas, I would like to take this opportunity to remind you of the ongoing classes and workshops available to you each and every day. As Captain Masterson mentioned, you will find them listed on the reverse page along with a map showing classroom locations.

For the musically gifted, it's not too late to join the Wisteria Orchestra or the Brides' Chorus as both rehearse American tunes for our nightly concerts as well as the patriotic concert scheduled for our last night together. Come one, come all!

For the beauties amongst us (don't be shy!), don't forget to enter our Beauty Contest to be held Friday evening, 8 February. Consolation prizes for the two runner-ups and a grand prize for the lucky girl crowned Most Beautiful!

But wait! Move over, Mummy. We haven't forgotten the darling babies on board. On Saturday afternoon, 9 February, we'll all enjoy our Beautiful Baby contest.

Categories determined by age: newborn to 18 months; 18 months to 2 years; 2 years and above. Is your baby the cutest? Find out Saturday!

I'm quite confident that every bride on board will enjoy this headline from America: "Hundreds of Yankee Husbands Await War Brides' Arrival." *The SS Argentina, the first official "War Bride Ship," which departed from Southampton on 26 January, is scheduled to arrive at New York Harbor on Monday, a day late due to a fierce storm encountered approximately 1,000 miles from American soil. The Argentina charts the course with 452 war brides and 145 babies on board, commencing "Operation Diaper Run" which will transport thousands of English, Scottish, Irish, and Welsh brides to their new homes in America. These anxious American husbands will be joined by the Mayor of New York, a band, and hundreds of news reporters and cameramen.*

Let's hope they'll give the Wisteria the same warm welcome when we arrive next week!

While the Americans prepare for the arrival of the Argentina, back in Southampton today, the Queen Mary will board her first war bride passengers, expecting over 2,400 to follow our voyage across the icy Atlantic.

Now for a final word. We're all anxious to see our husbands and explore our new land, but until we do, let's all make a special effort to get to know each other. If one of your cabinmates is a bit shy, include her in your activities. If she's feeling ill, do the right thing and help her out. If she's a bit fatigued from caring for her child, why not give her a break by offering to watch her little one for a while or suggesting she take little Robert or Mary to the ship's nursery? We're all in this together, ladies, so let's be good neighbors to one another.

Elizabeth Corbett, Editor

* * * * *

Have You Made Your Appointment?

The Wisteria Beauty Shop still has a few openings for hair styling and manicures before we dock in New York. Look your best for your American husband! Let the professionals help you look "shipshape" when you step off the Wisteria!

<u>Today's Lectures and Workshops</u>
Sewing Basics
Cooking American Style
American Fashion
Raising Children in America
Understanding the Government of the United States
"What Did You Say?" – A Study of
English vs. American English Colloquialisms
"Where's That?" A Brief Overview of the American States

<u>Books Available in the Library</u>
And Now Tomorrow by Rachel Field
A Tree Grows in Brooklyn by Betty Smith
Leave Her to Heaven by Ben Ames Williams
The Robe by Lloyd C. Douglas
Mrs. Miniver by Jan Struther
An Atlas of Infant Behavior by Arnold Gesell

I Never Left Home by Bob Hope
Our Hearts Were Young and Gay
by Cornelia Otis Skinner and Emily Kimbrough

<u>Tonight's Movie</u>
The Bells of St. Mary
Starring Bing Crosby and Ingrid Bergman

By Monday, most of Anya's cabinmates were feeling better, growing more accustomed to the ship's constant motion. Ruth still fought the dreadful nausea, unable to keep anything down. She insisted on staying in bed, moaning as she turned over and pulled the covers over her head. Worried about the fragile wisp of a girl, Anya promised to bring her something bland to nibble on.

The rest of them enjoyed a hearty breakfast including actual chilled oranges which they hadn't seen since the war began, and real eggs instead of powdered. Sautéed potatoes, pancakes with real maple syrup, and an assortment of flaky pastries rounded out the morning meal. Most of those who'd been especially ill took a pass on the sausage and bacon, but Gigi and Anya indulged themselves.

Afterward, they returned to their stateroom briefly to don coats and scarves before heading to the deck for some fresh air. Anya noticed Ruth's empty bunk, hoping that was a good sign. Maybe she was taking a hot shower or bath. With no more water rationing, everyone on board was raving about the sheer luxury of soaking in a nice hot bubble bath. Hopefully, Ruth was finding some relief. Anya left a wrapped pastry and orange for her on her pillow.

As they stepped out on the windy deck, Anya gazed up at the puffy white clouds dotting the perfect azure sky as the *Wisteria* cut her way through the rolling waves. She took a deep breath, savoring the tingling bite of frigid air as it filled her lungs.

Gigi joined her at the rail. "Don't you wish we could sleep out here instead of that smelly old stateroom?"

"Apart from the fact we'd freeze to death the first hour, I would say yes. It's a relief to breathe clean air again."

"Let's walk, shall we, girls?" Helen said as she came alongside Agatha. "Who knows if we'll have another chance to enjoy a pretty day out here."

"I'm so glad we weren't on the *Argentina,*" Agatha said. "I heard the seas were so rough, a baby was knocked out of its hammock. Rolled across the floor and back again before his mum could get to him."

"How awful," Kate said, glancing down at Joss in the pram. "That must have been ever so frightening. Did the child recover?"

"Just a bad bruise on his head, last I heard." Agatha arched her brows. "Want to know what else I heard?"

Gigi took the bait. "Do tell. What have you heard?"

"Well, rumor has it the girls on that ship have had to fight off the crew from unwanted attention, if you catch my drift. Apparently those guys have been at sea too long and were starved for female *interaction,* so to speak."

"Sounds like my kind of ship," Gigi teased.

Agatha's eyes widened. "No, not *that* kind of attention—against your will? Lots of assaults, from what I heard. Some happened right in broad daylight! They have so many crewmen locked up in the ship's brig now, there's hardly anyone left to help the girls disembark once they reach New York."

Anya stopped in her tracks. "That's the most ridiculous thing I've heard since we boarded this ship. Who told you such rubbish?"

Agatha stiffened, picking up her pace as she passed Anya. "I have my sources. And every word of it is true. You'll see. There are scads of news reporters on board with them. They'll spill the beans. Just you wait and see."

Anya slowly caught up with the others. "I doubt that seriously. The Army Transport would never put up with behavior like that. You shouldn't spread such rumors."

"Anya's right," Helen added. "You read the ship's paper this morning, Agatha. The *Argentina* is the first war bride ship to sail, which means they're in a publicity spotlight. My guess is the captain would nip that kind of behavior in the bud before it ever got out of hand."

Agatha's ample backside and short strides reminded Anya of a fairy godmother character in one of her favorite childhood books. A little busybody, bustling along, trying to keep up.

"I'm only telling you what I heard."

"Oh, don't be getting your knickers in a twist," Gigi teased. "Probably just some harmless flirting."

"Look there." Kate shadowed her eyes and pointed across

the starboard bow. "Are those icebergs?"

The rest of them turned to look. "I've never seen one before, but what else could it be?" Anya said. "Smaller than I imagined."

"That's because all you're seeing is the top of them," Helen said. "What lies beneath the water's surface is massive compared to what you see there."

"Maybe, but don't say the name of that other ship again," Kate cautioned. "No need to court a demise such as theirs."

"What ship?" Agatha asked. "You mean the *Titanic*?"

"Shush!" Gigi elbowed the girl's ribs. "Kate's right. Even uttering the ship's name could reap all sorts of peril and despair on us. I'll kindly thank the rest of you to guard against such thoughtless chatter."

Agatha snapped a salute. "Whatever you say, Captain Gigi."

They walked two full rounds of the deck before heading back inside for classes. Kate and Joss joined Helen for the "Raising Children in America" class. Gigi and another girl from their cabin chose the class about American fashion, while Agatha attended the study on British versus American colloquialisms. Anya decided a course on the layout of the American states might be helpful, hoping she might learn more about Chicago. The Red Cross workers made the classes fun and answered as many questions as the brides might ask.

The girls regrouped for the midday meal, dining over a choice of broiled salmon served with a lemon butter sauce or sugar-roasted ham with all the trimmings.

"Mmmm ... I'm beginning to think I never truly tasted food

until now," Gigi said. "It's like my taste buds are only now coming to life."

"We just forgot. That's all," Kate said.

As they ate, they discussed what they learned in their classes. Agatha had them in stitches sharing some of the differences between American English and their own British version.

"Like the expression *bugger off*. When we say *bugger off*, it's like saying leave me alone or stop bothering me! But in America, the word 'bugger' is what you find when you dig around inside your nose."

Gigi spewed the water she'd just sipped, making them all laugh even louder.

"If you're putting luggage into the back of an automobile, we say you stash it in the *boot*. Americans call it a trunk. And to them, a boot is a shoe similar to our galoshes. "

More laughter seemed to egg her on. "Oh, but this was my favorite. What do you say when you want someone to wake you in the morning?"

"That's easy," Kate said. "You ask them to knock you up."

"Yes, but in America if some fellow knocks you up, it means he got you pregnant!"

This time, their boisterous laughter drew stares from other nearby tables.

"Seriously?" Kate asked, still chuckling. "You didn't make that up, did you?"

"No, it's true! So be careful who you ask to knock you up, ladies."

After several more examples, Gigi finally stopped her. "Agatha, no more! We're doomed. We'll all sound like a bunch of fools every time we open our mouths."

"Oh, our Yanks will still love us," Helen added. "Don't you worry."

Later, several of the girls attended more classes while others visited the canteen, wrote letters, or roamed the ship to pass the time. Anya decided to skip the afternoon sessions and offered to take Joss for a while so Kate could have a break.

"Oh Anya, that would be *wonderful*," Kate said as they entered their stateroom. "I think I'll miss classes too and just rest here. I'm actually feeling a bit grotty after eating."

Anya reached for Joss. "Are you all right? Is there anything I can get for you?"

"No, I'll be fine. Taking Joss for a little while is more than enough." She gave her daughter a kiss on the cheek. "If you think you might take another stroll on the deck, be sure to take her coat and knitted bonnet. And here's her blanket to wrap around her."

"I think we might like another walk up on the deck, don't you, Joss?"

Kate helped Anya put the wool coat on the baby, then pulled the bonnet down over her ears. "There you are, sweetheart. You have fun with Auntie Anya while Mummy takes a lie-down."

Kate wasn't the only one needing a break. Anya had never been the sort to need constant companionship, and she ached for some time alone. She wondered if something might be wrong with her, this penchant preference for solitary over social. Not a loner, but surely more comfortable in less cramped and crowded surroundings. As she opened the heavy door and stepped out on the deck, a blast of cold air raced through her lungs again. She struggled to move Joss's pram through the door, then stooped to make sure the little one was wrapped snugly in her blanket. With her bonnet pulled low, all Anya could see were her sweet, smiling eyes filled with wonder and curiosity.

"Looks like it's just you and me out here, Joss. Seems we're the only ones brave enough to chance a walk. Feels good, though, don't you think?"

Jocelyn wiggled with pleasure, blinking as the cold air watered her eyes.

"We won't stay long. Maybe just one quick walk around. I wouldn't want to take you back to Mum all chilled to the bone."

Anya gazed up at the sky, disappointed to find a palette in shades of gray as far as she could see. Far off the starboard bow a spidery vein of lightning wobbled beneath dark clouds, followed moments later by a deep rumble of thunder. Yes, they could still make one trip around deck before the distant storm blew their way.

A distant storm. She recalled the note in *Wisteria's* newspaper about the gale storm that roughed up the seas and delayed the arrival of the *Argentina*. She hoped that wouldn't be the case for the *Wisteria*.

Undisturbed, Joss babbled happily in the breeze uttering a steady stream of nonsense sung in different pitches.

"Ba-ba-ba-ba-ba ... baaaaa."

"You're a funny one, little Joss."

"Ba-ba-ba-ba-ba ... baaaaa."

"Exactly. Couldn't have said it better myself."

As they rounded the stern, Anya noticed the bright red, white, and blue of the American flag flapping in the wind and changed her mind, deciding they should probably go back inside. But just as she picked up her pace to push Joss along, something caught her eye. A swath of fabric on the top rail in the far corner, fluttering in the stiff wind. Not flimsy like a flag. Something heavier. Something darker. A dark shade of navy blue or green—

Oh no... oh please no.

A stab of adrenaline shot through her, taking her breath. She turned to rush in that direction then stopped cold. She mustn't take Joss any closer to the rail. Not now with the wind blowing so hard.

With fresh tears stinging her eyes, she realized it was too late anyway.

40

"I can't believe it." Anya heard the quiver in her own voice. "I know in my mind it must have happened, but I just can't believe she jumped. Why now?"

Kate took a seat beside her on the lower bunk and took hold of Anya's hands. "I suppose none of us ever truly know what might be going on in someone else's head, Anya. Ruth was such a quiet girl. We can't begin to know what led her to think it was the only way out."

"You have to admit she was an odd duck," Agatha said climbing down from her bunk. "She said she was sixteen, but she looked more like a child if you ask me. And so quiet. Like a church mouse, she was. All pale and sickly."

"That's not helping, Agatha," Helen said. "Have a heart, will you?"

Agatha flipped a wrist. "I *have* a heart, thank you very much. I'm just saying what all the rest of you are thinking.

She was just a child and never should have made the trip. Better off home with Mummy and Daddy."

Gigi pulled a cigarette from her silver case. "Enough, Agatha. She's dead. Have some respect." She stopped to give Anya a hug. "I'm going to the lounge to have a smoke. Be back in a jiffy."

Agatha smirked. "Fine. If you all want to sit around and mourn someone you hardly knew, then fine. I'm going to the canteen for some chocolate."

"It's so terribly sad," Helen said. "Imagine surviving the war and finding the man of your dreams, then throwing it all away halfway across the Atlantic."

"All this time, we assumed she was just seasick," Anya said. "We should have helped her. That first day when we left Southampton, I found her weeping so hard up on deck. She said she'd made a mistake and shouldn't have come. I feel awful. I should have watched out for her. Paid more attention to her when she got sick and—"

"Stop, Anya," Kate said. "Just stop. As callous as it may sound, you weren't responsible for her. You barely had a conversation with her. You couldn't possibly have known she might do something like this."

"I know, but to think she felt so utterly alone and hopeless as to jump—"

Kate squeezed her hand. "Second-guessing your actions won't bring her back. She must have had deeper needs than any of us could have known." She wrapped her arm around Anya's shoulder and leaned her head against hers. "It's horribly sad and so heartbreaking. But it wasn't your fault."

She knew Kate was right. Anya barely knew the girl. She

glanced over at Ruth's empty bunk, at the wrapped pastry and orange exactly where she'd left them on her pillow. Anya remembered times when she too felt completely alone and hopeless. She'd been there too, not so long ago.

Later, a team of three Red Cross representatives came to collect Ruth's belongings. She was touched to see the compassion in their eyes and the respectful way they handled Ruth's things.

"Might someone notify her husband?" Kate asked as she lifted Joss out of her hammock.

"Yes, the captain wired the Red Cross in Ames, Iowa where her husband lives," the young man stated. "They'll send someone to the home to tell them."

"His name is Eddie," Anya said barely over a whisper.

"Yes, that's right. We're also sending some of our people to visit her parents back in Thorpe Abbotts. It's a heartbreaking day for all of them."

Anya could only nod. What if Eddie had already left for New York? The image of a young soldier waiting at the docks for his young bride clouded her mind.

"Thank you for attending to them," Kate said quietly.

The pretty redhead approached them. "Is there anything we can do for you? I'm sure this is so hard, being cabinmates and all. Especially when it should be such an exciting time in your lives."

They looked back and forth at each other. Then Helen asked, "Has this happened before?"

"You mean here? On the *Wisteria*?"

"Yes. Have there been others since we left Southampton?"

"Not that I know of. I certainly hope not." She paused,

glancing at Anya. "But obviously it's a large vessel. To be honest, if you hadn't seen the remnant of Ruth's coat on the rail, or hadn't recognized it as belonging to her, we might not have known she was missing at this point."

"So in other words, there could be others no one has noticed yet to be missing?" Anya asked.

"Yes, I suppose, but we shall hope and pray that's not the case."

"What about the *Argentina*?" Helen asked. "Do you know if they lost anyone?"

She glanced over her shoulder at the other two, then lowered her voice. "No, but we were told someone tried to jump during that horrid storm they encountered. Thankfully, her friends pulled her back to safety in the nick of time."

"Well, that seems to be all for now," the older gentleman said. "Our deepest condolences for the loss of your friend. Please let us know if there's anything we might be able to do for you."

The redhead offered a sympathetic smile then followed the men out the door.

That evening, Anya picked at her food and noticed Kate doing the same.

"Are you feeling all right, Kate?"

She pushed her plate aside. "No, not really."

"Still nauseated?"

Kate rested her head atop Joss's who was sitting on her lap. "Yes, I guess. Do you feel the boat rocking more?"

"Yes, but I didn't want to mention it."

Helen pushed back her chair and stood. "I'm feeling rather awful myself. I think I'll go for a bit of a lie-down."

"But wait—aren't you all coming to the concert tonight?" Gigi twirled a lock of her hair. "You can't all bail on me. I'm singing a solo with the chorus tonight. We've have a rehearsal in a few minutes."

"You sing?" Agatha asked.

"Yes, I do. And tonight I'm singing a popular American song. Gregory asked if I'd give it a go."

"Gregory?"

"The Red Cross chap who directs the chorus. Quite a musician, that one. And, I might add, easy on the eyes."

Anya and Kate shared a look. "There she goes again," Kate mused.

"Now, now," Gigi chided playfully. "I'm behaving myself. Nothing wrong with some last-minute flirting before we dock, and I commence on the straight and narrow. Nothing more, girls."

"Well, then," Kate said. "And not a minute too soon."

"So you'll both come, won't you? To the concert?"

They stood, shuffling trays to help Kate with hers. "We'll be there. Something to put our minds on, don't you think, Anya?"

"We'll be there, Gigi."

At first it felt strange, gathering for a concert so soon after such a sad day. A shudder passed over Anya as she dismissed the image of Ruth floating in the frigid waters. She glanced around at the bubbly crowd of women all smiling and enjoying themselves and wished she could summon that kind of carefree abandon.

"Ma-ma-ma-ma-ma-ma."

Joss's murmurs snapped Anya out of her malaise.

"Did you hear that?" Kate cried, her eyes sparkling. "Did I imagine it or did Joss just say Mama?"

"Yes!" Helen said. "I heard it too!"

"Oh, please," Agatha groaned. "She's just babbling. Babies babble. She doesn't know what she's saying."

"Whether she does or doesn't, it's a beautiful sound," Anya said.

Kate beamed. "Yes, and either way, I shall choose to believe she's cooing my name. So there."

"Kate, might I hold her a while?"

"Of course you can, Helen." She lifted the child into Helen's arms. "Let's hope her nappy stays dry."

"Not a problem. Good practice for me."

As the curtain opened, the all-girl orchestra played a jaunty tune, introduced by the handsome director as a tribute to the American flag. Behind the chorus, an enormous replica of the Stars and Stripes covered the back curtain.

You're a grand old flag,
You're a high-flying flag,
And forever in peace may you wave.
You're the emblem of the land I love,
The home of the free and the brave.
Every heart beats true
'Neath the red, white, and blue,
Where there's never a boast or brag.
But should auld acquaintance be forgot,
Keep your eye on the grand old flag!

It was impossible not to feel the energy and excitement filling the ship's theater as the snappy tune continued. Anya relaxed and smiled at the sight of the girls in the chorus, curious where they'd found so many red, white, and blue dresses. Gigi stood at the center of the front row, her blonde hair coiffed in a stylish victory roll like most of the other singers; her scarlet lipstick a perfect match to her form-fitting dress.

The concert continued with a string of unfamiliar American songs, each wooing their hearts for their new homeland. As the orchestra played the introduction for the evening's final number, Gigi made her way to a standing microphone beside the director and began to sing. The program listed the song as "God Bless America," a slow and impassioned prayer-like melody beseeching God's blessings on their new country. At first, Anya thought it a strange choice of songs for Gigi who seemed better suited to something more upbeat. As beautiful as the melody was, it was the purity of Gigi's voice that left Anya breathless.

Kate reached over and squeezed her hand; her own eyes pooled with tears. Anya returned the gesture, her heart filled to overflowing by the perfect blend of lyrics and melody. By the time the song ended, the entire audience was on its feet shouting, "Bravo!" The chorus gave a bow, then the director pointed his baton toward Gigi, and the crowd went wild with applause.

They might have insisted on an encore had the ship not suddenly lurched, almost toppling some of the singers off the risers. They grappled with outstretched hands as a sudden hush blanketed the crowd. Bewildered looks. A baby's cry. Then, a swelling murmur rolled across the room as the crowd surged toward the exits.

Anya watched as Captain Masterson hurried from a side entrance and made his way to the stage. He had a quick word with the director then tapped the microphone before speaking.

"Ladies, if I may have your attention?" When the chatter continued, he tried again. "Ladies! I need your undivided attention."

The ship rocked the other direction causing another rumble of chatter across the room.

"As you can tell, it appears we have entered a rough patch of weather. Not at all unusual this time of year, but we must respond with caution and diligence. When I conclude, I need all of you to remain calm and make your way back to your cabins in an orderly fashion. Under no circumstance shall *anyone* step onto the decks. Use the staircases and take proper care to hold onto the railings. I'm cancelling tonight's motion picture and asking that you help each other if needed. Now, let us all make our way to our cabins. Slowly, orderly, so all will be safe."

Agatha snorted. "If he knew we were heading into stormy seas, why didn't he warn us earlier? A fine kettle of fish this is. Look at everyone rushing and panicking!"

"Just stay together," Helen said as Kate took Joss from her arms. "Whatever happens we need to—" Suddenly, Helen leaned over, heaving most of her dinner all over the back of Agatha's dress.

"What the—" Agatha spun around just in time to have the front of her skirt splattered by a second heave, worse than the first. Through no control of her own, Agatha returned the favor, soiling Helen's dress. In seconds, a familiar chain reaction spread far worse than the previous bouts of seasickness.

"We have to keep moving!" Anya cried, scooping Joss out of Kate's arms just before she threw up. "We need to get back to our cabin. Kate, stay with me, okay?"

"Anya!" Gigi yelled as she caught up with them. "How can I help?"

"You stick with Helen and Agatha and follow us. We need to get out of here. Now!"

41

By the time they reached their cabin, Anya and Gigi swirled in the chaos, trying to help their friends and other cabin-mates settle down. A few were able to fight off the retching enough to help care for the others. But the ship's constant motion made it difficult to keep their balance for any length of time as they moved from one set of bunks to the next.

"Oh God, please make it stop!" Agatha cried.

Others sobbed, some cursed the day they met their Yanks, while others kept silent, gripping the rails of their bunk as the ship swayed back and forth, back and forth.

Anya lost track of time, only stopping to rest for a few minutes at a time. She closed her eyes and did whatever she could to dismiss the smells and groans roiling through their cabin.

"Anya?"

"Hmm?"

Someone tapped on her shoulder. "Anya, wake up."

She startled, not realizing she'd fallen asleep. She slowly sat up and wiped the sleep from her eyes.

"Anya!" Gigi whispered urgently. "Listen. Something's wrong."

She turned to see Gigi sitting cross-legged on the top bunk next to hers. "What?"

"They've cut the engines. We're not moving anymore, except for the waves rolling us. It's like we're dead in the water."

She rubbed her face and ran her fingers through her hair. As the fog evaporated from her mind, she stilled. "How long?"

"I don't know. I just woke up a few minutes ago."

"Are you sure?"

"Yes. And keep your voice down. We don't want to wake the others now that they're finally sleeping."

She nodded then yawned while stretching her arms over her head.

Gigi moved to the edge of her bunk and started climbing down. "I'm going to go see what I can find out."

"Do you want me to come with you?"

"No, one of us should stay here in case any of them wake up."

Anya nodded again. "But don't go far, all right?"

"I won't."

As Gigi slipped out the door, Anya leaned back against the wall and closed her eyes. She carefully breathed through her mouth to avoid the reeking stench still permeating the room. She was too tired to think or even imagine what could have stopped the ship's engines. All she wanted was to get to America. After everything else, was it really so much to ask?

She stuffed her pillow behind her head and wondered if she

might still be asleep and dreaming. *Maybe we never left Southampton. Maybe I'm still sleeping in the frigid barracks at Camp Tidworth. Or the room above Patrick's pub. Maybe I only imagined my wedding. Maybe I never actually met Danny? Could it be possible?*

"Anya? Are you awake?"

She opened her eyes to find Gigi climbing back up to her bunk.

"That was fast."

"Hardly. It's been over half an hour since I left. You must have fallen back to sleep."

"Really? I could have sworn you just left."

"Shhh! Keep your voice down." Gigi rolled onto her stomach, propped up her elbows, and wrapped her arms around her pillow. "I can't bear the thought of cleaning up any more sick."

Anya followed her lead, stretching out on her stomach, elbows propped. "What did you find out?"

"There was a fire in the main engine room."

"What?!"

"Shhh!"

"Sorry. Can they fix it?"

"I'm not sure. Gregory didn't sound very optimistic."

"Gregory? The choir director?"

"Yes. I bumped into him as I was going up the grand stair-case. He had just been to the bridge to find out what was going on. They told him a fire broke out about an hour ago. They said they've got it mostly contained—"

"Mostly?"

"Yes, but unfortunately, it caused damage to the ship's

primary genny which is why we're on backup now. The lights are dimmer in the corridors. Until they repair the main genny, we're dead in the water with no motors or 'ballast corrections'—whatever that means."

"It means we're in for a very rough time with this storm."

"Even worse, with the system down, they can't communicate or wire for help or send out an SOS."

"But surely they can fire off flares or something?"

"Yes, but it's storming outside, so visibility would be limited. Besides, if no other ships are in range, what's the point?"

They stared at each other. The implications ran through Anya's mind, none of them good. She glanced around their cabin. "Thank goodness the rest of them are sleeping through it. At least for now."

"Pretty amazing considering how much we're bobbing about. At one point, I started to fall down the stairs. Thank goodness George caught me."

Anya studied the dreamy smile on Gigi's face as she twirled another blonde curl.

"Why are you staring at me like that?"

"Like what?" Anya asked.

"Don't give me that."

"It's nothing."

Gigi leaned her head to one side. "Go on. What is it?"

Anya paused for a moment, thinking how to ask. "I just can't figure you out. Why do you flirt like you do? I try to understand, but I can't."

"Oh *that*," she whispered back, giving a flip of her wrist. "It's second nature to me. I don't know *why* I do it. I just do it. It's all perfectly harmless."

"I don't see how it can be. You're married, Gigi. What would Paul say? How would you feel if he flirted with every pretty girl he met?"

She snorted playfully, then clapped her hand over her mouth. "Oh, trust me. He does. How do you think we met?"

"Really?"

"Oh, sure. All the chatting up and carrying on? Think of it like a game, Anya. And Paul and I, we're both so skilled at it, we were naturally drawn to each other. Two peas in a pod, Paul and me."

"So he doesn't mind that you still flirt with other guys, even now that you're married?"

"Well, I'm sure if he were *here*, he wouldn't like it. Same as I wouldn't want to stand by and watch him chatting some girl up."

"Then why do it?"

Gigi narrowed her eyes. "What are you getting at? Why all the questions?"

"Just curious, I suppose. I grew up as a minister's daughter, so I guess our childhoods must have been quite different."

Something drifted through Gigi's eyes and with it, the last remnant of her smile.

"I'm sorry. Did I say something wrong?"

Gigi shrugged. "Don't be silly. Of course not."

"I didn't mean—"

"Anya, not all of us had the privilege of growing up in a perfect family, in a pretty house, with all that happily-ever-after nonsense."

"Gigi, I—"

"So before you sit there and judge me—"

"I'm not judging you!"

Gigi stared at her, her eyes ablaze. Then without warning, her face crumbled.

Anya reached for her hand. "Oh Gigi, I'm sorry."

Her voice cracked as she dropped her head. "You have no idea."

"Then tell me. Please? What's this all about?"

The ship pitched again, and this time Anya felt her stomach ride its wave. She hoped the others would sleep through it.

"Gigi," she whispered. "If you don't want to talk about it, you don't have to."

She nodded a couple of times without looking up, yanking a hankie from her robe pocket. She tried as best she could to wipe her eyes and find her voice. Anya waited patiently, alarmed to see such unguarded emotion from her friend. Not once in all the time she'd known Gigi had she seen her like this. Not even close.

"I've never told anyone this before."

Anya said nothing, just waited.

Then, in a hushed whisper, with her eyes focused on the wrinkled handkerchief she worked in her hands, she told her story. That of a young girl raised by her father after her mum died in childbirth. Theirs was a poor and loveless home. Her father knew nothing about raising a child, much less a daughter, but was much too proud to ask for help. Long before she was old enough for such responsibilities, she learned to cook and keep house and care for the man who cared nothing for her. But mostly she learned to stay out of her father's way. Especially when he was drinking.

When she was twelve, he took in a boarder named Fletcher to help pay the rent. A strange man with white-blond hair and bloodshot eyes just like her father's. Some might think him handsome, but for his mouth overcrowded with oversized, crooked yellow teeth. Whatever extra income his rent provided disappeared in pints of ale and bottles of rum, and more work for her.

One night, two weeks after Fletcher moved in, he crawled into her bed. With his large calloused hand firmly clamped over her mouth, he whispered what would happen if she cried out or spoke a word of it to anyone. She gagged as the smell of sweat and rum filled her nostrils while his filthy, disgusting mouth assaulted hers. He stole her innocence that night, hurting her and forever altering her life, both physically and emotionally.

In the months to come, he grew more demanding, always raising his threats to keep her silent. She wanted desperately to tell her father and make him get rid of the horrible man, but she couldn't risk it. She was only twelve! Who would believe her?

She was terrified to think her father might know what was going on. Then one morning, as Fletcher cracked the door to leave her room, she locked eyes with her father through the narrow opening. Sitting at the kitchen table, he sipped his coffee without a single shred of concern.

No shock. No alarm.

Nothing.

Gigi hoped and prayed he would do something, but he

never did. Then one day she realized something strange was happening in her body. From that day forward, her father would have nothing to do with her. Not that it mattered anymore. When she started to show, she packed some clothes, stole money from her father's hidden stash, and ran far, far away.

Anya was too stunned to speak. Gigi wiped her eyes again, took in a deep breath and slowly blew it out.

"I couldn't stand the thing growing inside me. When I finally reached London, I found a doctor who helped me get rid of it. I never once regretted it. Not ever."

Anya pulled her knees beneath her and sat facing her friend. With trembling hands, she reached for both of Gigi's hands and held them tight. "I'm so sorry, Gigi. So sorry ..."

Gigi shrugged and tried a weak smile. "It's over and done with. Ancient history."

"Maybe so, but—"

"So you see, my childhood was nothing like yours, Anya." She pulled a hand free and dashed the edge of her eyes with her wrist. "While you were learning about right and wrong, I learned how to survive. And for me, that meant learning how to play the game *my* way. I learned how to use men. How to stay in control of them and never again allow myself to be a victim."

"So that's why you—"

"Yes, that's precisely why I flirt with men. Lots of men." She straightened, pulling her other hand free. Her tone changed. "I let them know from the moment we meet that I'm the one calling the shots. I'm the one who gets to say what we will or won't do together. Sometimes I flirt just because I can, not because I have any interest."

Anya didn't respond. Nothing she might say would matter. Then she wondered. "What about Paul? Things were different with him, weren't they? If you married him, you surely care for him, don't you?"

Her expression softened with a genuine, easy smile. "And then there was Paul. He was handsome and fun and exciting ... and also very, very *rich*. I adore him. I really do. But more than anything, he was my ticket to America. And I think he knew. I know he loves me, and I'm madly in love with him. Will it last? I don't know. Maybe. I'd like to think so. But I'm damaged goods, Anya. And nothing can change that."

"Why can't it? You're about to start a brand new chapter in your life, Gigi. In a new country, with an American husband, and new friends and family. With so many possibilities, why wouldn't you want to change?"

Gigi stretched quietly. "Oh Anya, I don't want to talk about it anymore. I'm tired."

Whatever window of transparency Gigi had opened into her soul now closed, and Anya backed off.

Suddenly, Gigi grabbed her wrist. "But Anya? You must never tell another soul what I just told you. Promise me that. Not even Kate."

She nodded. "I promise, Gigi. You have my word."

Anya and Gigi had slept only an hour when the ship rocked so hard it nearly threw all of them out of their bunks, then quickly rocked back the other way.

"What's happening?"

"Not again, noooo ..."

"Oh, please God, make it stop!"

Something thumped hard. A loud and agonizing groan followed.

"Agatha! Someone turn the lights on! She fell from her top bunk!"

Anya hustled down the bunk ladder, willing her eyes to adjust. "There aren't any more lights. Just these backups."

"What do you mean there aren't any more lights?"

"The power's out." Gigi hurried down, jumping the final two ladder steps. "The ship's on backup gennies. That's why we're not moving."

"But we *are* moving! Back and forth and back and forth—oh, please make it stop!"

Anya grabbed the nearest pillow and stuffed it carefully under Agatha's head. "Agatha? Can you hear me?"

"My head ... what happened?"

"You fell from your bunk. Can you move?"

"Ahhh ... my shoulder ... I can't—"

The ship lurched again, farther and harder this time tossing them like rag dolls across the floor.

"Ahhh!" Agatha cried.

Anya scrabbled across the floor and found Agatha rolled up against a lower bunk, her forehead bleeding where it slammed against the bed rail.

"I'm here, Agatha, I'm here," Anya said. "Gigi, toss me that pillow."

The ship slammed hard the other way. Cries and wails

filled the dimly-lit cabin.

"Oh GOD, just kill us now and BE DONE WITH IT!"

The others shouted back, bellowing against the one who'd said it.

Anya shoved the pillow back under Agatha's head and gripped the bed rail, using her own body to wedge the girl securely against the bed. She held tight as they rocked the other way.

The ship keeled hard again, the cries in their cabin rising with each movement. Another bride fell from her top bunk, landing on top of Anya. The blow knocked the breath from her as the girl cried out in pain. Anya tried to find her breath again, then rolled the girl off her.

"Are you all right?"

"No, I can't—"

Another hard slam. More cries.

"JOCELYN!"

The baby's scream suddenly stopped. Kate crawled toward her, her hysterical pleas silencing the others.

"I've got her!" Gigi shouted, taking the baby in her arms. "I've got you, Joss! I've got—"

Kate scooped the child from Gigi's arms. "Oh sweetheart, I'm so sorry! Joss? Jocelyn? Breathe, sweetie!" Kate patted Joss on her back. "Oh, Joss, BREATHE!"

A split second passed before the baby's wail filled the cabin.

"Kate, is she all right?" Anya shouted.

"I don't know! I should've left her in the hammock, but I—"

The ship slammed hard again, sending mother and child rolling across the floor. The bedlam continued, and with each jolt, more cries and groans and hysteria. Helen crawled to the door and opened it.

"HELP! We need help! Somebody—"

"Helen, go find help!" Anya shouted. "I think Agatha's unconscious!"

Helen turned back. "Everyone's rushing down the corridor! I don't even know where to go or who—"

Joss screamed again, her blood-curdling cry obliterating all other conversation.

Helen grabbed one of the girls running down the corridor. "Please help us! We need a doctor!"

"No! There's no time!" The girl pulled her arm free. "They're lowering the lifeboats! Get out now! Get out!"

"What?!"

"We have to get out before—"

The ship banked hard again, knocking the girl to the floor and sending them all sprawling.

"You have to GET OUT!" she screamed as she got to her feet and tumbled out of sight.

"Oh God, save us!"

"We have to go!" Helen cried. "Anya! Gigi! Kate! We have to go before it's too late!"

Suddenly, the ship rolled back the other way, rolling them again before pitching hard the other direction.

"Oh God! Oh God! Please help us!"

Part IV

42

6 February 1946

Chicago, Illinois

Danny leaned into the bitter cold wind gusting off Lake Michigan as he hurried to catch the train. A heavy snowstorm had blasted the state overnight knocking out power throughout the greater Chicago area. He'd awakened with a start, almost an hour late thanks to his lifeless alarm clock. After hustling to get ready, he almost collided with his mother downstairs as she padded her way toward the kitchen.

"I'm sorry I didn't make some coffee in time before you go, Danny." She tightened the belt of her chenille robe. "Power must have gone out hours ago, so my alarm clock didn't go off. The house is chilled from top to bottom."

He pulled on his snow boots and quickly laced them. "No problem, Mom. I'll get some on campus." He climbed into his coat and placed a noisy kiss on her cheek. "Gotta run. See you tonight."

"All right, honey. Have a good day. Be careful out there. I love you."

"Love you too, Mom."

He hurried, shuffling his way carefully along the snow-covered sidewalk. Out of habit, he glanced across the street at Mrs. Martello's house and her sister's next door. A lifetime ago, on snowy days like this, he cleared the sidewalks for the two elderly ladies and most of the others on his street. He could hardly remember the kid he'd been back then, so young and naïve. Back then, his life revolved around school, the Cubs, his part-time jobs, and his dog Sophie. Then came college, the war, and Anya.

After a quick trolley ride, he arrived at the crowded station to wait for his train. Apparently his wasn't the only dead alarm clock on the south side. He squeezed onto the next train, grasping the leather strap to keep his balance as it pulled out of the station. He closed his eyes and tried to regroup. Once he chased away the fog, he relaxed, thinking of Anya and how soon he would see her again.

Three days. Just three more days.

He could hardly believe it, after all these months. Eight long months. An eternity. They'd had so little time together in England, but never in his wildest dreams would he have imagined it would take so long for her to join him here in America. He'd kept his focus on his studies, trying to bury his restlessness. He'd worked as many hours as the campus library would give him, and filled in the gaps by helping Joey at the theater. But staying busy only kept his thoughts of Anya at bay for short snippets of time.

I should never have left her behind.

How many times had those words trampled his mind over the past eight months? He should have stayed until she could travel to the States with him. Charlie pulled strings and remained in Framlingham. Why hadn't he?

Surely there was some loophole he could have uncovered to either stay with her in England or fly back over to get her? The regrets stockpiled themselves on his heart again. He shook his head, too tired to think about it.

Later, he dashed across campus, aggravated that he'd missed his first class and anxious to make his second. As he took the steps of the classroom building, he noticed the sign on the door:

CLASSES CANCELLED DUE TO POWER OUTAGE

"Well that's just great." It never occurred to him the campus might be affected. He'd been so preoccupied, he hadn't even noticed the sparse clusters of students milling about.

"Danny?"

He turned at the sound of Beverly's voice, grateful that it no longer gave him pause. He rarely saw her anymore. He'd intentionally avoided her since that strange night a month ago when she broke down. Life was too short to risk another of her emotional meltdowns.

"Hello, Beverly."

"Kind of strange, the campus all but deserted, isn't it?"

"Yeah, I didn't even notice until I saw the sign on the door."

"We're working by lantern light in the admissions office. A bit surreal. They keep telling us they should have the power restored any time now, but here we are."

"Does that mean I should hang around for my other classes?"

"No, it's an official snow day so classes are cancelled."

"Library closed too?"

"Yes, everything but administration. Lucky me."

"Then I guess I'll head back home."

She caught his elbow. "I'm glad I ran into you, Danny. I've never apologized for my horrible behavior that night—"

"That's okay, Beverly. No need."

"I feel awful about acting like that, but I want you to know I'm sorry, and I'm also doing much better now. Mostly, I just wanted to thank you for being such a gentleman. I truly appreciate that." She gave a funny smile, obviously embarrassed, but he could tell she was sincere.

"Not a problem. It's forgotten." He turned to go, and she fell in step with him.

"I heard about those war bride ships, and thought about Anya. But she's already here, right?"

"No, her ship is scheduled to arrive on Saturday in New York. In fact, I'm heading there as soon as classes are over on Friday."

She started to say something, then stopped.

"What?"

"Uh," she paused again, offering a tentative smile before glancing away. "Did you see the paper today?"

"No, I was running late and—why do you ask?" He stopped and stared at her.

Something flickered in her eyes. "I ... well, you should probably find a copy and—"

435

"Beverly? What is it? What do you know?"

"I just assumed you knew already. There was an article about some of the war bride ships hitting some pretty bad storms—"

Relief washed over him. "Oh, you must be talking about the *Argentina*. It ran into some bad weather and was a day or so late arriving in New York."

"No, not that one. These are some that hadn't arrived yet. The article said a couple of ships—or maybe it was three. I can't re—"

"What ships? Did it give the names or where they were sailing from?"

"No, the article said the Army Transport office wouldn't divulge the names of the ships until all the next of kin were notified."

He felt sucker punched. "Wh—what? Next of kin? You mean the ships are lost at sea?"

Beverly reached for his hand. "No! I just meant ... well, I don't really know. That's all it said. But I'm sure you would have heard by now if—"

He pulled his hand free and left her mid-sentence, racing back the way he had come, careful not to slip on any patches of ice. When he finally made it to the train station, he bought a copy of the *Chicago Tribune* and found the short article just under the fold on page one. There wasn't much beyond what Beverly had told him. He ripped the article off the page and dumped the rest of the paper in a trash bin.

Ten minutes later, he found a seat on the train bound for home. The slow burn in his gut volleyed with the images floating through his mind. The *Titanic* sunk more than a decade before he was born, but he'd learned about the disaster in school. How well he remembered reading about the horrors some of the survivors lived to tell about. Is it possible the *Wisteria* hit an iceberg? Had rough seas caused the ship to capsize? If not, were there enough lifeboats? Anya was a fighter. He knew she'd never go down without a fight. Never.

He'd been staring at nothing in particular as the thoughts wrestled in his mind. He noticed both of his knees bouncing faster than he thought possible. He stilled them, dropped his head in his hands, and closed his eyes.

God, no. Not this. Please, not this. Not after everything Anya's been through. Whatever's happened, wherever she is right now, at this moment, please hold onto her. Give her courage. Give her strength. Whatever she needs, please give her. Oh God …

He would have sworn the ride back home was twice as long. By the time his train arrived at the 59th Street Station, he was standing at the door, ready to bolt the minute the doors opened. After a quick ride on the trolley, he sprinted home, and carefully rushed up the porch steps. His mother opened the door, her face etched with concern.

"Oh Danny! I've been praying you'd come back home. Did you hear?"

"Yes. Has anyone called?" He stomped the snow off his boots before pulling them off. "Anything on the radio about the ships?"

"No, nothing. Our paperboy was late this morning, so we just saw the article about an hour ago. About the same time our power came back on. I tried to call the campus to see if there was any way to reach you, but the switchboard said—"

"Classes were cancelled. I know, Mom." She closed the door behind him as he shrugged out of his coat and hung it on the hall tree, then dropped his satchel beside it. "I need to find a telephone number to call. I've got to find out if one of those ships is Anya's." He took the stairs two at a time, pulling his sweater over his head.

"How can I help, Danny?"

He stopped and looked over his shoulder at her. "Just pray, Mom."

"Sweetheart, I've been praying since the moment I read the paper."

"Good. Then just keep them coming." He continued up the stairs just as Joey opened his bedroom door.

"Danny! Thank God you're home. So you heard?"

"Yeah. I've got to find the contact information and start making calls."

"What can I do?"

"I don't know yet. Give me a minute, okay?"

"Coffee?"

"That would be great."

He yanked open his desk drawer and found his folder of forms and letters from the Army Transport Company. He tucked the folder under his arm and hurried back downstairs where he pulled up a chair by the telephone in the front hall. He shuffled through the papers, wishing he'd kept them organized. When he finally found a number for the Army Transport Company, he dialed it. Busy tone. He dialed again. Another busy tone.

An hour later, he slammed the receiver down and banged his fist against the wall. "This is madness! How can the line stay busy this long? How am I ever going to get through?"

His mother appeared at the kitchen door, drying her hands on her apron.

"Danny, honey, just take a moment and relax. I know you're frustrated, so why not take a deep breath and—"

"Mom, I can't! I have to get through. I have to find out where she is right now. Right this moment. I can't just sit back and relax, don't you see?" The tone of his voice shamed him instantly.

She said nothing, just watched him, but Danny could see the concern in her eyes. She was only trying to help. A troubled sigh deflated his angst as he walked to her and draped his arm around her shoulders. "I'm sorry, Mom. That was out of line."

"It's all right, Danny. I know you're upset. We all are."

"Even so, I had no reason to snap at you like that. And you're right. I need to take a giant step back and try to think what else to do."

"What about that fellow at the embassy?"

They both turned toward the family room where Dad sat in his favorite chair, hidden behind the newspaper. Joey joined them as they drifted into the room.

"Who do you mean, Frank?" Betty asked.

He lowered the paper just enough and glanced at them over the top of his glasses. "That fellow who helped Anya and her friends. The one who was there on Christmas night when they almost burned down the house."

"Oh yeah," Danny said. He pinched the bridge of his nose. "What was his name? Paul? No, that's the other girl's husband."

Joey joined them in the living room with Millie and Jimmy right behind.

"Phillip!" Danny snapped his fingers. "His name is Phillip, but I have no idea how to find out what his last name is." He raced out of the room and started up the stairs. "Maybe Anya mentioned it in one of her letters."

"Can you call the embassy?" Millie asked.

He stopped and turned toward his sister-in-law. "You mean the American Embassy in London?"

"Just a thought."

"Good idea. I'll keep dialing. You go up and see if you can find his name."

Danny turned again. "Right—"

"They can't call in if you keep the line tied up."

They glanced back at Frank, hidden again behind the paper, then stared at each other as the truth registered between them.

Danny froze. "Oh, good grief. It never even dawned on me. All this time, if they tried to call, they've been getting a busy signal just like I have. "I'm such a—"

"Joey, why don't you run down to Aunt Lara's house and use her telephone," Millie suggested.

"That's it!" He gave her a loud kiss on the lips. "Another brilliant idea from my gorgeous wife." He dashed back to the hall and reached for his coat.

Danny held it up for him. "If you get through, just say you're me and find out what's going on, okay?"

"Right." He pulled his cap over his head and wound a wool scarf around his neck.

Danny clapped him on the back. "Let us know the minute

you hear anything, okay?"

"Will do. Same for you."

Danny hustled back upstairs and pulled the cigar box from the lower shelf of his bedside table. When he found Anya's most recent letters, he scanned them for mention of the American lieutenant who worked at the embassy in London. In her letter of 29 December, he found it. *Powell. Lieutenant Phillip Powell.* He stuffed the letter back in its envelope and slipped it into his shirt pocket.

A few minutes later, he knocked on the Zankowski's door then updated Joey and Lara. After a long series of dead-end calls, he finally got a number for the embassy in London.

"Yes, I'm trying to reach a Lieutenant Phillip Powell."

"Hold, please."

For the first time that day, Danny felt a sliver of hope as he waited for the connection. He would gladly reimburse Lara, but at the moment he didn't care how much the calls were costing; he just needed to talk to someone—anyone— who might be able to tell him what was going on.

"Lieutenant Powell," he answered.

"Lieutenant! This is Danny McClain, Anya's husband, calling from America."

"Yes, Mr. McClain—I mean, *Lieutenant* McClain, right?"

"Yes, but please just call me Danny. I'm hoping you can help me concerning news of the ship Anya's on—"

"Yes, we've been monitoring the reports of the *Wisteria* and the other vessels caught in the storms. I was actually about to call you, when I was called into two back-to-back meetings."

"So it's true? Anya is on one of the ships?"

"I'm afraid so. We lost contact with the *Wisteria* late on

441

Sunday eve—"

"Sunday?! Why wasn't I notified? That's been three whole days!"

"Lieutenant—I mean, Danny. I understand your frustration. But please understand, we've tried to make absolutely sure we had all our facts straight as there have been so many unfounded rumors and unsubstantiated newspaper stories covering these ships. Case in point—the rumors that one of our war bride ships was attacked by a German sub drowning all souls aboard. Utter nonsense, but it took massive amounts of manpower to put out the firestorm it caused. Which is why we have to—"

"I understand, Lieutenant. That makes perfect sense to me. I had no idea that sort of thing was going on. But is there *anything* you can tell me about Anya's ship? How can a luxury liner lose all contact? Aren't these boats equipped with telegraphs?"

"Yes, but their range only covers a few hundred miles to the nearest vessel. Then those vessels pass along information to other vessels. A relay system, if you will. The last message from the *Wisteria* reached a Canadian ship called the *Newfoundland* that was approximately 350 miles from them. The *Wisteria* issued a CQD wire at 11:30 that night—"

"CQD?"

"It's the British version of SOS. A Morse code signal alerting 'All Stations, Distress,' requesting all other sending and receiving be stopped in order to leave the wireless channel open. The *Newfoundland* responded that they too were fighting treacherous storms. The *Wisteria* telegraphed them saying they'd had a fire in the engine room and needed assistance. Unfortunately, the message was cut off before *Wisteria* gave her coordinates, and they have not been heard from since."

Danny felt a knot tightening in his gut. He turned around to look at Joey and Lara and noted the worry etched on both their faces. He slid down the wall, landing clumsily on the hardwood floor.

"Danny? Are you still there?"

"Yes, I'm here. Lieutenant, do you think there's any chance ... I mean, is it possible Anya's ship ..." He pulled his knees up and dropped his forehead on them. "Oh God."

"Danny?" Lara whispered.

"Danny, listen to me," Powell insisted. "Do not jump to conclusions. For all we know, the *Wisteria* is limping its way to New York as we speak."

"Or sinking like the *Titanic*."

"I refuse to believe that, and we have no proof whatsoever of anything like that happening. Fires happen on board ships like this all the time. Sometimes they're minor; sometimes they cut the power. But there's no reason to think the worst."

Danny heard a voice in the background. Someone talking to Powell.

"Danny? You still there?"

"Yes, I'm here."

"Look, I'm late for another meeting. I've got your number right here, and I promise I'll let you know as soon as I hear anything."

Danny asked him to take down the Zankowski's number as well. Powell offered him a few more words of encouragement then said goodbye.

As he stood to hang the receiver back on the phone, a rather large boulder settled on his chest, nearly suffocating him. He slid back down the wall and prayed as hard as he knew how.

43

Around three o'clock the next morning, creaking footsteps on the stairs woke Danny from his restless sleep on the sofa. He watched his father's silhouette pass by and heard the shuffle of his slippers heading down the hall. He raked his hand through his hair and sat up, suddenly cognizant of the fact he'd had no calls through the night. The boulder still weighed heavy on his chest as the facts filed back into his muddled mind. He uttered another silent prayer for Anya and everyone else on the *Wisteria* as unsolicited images flashed through his mind. English war brides and babies huddled on lifeboats, shivering in the bitter cold. Muffled groans and whimpers. A baby's sudden piercing cry, rousing cries from other children. Everyone cold and hungry and frightened.

Stop. Just stop it.

He rolled off the sofa and gave his face a rough rub. This would not do. He had to stay positive. Hopeful. He couldn't give up. Anya wouldn't. Neither would he.

Thoughts peppered his mind as he padded down the hall, compelled by the scent of strong coffee. He found his father taking a seat at the kitchen table, his familiar red and black plaid bathrobe wrapped loosely around him.

"Mornin', son."

"Dad." He took a seat and let out a weary sigh.

"You get some sleep?"

"Some. Not a lot."

"Holding up?"

Danny stretched with a yawn. "Not really. I keep thinking it's all some horrific nightmare, and I'll wake up from it."

"No surprise there."

They sat in silence for a few moments; the percolator's rumbling rhythm at odds with the ticking of the clock on the wall. When the coffee finished brewing, Danny poured a cup for his father and one for himself.

"Dad, what would you do if you were in my shoes?"

"What do you mean?"

"I'll lose my mind if I have to sit around all day and night waiting for the telephone to ring. Or *not* ring. Or grasping at some scrap of news on the radio or in the paper. I need to do something, but I don't know what. If you were me, what would you do?"

His father stared at him over the rim of his reading glasses. He blew on his steaming coffee, then took a cautious sip before setting it back on its saucer. "Well, son, I don't suppose it matters much what I might or might not do."

Danny sat up straighter. "Yes, it does. I'd like to know. I'm so tired and frustrated, I can't even think straight. So tell me what you'd do. Please."

Dad waited a few moments then rested his elbows on the table and warmed his hands around his cup. "Pretty sure I'd be confused, too. But I'm not much good at sitting around waiting for news, good or bad."

"I remember when Pearl Harbor was attacked, and we had to wait around all those days and nights wondering if Joey was still alive."

His father's eyes misted then narrowed as he looked away. "Those were awful days."

"I remember you'd get so upset, you'd storm down the stairs to the basement and hammer out your frustrations for hours on end. What were you working on down there all that time?"

A slight smile tugged at his dad's whiskered face. "Nothing."

"Nothing?"

He shrugged, shaking his head. "Just a box of nails I had a hankering to pound on."

Danny slowly nodded. "Makes sense to me. Maybe I should go down and hunt for a box of nails."

"What works for one doesn't necessarily work for another."

"I guess that's true."

They sat in silence again, sipping coffee, minds wandering.

Later, after refilling both their cups, Danny floated an idea by his dad.

"What if I hopped on a train for New York? At least that way I'd be there when her ship comes in. *If* it comes in."

His father stared at him, his brows slowly inching up his brow. "You'd be out of touch for quite a while, wouldn't you?"

"I could call from time to time, whenever we stop along the

way. I'm guessing it would take around sixteen, maybe seventeen hours by train?"

His father shrugged again. "I suppose. Sure you wouldn't rather just sit tight until you hear from that Powell guy in London?"

Danny blew out a huff. "I'm not good at sitting tight. Remind you of anyone?"

His father nodded. "I see your point."

"I'll let Lieutenant Powell know my plans. Then if he should call—or anyone from Army Transport, for that matter —you can just relay the message to me when I call. Sure beats sitting around drumming my fingers day and night." He took a slow sip of his coffee.

"Yes, I suppose it would."

"I can't stop thinking about Anya and this whole mess trying to get her over here, Dad. When that ship docks at the pier in New York, and she first steps foot on American soil ... I wouldn't miss that for the world. I want to be there. I *have* to be there."

"I can be packed in an hour."

They both looked up to find Mom standing at the door. "When do we leave?"

Danny and his mother boarded the *20th Century Limited* at half past five that evening at the LaSalle Street Station. He'd debated the last-minute choice of the express passenger train which would make no stops until arriving at Grand Central

Station in New York. But the speed of the sixteen-hour ride—
most of it overnight—appealed to his underlying urgency to
get there. After a quick call home to let them know, he and
his mother made their way to the platform to board what was
known as the world's greatest train.

Several hours into their trip, the moonlit landscape
flashing by did little to calm Danny's nerves. Once he'd made
the decision to make the trip, the day had vanished as he and
his mother set the plan in motion. He would never have
thought to ask her to come, but had to admit he appreciated
her presence. He gazed over at her, grateful for her company.

She looked up, meeting his eyes. "What is it, honey?"

"It just occurred to me that some things never change. I'm
not a little kid anymore, yet here I am, riding the train with
my mother along to help find my bride." He slipped his hand
over hers. "Now that you're here, I can't imagine doing this
without you. It's a tremendous comfort to me, Mom."

She shook her head, her face warmed with an easy smile.
"If you must know, I'm a bit surprised to be here."

"Really? You didn't offer to come out of the mere goodness
of your heart?" he teased.

"No, I'm afraid not. I was told to come."

"Dad? Did he—?"

"No, not your father. *Our* Father." She took off her glasses
and turned slightly in her seat to face him. "I must say, it
was the strangest thing. I didn't sleep much last night either.
But when I woke up, the first thought that came to mind was
to get down on my knees and pray for Anya. So I slipped from
beneath the covers and knelt beside our bed. I asked God to
comfort and strengthen her and all the other brides and

children on that ship. I asked Him to use whatever might be happening to draw Anya back to Him. And no sooner had those thoughts crossed my mind, than I heard Him say, 'Go with Danny.' It wasn't audible, mind you, but such an intense and specific impression on my heart that I knew it could only have come from God.

"Of course, I didn't have a clue what that meant at first. I was still a bit foggy and trying to wake up. But when I came downstairs and overheard you talking with your father about taking the train to New York, I knew immediately that was what God was telling me to do."

"Whoa ... I'm not even sure how to process that. I hadn't even thought of going until I sat down at the table with Dad. And even while I was explaining my reasoning to him, I thought it sounded impractical. I knew I'd be out of touch if Powell tried to reach me. But at the same time, I knew I had to get to that pier. I can't it explain it. I just *knew*."

"Then it seems we both had a bit of a holy nudge to get on this train. Would you agree?"

"Absolutely."

"Though I must also say, I feel a bit odd to impose myself on the two of you at a time like this."

"Don't be silly. How could you possibly impose on us, Mom?"

A sheepish grin accompanied her response. "I'm not so old as to forget what it was like to be a newlywed."

Danny felt his face warm. "Oh. That. Well ..."

"So once Anya joins us, I will give you as much privacy as I can. Whether at the hotel or on the return trip. Or if you'd prefer to stay in New York for a while after she arrives, I'm perfectly capable of riding the train home by myself."

Danny leaned over to whisper, "I didn't think it was possible to blush at my age, but I'm pretty sure my face—"

"—is quite a lovely shade of crimson. Yes, it is."

He rubbed his face with both hands. "Okay, then. I think it's time we change the subject, don't you?"

"Whatever you say, son."

"Good. Fine. Well, then. What would you like to talk about?"

"Let's talk about Anya."

"Yes. Good idea. What would you like to know?"

"Let's think through what it's going to be like for her once she arrives."

He nodded slowly, his thoughts jumbled. "I hadn't thought that far ahead. I'm still focused on hoping the ship didn't capsize. That it actually makes it to New York, and she's still alive."

"Oh, I think if the ship had capsized or gone down, we would have heard about it by now. Anya's friend at the embassy in London would surely have told you."

"I'm not so sure about that. I'm not ready to take anything for granted at this point. Particularly with Anya. She's had such a rough time for so long now. Sometimes I find myself starting to think like a pessimist. Almost expecting more to go wrong. It's like every time she turns around, something bad has happened to her. It's just the way her life seems to be playing out."

"Danny, don't let your mind stay on thoughts like that. Doesn't help her, and it certainly doesn't help you."

"But face it. I assumed once the war ended and we got

married, everything would start falling into place. Yet here we are, almost eight months to the day since I said goodbye to her in England and flew home. If you had told me the day I left that it would take eight long months before I'd see her again, I would have laughed in your face."

"I know, honey, but war has a way of tainting everything it touches, including something as simple as the logistics of travel. And it's not as if Anya is the only war bride needing passage to America."

"I know." Danny leaned his head back and closed his eyes. "But I'm only concerned with *one* of those brides."

"I understand."

They sat in silence for a few minutes until Danny opened his eyes again. "Mom, you said you wanted to talk through what it'll be like when Anya arrives. In what way?"

"Only that we can't pretend everything will simply be business as usual once she's come to live with us. We will all need to be especially patient and understanding. Whenever I'm praying for Anya, I have a sense that I'm praying for a wounded little lamb. Sounds silly, I suppose, but that's the image in my mind. I know you've told me she can be tough at times, but—"

"That's an understatement," he said. "She's been that way since she was a young girl. Hans used to tell me all kinds of stories about the mischief she'd get into. And I remember him telling me they always knew where to find her if she'd done something wrong. She would disappear for a few hours, hiding up in a tree behind their home. Whether she was hoping to evade punishment or plotting her next deed, who could tell."

"Oh dear," she said with a twinkle in her eye. "We don't have a single tree worth climbing and no time to plant one now."

"We'll have to remember that come spring."

"Yes, we will. The thing is, she may have been a rough and tumble child—and more than likely, that's what helped her survive these past few years. But I would imagine her war wounds run much deeper than any of us can imagine."

"I know." His mind hobbled from one scene to another, stories of her journey from childhood to her years with the Dutch Resistance, to the girl he married in Framlingham. "Little by little, I've seen some of those emotional wounds begin to heal. But I'm sure there's much more she hasn't told me. Hasn't told anyone."

"Yes, and that's why we must all be prepared to give her a safe place to recover. You and Anya are welcome to stay with us as long as you like, son. You will always be welcome in our home. And while I want desperately to help in any way I possibly can, I want you to know that your father and I will respect your privacy. We're available if you need us—and especially if Anya needs us. It's been my prayer for some time now that our home will be a haven of rest for her soul."

"I appreciate that, Mom. Guys can be real blockheads when it comes to emotions, so I hope you'll let me know if you notice I'm being oblivious to Anya's needs."

"Oh, you'll learn soon enough. Besides, I'm guessing Millie will be a good friend to Anya. It will be good for her to have another young woman her age living in the same house."

"Millie's great. Though what she ever saw in my brother, I'll never know."

"The same could be said for Anya," she volleyed.

He smiled. "True, true."

"I'm just teasing. Both you boys have been blessed beyond measure. Since you were little babies, I've prayed for the girls you might marry."

"Seems God answered those prayers." Danny patted her hand." I'm glad you're here, Mom. I'm glad we've had a chance to talk."

They sat in a comfortable silence for a while before the rhythm of the train's motion lulled Danny to sleep. He gladly surrendered, giving in to the fatigue that had dogged him the past couple of days. Besides, sleeping would make the trip go faster.

The next morning, after a hot breakfast in one of the dining cars, they returned to their seats and watched an early-morning snow falling on the farmlands they passed by. Danny checked his watch again. Seven-thirty. Only an hour or so until they would pull into Grand Central Station and hail a cab to take them to their hotel. From there, he would make as many calls as necessary to find out what happened to the *Wisteria*.

Hold on, Anya. I'm coming. Just hold on.

44

New York City

After checking in to their hotel not far from New York's harbor, Danny and his mother rode the elevator up to their room on the sixth floor. While she rested, Danny placed a call home. As soon as the operator connected him, Joey told him they'd had a call about an hour earlier from Lieutenant Powell.

"Ready for some good news, Danny?"

"Yes! Tell me!"

"Anya's ship has been repaired and is heading as we speak to New—"

"YESSSS! THANK GOD!" Danny closed his eyes, savoring the news and letting it penetrate his anxious heart.

His mother sat up. "What is it, Danny?"

"Her ship is on its way here again!"

"Oh, sweetheart, that's wonderful!"

"Joey, that's GREAT!"

"I had a feeling that might cheer you up. We've all been celebrating ever since the call came through."

"Oh, my goodness, I'm not sure I can even breathe right now!"

"Take your time, baby brother. You've been waiting for this for a long time."

"I just can't believe it's finally happening. Okay, let me think ... wait, did Powell say if he'd had any direct contact from Anya? No, wait. She wouldn't have wired him. Did she send a telegram there? Do you know if she's—"

"Look, all he said was that the ship was sailing again. Apparently they got hit with some awful weather while they were trying to deal with that fire in the engine room."

"Was anyone hurt?"

"Yes, I'm afraid so, but he didn't know the specifics."

"So he didn't say if any of the brides or kids were injured?"

"Yes, but he had no names or even how many were hurt for that matter. But I'm sure Anya's fine, Danny. The odds are in her favor. Don't forget that."

"Yeah, but her odds aren't always 'in her favor' as such."

"Still, you've got to go on the assumption that she's fine and just as anxious to see you as you are to see her."

"I sure hope so."

"Oh, I almost forgot," Joey continued. "Because the *Wisteria* is running behind schedule, Powell said it will be docking on Sunday, the same day as the *Queen Mary*, so you'll have to check and find out which pier. Powell said he wished he knew specifically, but everything's still up in the air, as you can imagine."

"Did he say where I can find out?"

"His best guess was the Red Cross Center on Lexington Avenue there in New York."

"Okay, I'll start there. Ah, this is great, Joey! Thanks so much. Let me give you the number of the hotel where we're staying in case you need to reach me."

After he finished his conversation with Joey, he and his mother celebrated the good news and spent a few minutes in prayer, thanking God. They decided to leave in an hour or so to have some lunch before heading to the Red Cross.

The hustle and bustle of the city invigorated Danny as they made their way to a café around the corner from the hotel. They took a seat in the front near the windows, placed their order, then relaxed while they waited.

"Almost feels like Christmas, doesn't it?' Danny said. "Especially with the snow falling."

"Yes, it does. And in a way, I guess it is ..."

"Mom?"

She blinked a couple of times then waved him off. "Oh, nothing. Just some rambling thoughts bouncing around my mind."

"Care to share?"

She shook her head with a strange nonchalance, then glanced back outside.

"Are you sure?"

"Oh, don't mind me. I suppose I'm still a little tired from the trip."

"Why don't I walk you back to the hotel before I head over to the Red Cross?"

"Absolutely not. I wouldn't miss a moment. Until Anya

steps off that ship, you're stuck with me."

After lunch, they hailed a cab to take them to the Red Cross Center. As the taxi turned the corner onto Lexington Avenue, they noticed a huge crowd of people and asked the driver if he knew what was going on.

"It's been like this for a few weeks now. Mostly GIs trying to find out when their war brides will arrive."

Danny and his mother shared a look, then paid the driver and joined the throngs huddled in clusters. They found their way to the end of a long line more than a block from the entrance.

"Mom, are you sure you want to wait with me? Maybe there's a coffee shop where you could—"

"I'm fine, son." She tightened the wool scarf around her neck. "Let's see how the line is moving along. If I get too cold, I'll tell you."

As the snow continued falling, Danny picked up bits of conversation in front and behind them. Most were expecting their wives on the *Queen Mary,* which was scheduled to dock on Sunday morning. Not a single one of them had mentioned the *Wisteria*, which made him wonder. Half an hour later, they finally stepped inside the center to find another long line winding back and forth around roped stanchions.

Danny groaned. "Great. Just great."

"At least it's nice and warm in here," his mother said. "I'm going to see if I can find the ladies room."

"Take your time. In fact, why don't you find somewhere to sit down while I wait my turn? No need for you to stand and wait with me."

"Sounds like a good idea. How will you find me?"

"Don't worry. I will."

Another half hour passed before Danny made it to the front of the line. A uniformed Red Cross girl motioned him toward her.

She smiled. "How may I help you today?"

He took off his hat. "My wife is on the *Wisteria,* and I need to know what time it's scheduled to arrive on Sunday and where it will dock."

Her smile diminished briefly. "Yes, I can help you with that. Are you aware the *Wisteria* ran into some problems?"

"Yes, I have a contact with the embassy in London who told us about the fire on board and the storms they encountered."

"Good. I'm glad you're up to date on that. I'm guessing you must not have received the telegram sent to all husbands asking they not come to New York?"

"What? No. But I'm—"

"No, it's all right." She raised her hand, still smiling. "And I'll do whatever I can to help you."

"No, you see, once I heard from my contact in London, I hopped a train to come here. Why would they tell us not to come?"

"There has been a great deal of confusion, which is to be expected in situations like this. The Army Transport Division made the request as an attempt to alleviate the confusion and these long lines. But you're here, so we'll do whatever we can to help you find your wife."

"I appreciate that."

"Good. What is your name and your wife's name?"

He gave her all the information requested, including the

telephone number of the hotel. After she confirmed Anya's name on the *Wisteria's* manifest, she explained the situation further.

"Right now, it looks like the *Wisteria* will dock mid-morning on Sunday. As you probably know, the *Queen Mary* will be docking on Sunday as well, which means the dock area will be quite congested. At this point, we haven't been told which of the piers the two ships will be docking, but we'll have Red Cross workers working the area. When you arrive, simply look for one of us and we can tell you more then. For now, I will put your name on the list so that you'll be allowed in the queue at the appointed pier waiting for your wife's name to be called."

"That's great. Thank you so much."

"You're welcome. I'm sure you're anxious to see her again."

"You have no idea. Oh, I wonder—my mother is here with me. Would it be possible for her to join me in the queue?"

She paused for a moment, then, "Sure, why not?"

He gave her his mother's name and waited as she added her name to the list.

"Now, here are your passes for the main entrance. We'll have tables set up at the foot of the gangways. Each bride will have a printed landing card indicating the city or town where she is ultimately headed. That means your wife will be grouped with those heading to Chicago. It's important that you're there to hear her name called. Otherwise, I can't rule out the possibility that she'll be bussed to another location or even put on a train bound for Chicago. These disembark-kations are quite an undertaking and take several hours, as I'm sure you can imagine. Hopefully, there won't be a problem, but I wanted you to be aware of the possibility. If that should happen, we'll do our best to let you know how to catch up with her."

"All right. Thank you for your help, miss."

"Thank you. Best wishes to you and your wife."

He tucked the pier passes in his suit coat pocket then skirted the crowded area to find his mother.

After an early dinner at the same café where they had lunch, Danny and his mother took the subway to Times Square. The neon lights dazzled the snow-filled sky as theater patrons, moviegoers, and tourists packed the busy sidewalks. Here and there, musicians played jazz and entertainers danced a jig as a host of others sold souvenirs piled high on tables.

"I've never seen anything like it," she said, her hand on her hat as she gazed up at the bright marquees. "If you told me we were on another planet, I couldn't be more surprised."

"You've got that right."

When they passed a small jewelry shop, Danny glimpsed something in the display window. He steered his mother out of the crowd and stopped for a look.

"A welcome gift for Anya?"

"To be honest, I hadn't thought about it, but see that charm bracelet?"

"Yes, it's lovely."

"I gave her one when we were on our honeymoon in England. And that Empire State Building will make a nice addition to it, don't you think?"

A few moments later, they left the shop with the gift box tucked in Danny's coat pocket.

"I don't know about you, but I'm starving. How about an early dinner?"

"Sounds wonderful, son."

They dined at a busy restaurant just off Times Square and finished their meal by sharing a piece of cheesecake.

"Oh my goodness," his mother said, savoring her last bite. "I would love to have their recipe. Isn't this divine?"

"I'd order another slice, but I'm stuffed. How about you?"

She sat back with a happy sigh. "No, I couldn't eat another bite."

After paying the waiter, he asked where she'd like to go.

"Oh, honey, if it's all right with you, I'd like to go back to the room and go to bed."

"That works for me."

"Are you sure?"

"Absolutely. Let's call it a night." He helped her into her coat.

As he opened the door to exit, he added, "Just promise me one thing."

"What's that?"

"Let's not tell Dad or Joey how early we tuckered out in New York City."

She chuckled, following him out to the curb. "Not a word. My lips are sealed."

Danny raised his hand. "Taxi!"

45

10 February 1946

On board the SS Wisteria

"Anya! Wake up!"

Someone shook both her shoulders, rousing her from another restless night's sleep. She lifted her head and found Gigi sitting up on her adjacent bunk.

"Gigi? What are you doing? What time is it?"

"It's almost five. Get up!"

"Five in the morning? Are you out of your mind?"

She ruffled Anya's hair. "Come on, sleepyhead! We have to get dressed so we can be up on deck in plenty of time to see the Statue of Liberty!"

Somewhere in her fog-filled mind she remembered reading about the brides on the SS *Argentina* lining the rails of the deck to see the famous statue as their ship pulled into New York's harbor. But Anya was so tired, she couldn't care less about some silly statue.

"Anya, come on! You don't want to miss this!"

Anya pulled the pillow over her head. "Just take a picture. You can tell me all about it later."

Gigi yanked the pillow off her head and tossed it out of her reach. "Not a chance. I'm climbing down to knock up—" she giggled, "I mean, *wake* up Kate. Don't you make me come up here again."

Anya rolled onto her back again with a weary groan, realizing she'd never get back to sleep if Gigi had anything to do with it. As the cabin slowly came to life, she closed her eyes for a moment, trying to get her bearings. She couldn't quite grasp the fact that they might actually be that close to America. In American waters?

After enduring the past few days stuck on this big gray bucket, she could hardly believe they were almost there. What a journey. The war had taught her to expect the worst, but nothing could have prepared her for the sheer panic that swept through the rolling corridors of the *Wisteria* the night it lost power. Rumors of the call to abandon ship had sent them all scrambling up the stairs in search of lifeboats. Thankfully, the crew blocked all the deck doors, shouting for them all to return to their cabins even as the captain made stern announcements over the public address system debunking the rumor. But with hundreds of women and children, most of them sick and in a state of utter panic, the scene was like something out of a horror cinema. Once again, she witnessed the tremendous calming presence of the Red Cross and their assistance in emergency situations. Had it not been for their compassionate, assertive help that night, who knows what might have happened.

She closed her eyes, hoping Gigi would let her rest a few more minutes. *Dear Gigi.* Last night's talent show had played to a small group of those able to attend. Gigi won with a warm rendition of "There Will Always Be an England," a heartfelt patriotic song that stirred a strong emotional response from all the English brides in the room. To be fair, Gigi had little competition with so many of their shipmates still bedridden with the dreadful seasickness. The event probably should have been cancelled, but Anya had to give the staff credit for their valiant efforts to keep up morale among the few who came.

Over the past few days, she and Gigi had been the only ones able to help the others in their cabin who'd been so sick. Kate had fared better than most, but she stayed out of the cabin as much as possible for Joss's sake. Thankfully, the little one hadn't been sick again.

Anya had cleaned up more vomit than she'd ever seen in her entire life. She wondered if she'd ever get the stench of it out of her nostrils. She still had no idea how she avoided getting sick herself. What a wretched way to travel. Still, she mustn't complain. Rumors of deathly ill passengers—or worse, those who had considered jumping overboard—had swirled down every corridor like a string of harrowing tornadoes. And while Anya hoped they were nothing more than rumors, it grieved her to think otherwise. To be so close to America's shores ...

She shook off such thoughts, grateful she and her friends had survived, and thankful the ship was no longer being tossed about.

In fact, it was quite still now. *Too* still. She sat up suddenly.

"Gigi, why are we stopped? What's going on?"

Gigi brushed her long blonde curls. "I snuck out before I woke you and asked one of the stewards. He said there was a boatload of reporters and Red Cross workers boarding us. I suppose they'll make an announcement. Then at some point a tug will take us in the rest of the way."

"But I thought someone said the tugboat workers were on strike?" a groggy Kate asked from below.

"They are. The steward said the U.S. Army Transport arranged for army tugs to help us dock. C'mon, girls. Get up!"

Anya pushed her hair out of her face then slowly climbed down the rungs from her bunk. "Why do we need more Red Cross workers if we're about to dock?"

Gigi pulled on her dress and wiggled into it. "Yesterday someone said we'd have to get all checked out again before we can disembark."

Anya groaned. "Surely that doesn't include another physical?"

"How would I know? Kate, hurry up and get dressed so we can go up top!"

Joss whimpered from her hammock as Kate lifted her out. "You all go without us. I have to nurse Joss."

Gigi pulled on her stockings. "Don't be daft. You have time. We won't leave without you."

"But it will take me a while to get dressed properly. I don't want Joe to see me like this. And I'll want to freshen Joss a bit more before she sees her daddy for the first time."

Gigi folded her arms over her chest. "Kate, we're just going up to see the Statue of Liberty. They told us it will take most of the day to get us organized to disembark. Just feed Joss then throw on some clothes and come on. We can all doll up later."

Kate positioned Joss against her breast. "Joss, has anyone ever told you how bossy your Auntie Gigi is?"

Anya snorted. "Gigi bossy? Isn't that like saying Hitler could be a bit rude at times?"

"Hey!" Gigi pinched Anya's arm playfully. They tussled like a couple of schoolgirls until Anya locked her arm around Gigi's neck, trying not to laugh.

"I give up! I give up!" Gigi raised both hands. "Let me go! Mustn't harm the goods before I see my handsome husband."

"It's a wonder we've made it this far," Kate quipped from her bunk. "I feel like I've had *three* children instead of one." She leaned down to kiss Joss as she nursed. "Never you mind those two, Jocelyn. Just a few more hours and we'll be safe in our new home with Daddy."

When neither of her friends responded, Kate looked up at them. "What is it? What's wrong?"

Gigi looked back and forth between them. "It's just that ..."

Anya blinked. "It's just that we've been ..."

"Family," Gigi whispered.

"Yes." Anya nodded, her smile waning. "We've been family."

"And now we'll be going our separate ways," Kate said quietly, understanding.

Gigi took hold of Anya's hand. "Surely we can plan a visit? Once we're all settled?"

"How?" Anya asked. "You'll both be in New York, but won't I be such a long way from you?"

"Anya's right," Kate said. "America is ever so much bigger

467

than England."

Gigi's voice graveled with emotion. "Then we must insist on a meeting place. We simply must. I can't bear to think of us not being together again." She pulled Anya into a hug and held her tight. "You're more family to me than I've ever known."

"Oh Gigi, please don't cry, love," Kate said. "You'll have us all in puddles."

"You heard her," Anya said, dashing at her tears. "And don't go staining my blouse with all those cosmetics you cake on."

Gigi laughed as she reached for her hankie. "Now look what you've done. I'll be all splotchy and drippy when Lady Liberty sees me."

Kate refastened her bra and lifted Joss from her lap so she could stand and join them. "Look at us. Happiest day of our lives, and we're all three in puddles."

It felt so strange to Anya, this unexpected sense of sisterhood. And with it, a palpable sadness. First Sophie. Then Sybil ... *poor Sybil.* Now Kate and Gigi and sweet little Joss. Friendships she never would have imagined; friendships she couldn't imagine living without now. So many new beginnings on the heels of so many goodbyes. Oh, how she would miss them.

Chatter rose as others in the cabin got up and dressed. At a pause in the excited conversations and laughter, they turned at the sound of sobbing from the corner of the cabin. The girl named Tilly had suffered terribly from seasickness from the first day they sailed. Then, last night, she'd become so distraught, her friends had asked the crew to allow her to make a ship-to-shore call to her husband. Others had placed calls, and they thought the sound of her husband's voice might reassure her and give her hope.

The crew obliged. When she finally got through to her husband's family home, she'd been told her husband had their marriage annulled a week ago, then quickly married someone he'd just met and moved to California. The news nearly put her over the edge. Her friends hadn't left her side, fearful she might try to do something desperate.

The shocking news spread through the ship like a raging wildfire causing most all the brides to wonder. Would they arrive in America only to find no husband waiting for them? A long queue formed at the communications office, but eventually the crew turned them all away. Perhaps they knew best, Anya thought. A ship full of unwanted war brides could get ugly in a hurry.

She watched the girl as she wailed, then turned back to Kate and Gigi.

"We have to believe," Kate said quietly. "And believe with all our hearts."

Gigi straightened. "Yes, and we need to go. Now."

It took a while for them to make their way to the deck with all the others heading the same direction. Anya noticed that many of them looked as haggard as she felt. Theirs had hardly been the luxury cruise they'd all dreamed of. Far from it. But now, so close to their destination, the sparkle had returned to their eyes, and their voices rang with joy again as they eagerly made their way outside to see the Statue of Liberty.

"Fancy that—it's snowing!" Gigi giggled. "Oh, isn't it lovely?" She tilted her head back and tried to catch snowflakes on her tongue. "Oh, girls! It's like we've been given another go at Christmas!"

"I certainly hope it's better than the one we just had," Kate mused. "I shouldn't like to see any Christmas trees burn down the house again."

"Kate, why did you have to bring that up now?" Gigi moaned. "Don't spoil our fun! Nothing but happy days ahead now, so leave all that behind, will you?"

"Yes, but I wish Sybil was here with us," Anya said, shielding her eyes from the snowflakes dancing all around them.

Kate sighed, holding Joss close. "Dear Sybil. I hope she's well. We must all write to her as soon as we're settled."

Gigi rubbed her hands together and stomped her feet to stay warm. "Yes, we must. I hope that handsome lieutenant is watching over her. Such a nice fellow, that one."

"Yes, he is," Anya added, "and she deserves someone who'll be good to her."

"Then let's pretend they're already in love," Gigi said. "Remember, nothing but happy days ahead of us now. And that goes for Sybil, too."

"Gigi, you're the eternal optimist, and I love that about you." Kate reached for her hand and squeezed it. "Now please tell us where that statue is. Joss and I are shivering!"

Ripples of conversation floated forward and aft as they all searched the early-morning waters for a glimpse of the famous statue. No sooner had they settled in than a noisy group of men spilled out of the doorways onto the deck. Photographers started snapping pictures as reporters huddled close vying for a chance to interview anyone who would look their way.

Anya and Kate laughed as they watched Gigi draw them in.

"Hey, boys! What's a girl got to do to get a little attention?"

"Like moths to a flame," Kate quipped. "They can't help themselves, can they?"

They surrounded Gigi as flashbulbs popped off in rapid succession and the eager reporters barked questions faster than she could answer.

"So how does it feel, finally getting so close to America?"

"What's the first thing you'll say to your husband?"

"He's a lucky one, your husband!"

"Ain't she a beauty!"

"How long since you last saw your husband?"

"Where did you meet?"

"What's your name and where are you headed?"

Gigi raised her hands. "Boys, boys! Give a girl a chance, will you?"

Their hearty laughter filled the deck.

"How does it feel to finally reach American waters?" she repeated the question. "It feels *wonderful*, doesn't it, girls?"

All the girls cheered as they crowded in closer, jostling Anya and Kate as they joined in the fun.

"First thing I'm going to say to my husband? Well, let's see now. Let me think." She gazed up into the snow-filled sky as she tapped a red-nailed finger on her chin. "First, I'll ask him for a great big, juicy kiss—"

Whistles and catcalls drowned her out.

"—then I'll ask him to take me to Saks Fifth Avenue! Time for some new clothes. Wouldn't you agree, girls?" she asked, tossing the question their direction.

The crowd of girls cheered again as the men guffawed.

Anya and Kate shared another laugh.

"Will you look at them?" Kate shouted. "They're practically eating out of her hand!"

"Tell us, doll, what's your name?"

Gigi turned toward a handsome reporter as he pushed the brim of his hat up off his forehead. "It's *MRS.* Williams. And don't you forget it!"

"Where are you headed with Mr. Williams?" he asked, playing along.

"Wouldn't *you* like to know!"

The banter continued as the reporters spread out to talk to others, the bulbs flashing one after another. Then, suddenly, a voice from the ship's loudspeakers hushed them.

"Ladies, this is Captain Masterson speaking. It seems we have almost completed our journey, and it is my distinct honor to invite you to take a look off the port bow, where you will see the Statue of Liberty welcoming you to your new home."

"That way!" someone shouted, pointing forward.

They all turned to look, crowding the rails for a chance to see her.

"LOOK!" someone else shouted. "There she is!"

"Oh Anya, look!" Kate cried, pointing across the rail. "Have you ever seen anything so beautiful?"

And there she was, aglow in the early-morning darkness, washed in spotlights from every direction. Lady Liberty, her torch raised high. Tears stung Anya's eyes. She never expected such a reaction, but gladly let them fall. Gigi hooked her arms through Anya's and Kate's as the three stood in silence. All around them others whispered in hushed reverence as the cameras clicked away.

"If you would allow me," the captain continued, "I would like to read to you Lady Liberty's greeting. These verses, from a poem called 'The New Colossus,' were penned by a Jewish Portuguese immigrant named Emma Lazarus in 1883. They are engraved on a bronze plaque on the base of the statue.

"Not like the brazen giant of Greek fame,
With conquering limbs astride from land to land
Here at our sea-washed, sunset gates shall stand
A mighty woman with a torch, whose flame
Is the imprisoned lightning, and her name
Mother of Exiles. From her beacon-hand
Glows world-wide welcome; her mild eyes command
The air-bridged harbor that twin cities frame.
'Keep, ancient lands, your storied pomp!' cries she
With silent lips. "Give me your tired, your poor,
Your huddled masses yearning to breathe free,
The wretched refuse of your teeming shore.
Send these, the homeless, tempest-tost, to me
I lift my lamp beside the golden door.'"

Anya knitted her brow and turned to find Kate and Gigi's expressions reflecting her own.

"Did he just call us 'a wretched refuse?'" Gigi whispered.

"I have no idea," Kate answered, "but we've certainly been 'tempest-tossed'—"

"And now, ladies, if you'll listen closely as we draw closer, you should be able to hear a grand welcome by members of the United States Army Band, who wish to serenade you from the base of Lady Liberty."

Smiles and laughter broke out as the brides recognized the melody of "Here Comes the Bride," followed by "Sentimental Journey."

"Oh, isn't it wonderful!" Gigi cried. "We made it! We're finally here!"

46

After a hot breakfast, Danny and his mother took a cab to the New York Harbor, arriving just before 7:00 that morning. The Red Cross worker had said the *Wisteria* would arrive mid-morning, but he wanted to be there early. Even before they rounded the corner to the piers, they could hear a band playing John Phillip Sousa's famous march, "Stars and Stripes Forever."

"I don't believe it! Mom, look—she's already docked! The *Wisteria* is already here!"

Danny broke free and raced in the direction of the ship's pier. He was twenty paces away before he remembered her and sprinted back to find her laughing.

"Sorry!" He smothered her in a bear hug then tugged her along beside him. "Guess I got carried a little away—"

"Oh Danny, isn't it exciting?" she shouted over the music. "She's here! Anya's finally here!"

They hurried along, weaving their way through the huge

475

crowd. A long line had already formed at the entrance to the pier alongside the ship. They took their place at the end, but Danny kept his eyes on the ship's rails above.

The decks were lined with hundreds of young women, many with young children, all waving and cheering, though the music overpowered their voices. He scanned the faces and wondered how he would ever spot Anya from where they stood. Unless she was standing on the port bow, he couldn't possibly see her.

"Can you tell if anyone's come off the ship yet?" his mother asked.

The young man in front of them turned around. "They haven't let any of them disembark yet. Apparently the Public Health people went aboard to give them another physical."

"What?! Why? My wife said they had physicals back in England before they left. Several, in fact. Isn't it kind of late to be doing that now?"

"Someone said it's a final check for lice, but who knows. I'm just telling you what I heard. The Immigration and Customs folks also boarded once they docked. Who knows how long all that might take."

An hour later, they were next in line to check in at the table beside the gangway. With that accomplished, they finally joined the growing group in a designated area. By 11:30, Danny was at his wit's end. They'd been at the harbor for almost four hours. Four hours! The snow had stopped falling, but the blowing wind made the bone-chilling temperatures much too cold for his mother. She said she was fine, but seeing her teeth chatter, Danny insisted she go warm up in one of the coffee shops. When she returned half an hour later—and still no brides had come off the ship—Danny suggested she take a cab back to the hotel.

"Absolutely not. I came along to welcome Anya, and I'll not let you get rid of me just because there's a nip in the air."

"I guess I know where I got my stubborn streak," he teased. "All these years I assumed it came from Dad."

With a chuckle, she said, "Yes, and don't you forget it."

The Red Cross folks continually made the rounds serving coffee and donuts, not unlike those offered by the Red Cross girls at the 390th in Framlingham. Now, as the lunch hour approached, they returned with wrapped sandwiches.

"Please tell me we won't still be here for dinner," Danny growled.

"Not a chance, son. We'll be seated in a nice restaurant along with your bride. My treat."

He wasn't so optimistic.

Another hour and a half later, the first of the brides came down the ramp as a groundswell of cheers rose from those waiting. Others followed, each stopping at the table near the gangway to give their husband's name which was then announced over the public address system. The band played quietly so the names could be heard, and with each one came a hearty shout from a waiting husband. The squeals and kisses of their reunions played much to the delight of the crowd.

The initial excitement began to taper off as the process crawled along at a snail's pace. Danny realized this could take all day and into the night.

"Stop that."

He looked at his mother. "Stop what?"

477

She touched a gloved finger to his jaw. "You're grinding your teeth. I can tell by the twitching of your jaw—"

"Mrs. Anya McClain. Wife of Daniel McClain."

"ANYA?!" He bolted from the crowd and rushed toward her.

"DANNY!"

"ANYA!"

And suddenly she dropped her bags and flew into his arms, kissing him and crying tears of joy. "Oh, Danny! You're here! You're here!"

"Oh sweetheart, I can't believe it! You're here!"

They kissed and laughed and cried, then kissed again.

She clung to him, her arms around his neck. "I thought they'd never let us off! I kept searching for you in the crowd, and couldn't see you and then I worried that perhaps you didn't—"

He silenced her with a kiss as he lifted her off the ground. "Oh Anya, it doesn't matter now. None of it matters! You're here in my arms, and I will never, *never* let you go."

"Move along now," one of the Red Cross workers said. He picked up the bags Anya had dropped and nudged them away from the congested desk area. "Here you go. Welcome to America," he said with a smile before disappearing into the crowd again.

Danny gathered her back in his arms. "I honestly can't believe it. You're finally *home*. Well, almost, anyway."

"I was beginning to think this day would never come. And yet, here you are—"

"Yes, here I am with you in my arms." He kissed her again, oblivious to everyone else around them.

"Anya?"

Danny pulled back, allowing his mother to join them. "Oh, I almost forgot you, Mom! Anya, this is my—"

"Mrs. McClain? You came too?"

"Oh, Anya, dear, dear Anya." Betty gathered her into her arms. "We've waited so long, and now you're here. My dear sweet child, you're finally home. I can't possibly tell you how thrilled I am to finally meet you."

Her eyes pooled with tears, Anya tried but couldn't speak. Danny thought his heart would burst with joy. He wrapped his arms around both of them and couldn't have stopped his own tears if he tried.

When Anya pulled back, his mother held her face in her gloved hands, brushing aside the tears on her cheeks. "Anya, there are a thousand things I want to ask you and say to you, but for now, I first and foremost want to thank God for bringing you through your long journey home. Welcome to America, sweetheart. Welcome home."

Anya clung to her mother-in-law with such a profound sense of gratitude, she couldn't speak. From the moment Betty embraced her, she felt something so familiar and safe, it nearly overwhelmed her. As if she'd met a long-lost friend ... but no, it was more than that. Something similar, but at the same time different.

And then she knew.

A mother's love.

Familiar. Safe.

Oh, how I've missed it.

She couldn't fully comprehend the depth of such thoughts, and now wasn't the time. She pushed those emotions aside, and simply grasped the essence of meeting the woman who had prayed for her and loved her before they'd ever met. Without a word, Anya hugged her again, not quite ready to let go just yet.

"Anya!"

At the sound of her name, she dashed away her tears and turned.

"Here you are!" Gigi cried, pushing her way into Anya's embrace." Oh Anya, isn't it wonderful? Isn't it all glorious?!" She giggled and hugged her again before stepping back. "Anya, I want you to meet my husband, Paul."

He leaned in for a hug then stood back, his arm wrapped around Gigi's tiny waist. He was just as Anya imagined him from Gigi's photograph. Tall and handsome with the bluest eyes she'd ever seen. They exchanged the introductions, sharing hugs and handshakes all around.

Kate joined them too, her husband Joe carrying little Jocelyn. The introductions were repeated, including quite a fuss about little Joss. At times, they were all talking at once, so excited to finally be reunited.

When the time came to part company, Anya was surprised at the ache in her heart as they said their goodbyes. They'd already exchanged addresses and telephone numbers, but it would never be the same. That was as it should be, of course. But Anya was surprised by the bittersweet longing already seeping through her heart. A moment later, they were gone.

Danny pulled her to his side, wrapping her snug against him. "Are you okay?"

"Yes." She turned to look up at him. "I'm so glad you got to meet them, Danny."

"I am too, sweetheart. You ready to go?"

She stood on her tiptoes and kissed his lips. "I've never been so ready in all my life. Let's go home."

47

The snow was falling again as they left the hotel in a yellow taxi. Anya watched out the window as they passed block after block of high-rise buildings, masses of people walking the sidewalks, and seas of yellow cabs just like theirs. When it all started to blur, she turned to Danny, smitten by the smile on his face.

"It's a lot to take in, isn't it? The city?"

"All these buildings and all these people. I've never seen anything like it."

"Well, yes, New York is big, any way you look at it. And the population is something like seven and a half million, or there-abouts."

"Is all of America like this?" She turned to look up at the skyscrapers rushing by them. "I can't even grasp it."

"Oh, don't let it carry you away," Betty said. "The rest of the country, for the most part, is nothing like this."

She turned toward her. "Is Chicago as big as New York?"

"Heavens, no. Thank goodness!"

The taxi delivered them to a lovely restaurant where the three of them dined by candlelight just around the corner from Central Park. After dinner, they sipped steaming cups of coffee before the waiter brought their dessert. Danny and his mother chuckled as Anya savored her first bite of New York cheesecake. She closed her eyes, savoring the heavenly blend of flavors.

It was the strangest thing. She supposed others might begrudge the presence of a mother-in-law at a time like this, but Anya felt only gratitude. Through the handful of letters they'd exchanged, she knew Betty—as she insisted Anya call her—to be a godly woman who loved her family. Even now, sitting across from her in the cozy restaurant, Anya knew that without Betty's faithful prayers, she probably wouldn't be here.

They asked about her trip across the Atlantic, but she kept the conversation light, not wishing to dampen their first night together. She told them about Gigi and Kate and little Joss, and how they'd survived the long months together in London and the difficult voyage across the Atlantic. Danny asked if anyone special had come to see her off. Only then did she remember his part in Charlie and Sophie showing up the day they left Southampton. She thanked him for such a wonderful surprise. He asked how Sybil was doing, and she told him all she knew. As she did, the same bittersweet ache wrapped around her heart.

Betty reached for her hand across the table. "How nice to have friends you care about and who obviously care so much about you. We'll look forward to a time when they might come for a visit."

"I would love that."

Moments later when they stood to go, Anya swayed, nearly tumbling into Danny.

He grabbed her just in time. "Are you okay?"

"I'm not sure. It felt like I was back on the ship."

"You've had sea legs for a long time. You'll get your land legs back in a day or two."

"I hope so. I'm anxious to put all that behind me."

They hailed a cab and returned to the hotel. Betty had moved her suitcase to a room down the hall when they first returned from the harbor. As they stopped outside her door to say goodnight, she gave both of them a kiss on the cheek and a hug.

Danny escorted Anya down the hall to their room. Once inside, he reached for the *Do Not Disturb* sign and placed it on the outer doorknob. With a silly grin on his face and a wink of his eye, he closed the door.

As the morning light streamed through the window, Danny felt Anya roll over and snuggle close beneath the covers. He slid his arm around her, loving the warmth of her body so close to his.

He sighed happily as he kissed her forehead. "Good morning," he whispered.

"Mmm."

"You can say that again." He kissed her soft cheek.

"Mmm. Can't we just stay here all day? Do you think your mother would mind terribly if we skipped breakfast?"

"Oh, I'm sure she'd understand."

"Good."

"Good." He kissed the soft spot below her ear. "If she knows on our door, I'll let you get it."

"No problem. But I wonder ... do you think she'd mind if we skipped lunch too?"

"Why? Did you have something else in mind?"

"No."

"No?"

"Well ..."

"Well?"

She turned on her side and rested her head on his shoulder. "Well ... the thing is, I don't want to leave the room today. And if you must know," she added, barely above a whisper, "I don't want to leave this bed."

He turned, pulling her closer still. "I think that can be arranged." She kissed him gently with a soft sigh. "There's just one problem."

She looked into his eyes, a tiny crease forming between her brows. "What's that?"

He stared into the eyes he loved so dearly, hating to break the moment. He kissed her cheek, then inched his way up to whisper in her ear. "If you must know, I need to go ... brush my teeth. Yes. That's it. I need to brush my teeth."

"Are you sure?" She smiled and rolled back onto her pillow. "Because I'll probably fall back asleep and who knows how long I might sleep?"

He stared at her lips for half a second, debating. "Oh, don't you worry. I'll be sure to wake you when I return."

He kissed her cheek again, then rolled out of bed. He made his way to the bathroom, and when he flipped on the light, noticed an envelope had been slipped under their door. He picked it up and recognized his mother's handwriting.

"What's that?" Anya asked.

He turned back toward her as he opened it. "A note from Mom, by the looks of it."

"What's it say?"

"Let me see ... oh my goodness, she's gone."

"What?"

He wandered back toward the bed. "It says, 'By the time you read this, I'll be on the train heading home. You were so kind to let me tag along, Danny, but you and Anya need some time alone. Your hotel bill is paid in full for two more nights, so have some fun. I'll see you when you come home. Love, Mother.'"

"Oh, she didn't need to leave."

"I know, but I'm not surprised."

"You're not?"

"That's just Mom. Always thinking ahead, always anticipating the needs of others."

Anya stared at him a moment longer. "It's very thoughtful of her. She's just as I'd imagined her, Danny. So genuine, so kind. I can't tell you how pleased I was to finally meet her yesterday."

"She never had daughters, and if the way she treats Millie is any indication, she'll be spoiling you rotten too. Which is fine by me, in case you were wondering."

"I thought you were going to brush your teeth?"

"Oh. Right." He turned to go then stopped. "You won't fall asleep, will you?"

"I don't know. I suppose it's possible. So ..."

They didn't leave their room all day.

On Tuesday morning, they decided to venture out and see the sights. First stop, the world's tallest building—the Empire State Building in midtown Manhattan. With a brilliant blue sky as backdrop, the building's panoramic view of New York astounded them. The brisk wind stung their eyes as they looked far below at the golden rays of the sun dancing on the ripples of both the Hudson and East Rivers. Danny pointed out the Chrysler Building with its classic art-deco architecture and several other famous structures.

"It's so beautiful, Danny. But doesn't it seem odd compared to the bombing damage in London? I hadn't thought how strange it would look, literally unscathed by the war."

He stood behind her, his arms wrapped around her waist. "You're right. Hadn't thought of that either, to be honest. But I remember reading about a B-25 that crashed into this building just last year."

"Really?"

"Yes, it was a Saturday morning back in July and extremely foggy. The pilot got confused and flew right into it."

"How horrible."

"Surprisingly, only a dozen or so folks were killed. The

small crew on board the plane died, of course, and the others who were working on the floors where it hit. Since it was a weekend, there weren't as many casualties as there might have been."

"I didn't notice any damage to the building, did you?"

"No, come to think of it."

They made their way all around the observation deck, taking in the view to the north, east, south, and west. When the wind picked up, they headed back down the elevator. They rode the subway south, hopping off to take a stroll on the Brooklyn Bridge where they asked a stranger to take their picture with the famous structure behind them. Danny asked if she'd like to take a ride on the Staten Island ferry. She declined, saying it might be decades before she'd ever take another boat ride.

"I see your point. Well, what else would you like to see? Times

Square? A show on Broadway?"

She took hold of his hand again. "You know what I'd really like?"

"Surprise me."

"I'd like to have an early dinner at a quiet restaurant. Preferably one that serves cheesecake."

"I believe we can make that happen."

"Good. Afterwards, I'd like to go back to the hotel."

"Oh, I *know* we can make that happen." He kissed her soundly then raised his hand. "Taxi!"

48

13 February 1946

Chicago, Illinois

Anya spotted Joey on the platform as they stepped down from the train at the LaSalle Station shortly after seven that evening. She might not have recognized him apart from his waving hands as he dodged people and mounds of luggage to reach them.

"Joey!" Danny engulfed his brother in a hug, slapping his back.

"Hey, baby brother! But enough about you." He stepped back and elbowed Danny out of the way, opening his arms to her. "Anya! At long last we meet!"

She stepped into his embrace, surprised to find him taller than Danny. "Hello, Joey."

Joey released her, then reached for her hand. "If Mom hadn't come home gushing about her newly-arrived daughter-in-law, I would have thought you existed only in

Danny's imagination. But here you are!"

"Yes, here I am," she said. "I've heard so much about you through the years. I'm glad to finally meet you in person."

He narrowed his eyes toward Danny. "Don't believe half of it."

"It was all good. I promise."

"Somehow I doubt that, but let's get going." He reached for her bag and took another from Danny. "I'm on strict orders to hurry home with you two. Everyone's anxious to see you. Mom's been cooking all day, so I hope you're hungry."

He chatted nonstop as they made their way through the crowded station. Once they reached the car and stashed their luggage in the trunk, they climbed inside. Danny insisted she ride in the front seat with Joey to give her a better view of the city. He'd told her Chicago wasn't nearly as big as New York, but gazing up at the tall skyscrapers and the galaxy of city lights against the ink-black sky, she couldn't tell much difference until they left the metropolitan areas.

She warmed to Joey immediately, pleased to find him just as charming and funny as Danny had always described him.

"How's my nephew doing?" Danny asked from the back-seat.

"Oh yes," Anya added, "congratulations on the birth of your son. I can't wait to meet him. Danny tells me he's quite a handsome little guy."

"Oh, is he ever! Cute as a button and smart as a whip. Takes after his father, of course."

"Don't listen to him, honey. Jimmy's the spitting image of his mother. You'll see."

She glanced over her shoulder. "The spitting image? What

does that mean?"

Joey laughed. "Good question. And I have no idea where the expression came from, but it means there's a striking resemblance between two people. You'll see when you meet Jimmy. We're identical. Well, except for the age difference, of course."

A snort sounded from the backseat. "Behaviorally, they're remarkably similar."

"Nice one, Danny."

The teasing continued and with it, waves of laughter. It reminded her of the verbal jousting between Charlie and Danny. She found it relaxing, this warm relationship they shared. Much to her relief, she realized her silly worries about meeting Danny's family were evaporating.

Danny scooted forward and tapped her shoulder as they turned a corner. "Anya, look."

Most of the houses on the block were lit up with Christmas lights. Anya couldn't make sense of it.

"I don't understand. It's the thirteenth of February. Do all Americans leave their Christmas lights up all year?"

Danny patted his brother's shoulder. "Joey, Joey, Joey, what have you done?"

"Don't look at me. I'm just the chauffeur."

As they pulled in front of the house, Anya couldn't believe the crowd of people all bundled in the front yard, waving and cheering as they drew to a stop. She spotted a sign over the front porch that read, "WELCOME HOME, DANNY & ANYA!"

A flutter of butterflies troubled her stomach. "What's happening? Danny, did you know about this?"

"No, I didn't. Are you okay with this?"

She nodded. What else could she do?

He hopped out of the backseat and opened her door. The crowd raised their voices, all singing together for them.

We wish you a merry Christmas,
We wish you a merry Christmas,
We wish you a merry Christmas,
And a happy new year!

With Danny's hand clutching hers, they moved into the bustling crowd of well-wishers who hugged her and welcomed her. A moment passed until a path cleared for Danny's parents as they made their way to her.

Betty hugged her tight then stepped back, her eyes filled with tears of joy again. "Welcome home, Anya!"

Danny shouted above the chatter as he introduced her to his father. "Dad, this is Anya. Anya, this is my dad."

Mr. McClain held out his hand to shake hers, his eyes glistening in the glow of the colorful Christmas lights. He started to speak, then clamped his jaw tight, his smile wavering. Anya looked at his hand, ignored it and stepped slowly into his unsuspecting arms. Around them, lots of *ahhhs* accompanied the crowd noise and those still singing. He stiffened at first, then relaxed as he wrapped his arms gingerly around her.

They stood there for a moment unable to speak. Then, "It's nice to meet you, Anya. Welcome home."

Anya pulled back just enough to look into her father-in-law's eyes. "Thank you, Mr. McClain. It's pleasure to meet you."

Betty looped her arm through Anya's. "Oh, Anya. I can't believe you're finally home! I hope it's all right that we invited a few friends to welcome you."

"It's very nice. Very kind of you."

"Don't worry," she whispered in Anya's ear. "We'll shoo them all away in a bit. I know you must be exhausted."

"No, I'm fine. Thank you, Mrs—I mean, Betty. Sorry. I keep forgetting."

"You call me whatever you like, sweetheart. Now enjoy yourself. We have refreshments inside if you're hungry."

Before she could respond, Joey reached through the crowd for her hand. "Anya, there's someone here who wants to say hello. You too, Danny. An old friend of yours."

Anya and Danny shared a look.

Suddenly, a fiddler stood before them, his head bowed as he played "Here Comes the Bride."

"Cosmos?" Danny sputtered. "What are *you* doing here?"

With an exaggerated flair of his bow, he finished the song and took a deep bow. "Mr. Danny and Mrs. Anya, yes! It is I— Cosmos Francis Benedetto at your service!"

"But how—"

"How is it that I am here? I'm here at the request of your family, and most especially your brother Joey, who asked me to bring my fiddle to play for you and all these fine people, as we celebrate together the Christmas that the two of you were not able to share together."

Anya couldn't believe it. The same Cosmos who had "kept watch" over her in Framlingham after Danny left—here? In Chicago?

Suddenly, Joey popped up beside them, a mischievous grin on his face. "Surprised?"

Cosmos played another round as others joined to sing.

After the applause ended, he started to speak to them, then paused. He tapped his quivering mouth with the tip of his bow and tried to collect himself, then tried again. "It is with the utmost pleasure that I, Cosmos Francis Benedetto, accepted your brother Joey's invitation to join the two of you in this auspicious gathering of your friends and neighbors as we recreate the holiday ambience to welcome you both home. Especially you, Mrs. Anya, as you start your life here in the land of the free and the home of the brave."

The crowd cheered, "Here, here!"

"Oh, thank you, Cosmos," she said. "What a surprise to see you again. I'm ... speechless. Really. It's so kind of you to come."

He laughed heartily. "Merry Christmas, Mrs. Anya!"

He placed the fiddle beneath his chin and played a rousing introduction to "Joy to the World." He wandered off as the crowd joined in, their voices sending puffs of fog along the way.

Joey draped his arm around Danny's neck. "Nice homecoming, eh?"

Danny shook his head as he chuckled. "Never saw *that* one coming."

Anya stayed close to Danny's side. "What's he doing here? I thought he lived in New Jersey. Is that close to Chicago?"

Joey grinned. "No, not at all. But a couple days ago, the little guy showed up at the theater and said he wanted to take me up on my offer of a job."

Danny blinked. "You offered him a *job*?"

"Well yeah, but I never thought he'd take it!" He turned to Anya. "See, he came through town back in January to see

Danny. Actually, I believe we have *you* to thank for giving him the family's address?"

She felt the sheepish grin creep across her face. "Oh ... right. I forgot."

Danny narrowed his eyes at her. "You forgot. How convenient."

"Not a problem, though. Right, Danny?" Joey prodded.

He laughed. "The missus and I will talk about this later."

"Anyway," Joey continued, "that's when I met him, Anya. In fact, we spent a very interesting day with him while we waited for Danny to come home from his job at the library. Cosmos said he'd been traveling a lot and decided to stop by and see Danny while he was in Chicago. Then, as I said, he showed up a couple of days ago and told me God wanted him to live here in Chicago, especially with his dear friends here."

Danny smirked. "Oh, how I wish Charlie was here." He shook his head as he watched the feisty Italian playing his fiddle and dancing through the crowd. "Wow. I don't even know what to say."

"Nothing to say, brother. We'll all be one big happy family. You and Anya, Millie and Jimmy and me, Mom and Dad— and Cosmos."

They gradually moved inside. Anya marveled at the house so warmly decorated for Christmas. Fragrant garlands of pine gracing the banister. Mistletoe hung from light fixtures here and there. And in the corner of the living room, a Christmas tree glowing with colorful lights, and an angel atop with wings touching the ceiling.

"I can't believe you did all this for us. Have all these decorations been here since Christmas?"

Betty chuckled. "No, we put them up when I got back from New York. It was actually Danny who gave me the idea."

"Me? What are you talking about?"

"Yes you, though you didn't know it at the time. It was that first morning in New York after you heard Anya's ship was on its way again. You were so excited, Danny, and you said it was 'almost like Christmas.'"

"You're right. I did say that."

"That's when I got the idea to have another Christmas to celebrate Anya's homecoming. I called home and told Dad and Joey to find a tree and start decorating."

"Well, you couldn't have surprised us more."

She kissed his cheek. "Now, you two go get something to eat. We'll open presents after everyone leaves."

Neighbors came and went; everyone wanting to meet Anya until she thought one more smile would surely break her jaw. Many had helped with the spread of food, unlike anything she had seen since before the war. While sampling a cookie, she was delighted to meet Lara Zankowski—or "Mrs. Z" as Danny called her.

"I feel as though I already know you," Anya said, "from all Danny's letters telling me about his favorite teacher."

"Really? Well, teachers aren't supposed to have pets, but between you and me, Danny was always my favorite. He always shared my love of history, and what teacher doesn't love to have a student catch the passion for the subject matter?

"Now, Joey? That was a totally different situation. That young man didn't care one iota about his studies, but oh my, what a charmer he was. I lost count of how many girls vied for his attention in the classroom. But I loved him from the start. Which is a good thing now that I'm his aunt."

Danny caught Anya's eye, crooking his finger for her to join him in the kitchen.

"I'm sorry, but could you give me a moment? Danny's motioning for me."

"No problem, I need to walk home. School night, you know." She placed her hand over Anya's. "You tell that handsome husband of yours to bring you over for coffee once you get settled. All right?"

"Yes, of course. I'll look forward to it."

With a quick hug, she was gone. Anya worked her way over to the kitchen where Danny introduced her to Mrs. Martello and her sister Angelica. He told her they lived side by side in the two houses across the street.

"Are these the ladies whose snow you used to shovel?"

"Best snow boy we ever had!" Mrs. Martello said. "We haven't had a decent shoveling since he left." She took both of Anya's hands in hers and gave her a peck on each of her cheeks.

Her sister Angelica did the same. Anya noticed they both wore the same sweet fragrance.

The elderly pair gave them a large gift box wrapped in festive Christmas paper.

"Don't let the paper fool you."

"It's your wedding gift."

"Oh, how thoughtful," Anya said, motioning for Danny to help her unwrap it. As they lifted the lid, the overpowering scent of mothballs wafted from the box. Inside, wrapped in layers of white tissue paper, they found a knitted blanket.

Patterns of bright color on a black background. "Oh my goodness, what a beautiful blanket."

"It's an afghan, not a blanket."

"We crocheted it."

"Both of us."

"Started it the day we heard you two got married."

"Because every couple needs an afghan."

"How nice of you. Isn't it lovely, Danny?"

"It sure is. Thanks, ladies," Danny said. "We'll think of you every time we wrap up in it."

"Course, we had no idea it would take this long for you to get here."

"So we stored it in the closet."

Ah. Mothballs. Of course.

They continued the chatter, each finishing the other's sentences. They were adamant that Anya insist on having a "real" wedding now that she was going to live in America. She avoided eye contact with Danny, despite his silly antics behind the two sisters. She assured them she and Danny would discuss the matter.

Anya would never remember all the names, but did her best.

But she was especially drawn to Millie the moment they finally met.

"Oh Anya, I'm *so* pleased to meet you!" she said with a hug. "Welcome home!"

"Thank you, Millie. To be honest, I can't believe I'm actually here."

"I'm so sorry I wasn't out front to greet you, but just as you all drove up, Jimmy blew out his diaper. Wouldn't you know? I had to bathe him and then dress *both* of us again. But forget all that now. You're home!"

She hugged her again then introduced her to seven-month-old son Jimmy, his bib already soaked from the onslaught of drool which Millie attributed to teething. Nevertheless, the little guy smiled constantly, clearly enjoying all the attention.

She decided Jimmy was the "spitting image" of *both* Joey and Millie.

They talked like old friends, and Anya was touched again at the simple pleasure of friendship. With each passing moment, she felt the long months of apprehension and suppressed fear slipping away.

And the thought pleased her more than she could have imagined.

When the last of the neighbors took their leave, Danny and Anya joined the rest of the family around the beautifully decorated Christmas tree. Betty pointed out the ornament Anya had sent them from London, then distributed the gifts for the two of them. A soft pink chenille robe for Anya. A pair of leather gloves for Danny. A set of fluffy white bath towels and washcloths, and so much more.

Afterward, as the family relaxed over coffee and dessert, Danny sat back and enjoyed watching Anya and his family get to know each other.

She'd changed since he'd left her in England. He'd noticed

it as soon as they reunited at the dock in New York. Anya had never been comfortable in social settings. She'd always been guarded and slow to warm to strangers. Those first weeks in Framlingham, he'd noticed subtle hints of change as she and Sophie became friends. He would never be able to thank Sophie enough for welcoming Anya with such open arms. Her friendship had helped Anya in ways he never could.

After he'd flown home, she'd worked at the pub with Sophie and Charlie. Is that when she learned to relax around strangers? When she moved to London, had she grown accustomed to living with her roommates, all of them strangers for the most part? Did it happen overnight? Or had the weeks and months slowly eroded the carefully constructed walls around her heart? Seeing her with Kate and Gigi the day they arrived had astounded him, the bond of sisterhood as plain as day when they said their goodbyes.

He had not discussed these changes with her, merely observed them and thanked God for the work He was obviously doing in her spirit. But he also recognized the emotional fatigue, knowing the gathering of friends and family had been a bit much for her. Too much, too soon perhaps.

"Well, family, this was great." He pushed back his chair and stood, feigning a yawn. "Thank you for such a nice homecoming, but I'm ready to call it a night. I don't know about you, Anya, but I'm exhausted."

"Yes, I suppose I am." She stood and gathered their dishes.

"Leave those, Anya," Betty said. "We'll take care of them. You two go get some rest. We'll see you in the morning."

They said goodnight and made their way up the stairs.

As they settled into his room, Danny noticed something off but couldn't quite put his finger on it. He jumped when something scratched on their door, then laughed when he realized it was Sophie. He cracked open the door and in she came. She meandered over to Anya, sniffing at her feet and looking up at her with curious eyes.

Anya knelt to pet her. "Hi there, Sophie. I met you downstairs, remember?"

Her tail swished back and forth as she accepted Anya's scratch beneath her chin. When she'd had enough, she parked herself beside the bed and glanced over at Danny, uttering a quiet whimper. He picked her up and set her on the bed where she circled twice, planted herself in the middle, and let out a long sigh. Some things never change, he thought.

"Oh, I see how it is," Anya teased. "You're not used to sharing Danny with anyone, are you? And especially the bed?"

"Don't worry." Danny pulled his tie from his neck and hung it in the closet. "I'll give her the boot when we ... uh, when we go to bed."

"Yes, and we'll see how well she likes that." Anya reached over to give her a good scratch behind the ears. Sophie rolled onto her side, her leg jiggling in response.

Danny smiled. "You keep that up, and *I'll* be the one who gets the boot."

They took their time, making small talk as they unpacked. When they finished, Danny turned off the overhead light and took her into his arms as they stood at the foot of the bed. How long had he waited for this moment? Suddenly, he felt shy and wondered why.

"What?" she asked.

"What do you mean 'what'?"

"I don't know. There's an odd expression on your face. What are you thinking about?"

He shook his head and glanced away, knowing she was right but unable to make sense of it. "I'm not really sure—"

The patter of footsteps outside the door halted their conversation.

"Goodnight, Millie," Betty's voice sounded from the hall. "Thanks for your help in the kitchen."

They watched her shadow pass beneath the door.

"You're welcome, Betty. Good night," Millie answered down the hall. Two separate clicks of doors closing ended the interruption.

"Ah."

He looked back at her, curious at the smile on her face. "Ah?"

"It's this. Us. Here in your bedroom, under the same roof as your family."

Understanding washed over him. "You know, I think you're right. It's all a bit ... awkward, isn't it?"

"Yes, I suppose it is."

They stared at each other then snickered at the exact same moment.

Without taking his eyes off her, he nodded toward the bed. "Well, we don't have to—"

"Nonsense," she whispered with a smirk. "We'll figure it out."

A low growl from the bed distracted them. Anya snorted, startled by the sound of it. Danny covered his mouth as they both laughed.

"Sophie, believe it or not, you can't—"

She growled louder, raising her head but looking past them.

"Now see here, Sophie." Danny started toward her, but before he could reach her, she stood, the fur along her spine standing straight up. Her growling grew louder.

"Danny, do you think it's me?"

"I'm not sure. I've never seen her act like this before—" He paused, raising his hand. "Wait ... do you hear that?"

"Hear what?"

"Music."

She stood still, listening. A moment later, a smile of recognition. First hers, then his.

In the silence, they could hear music playing.

A familiar tune.

Played on a fiddle.

They moved toward the window and drew back the curtains. There, on the sidewalk below, silhouetted against the street light, Cosmos played for them.

Oh Danny boy ...

They couldn't help laughing at their discovery, such a sight at a time like this. Then they grew silent, listening to the melody so perfectly suited for them. Anya nestled herself against him, slipping her arm around his waist. He pulled her closer beside him, her head coming to rest against his chest.

He brushed his lips against her forehead then whispered in her ear.

"Welcome home, Anya. Welcome home."

About the Author

Born in Texas and raised in Oklahoma, Diane Hale Moody is a graduate of Oklahoma State University. She lives with her husband Ken in the rolling hills just outside of Nashville. They are the proud parents of two grown and extraordinary children, Hannah and Ben.

To date, Diane has penned thirteen books with several more projects vying for her attention. She and her husband Ken, who writes as McMillian Moody, founded OBT Bookz in 2011.

When she's not reading or writing, Diane enjoys an eclectic taste in music and movies, great coffee, and the company of good friends.

Visit Diane's website at dianemoody.net and her blog, "just sayin'" at dianemoody.blogspot.com.

Acknowledgments

I'm quite confident Danny and Anya might never have made it to the altar if not for the faithful encouragement of my husband Ken. On those days when I lost my way on the page, he was always, always there for me. Not to mention all the household chores he silently tackled so I could stay focused. I'm so humbled and honored that I get to do life with you, Ken Moody. How I thank God for these past 35 years and how they grow sweeter every year.

I never would have written *Of Windmills & War* if not for my dad, Glenn Hale. Many of Danny's experiences came from the pages of Dad's wartime memoirs. At 92 years young, Dad has enjoyed reading all the reviews and having more opportunities to tell his story. While Danny's post-war life took an entirely different path from my father's, I've relied on Dad's phenomenal memory to get my facts straight. Couldn't have done it without you, Dad. And please accept my condolences for your beloved Cubs. It's been 70 years since their last World Series appearance, and they sure came close this time. Darn that goat! But as you always say, when it comes to the Cubs, "there's always next century!"

Tremendous thanks to my wonderful editor Bev Harrison for adding her Aussie sparkle to my manuscript. I hope we have many more projects together, my friend.

To my daughter Hannah Moody for designing another gorgeous book cover. I am blown away by the gifts God has given you and the beautiful woman you've become. To the moon and back, sweetie.

Additional thanks to Lydia Kindred Kirk for help to give my English war brides the proper Brit-speak. I take full responsibility if I got it wrong, my friend. Thank you also for allowing me to "borrow" the newest member of your family—sweet Jocelyn Rose. I can't wait to meet her face to face.

To Lydia's parents, Peter and Kath Kindred, for your unwavering dedication to the memory of the 390th through the Parham Air Museum. Dad and I will never forget our visit with you and your incredible team of docents.

Special gratitude to Michele Edwards Thomas and all the wonderful folks at *The American War Bride Experience* website: www.usawarbrides.com What a fabulous resource of stories, photographs, ship manifests, and so much more. Thank you for keeping these amazing stories alive and well, and for use of a war brides photograph from your website for the back cover art.

And finally, a heartfelt word of thanks for my favorite war bride, Joan Van Spyker. Joan and her baby daughter came to America on the *Queen Mary* in 1945. (More about Joan in my tribute on the following page.) With the fondest of memories and gratitude, I dedicate this book to your memory. Oh, how we miss you, love.

In Memory of Joan Van Spyker

As I began my research for this book, I remembered a dear friend in Florida who had come to America as a war bride. Over the past few months, I enjoyed many long hours on the phone with Joan, loving every moment as she reminisced in her beautiful English accent. Much of Joan's story wove its way into the characters of my war brides in my book.

Joan was just thirteen years old when the war started in the skies over England in 1940. She told of walking along a road one day and seeing a bomber drop out of the clouds and coming toward her. She ducked into some nearby hedges and watched as a Messerschmitt strafed the middle of the road she'd been walking. She remembered wearing those tin pith helmets and hearing the shrapnel "ping" against it. Can you imagine.

In 1944, she was working in the offices of a Spitfire factory. After work, U.S. Army troop trucks would stop by offering the girls a ride to dances with American soldiers. One night, Joan noticed a handsome guy playing saxophone in the band. When they took a break, she walked right up and introduced herself. His name was Joe Solerno, an Italian-American from Long Island, New York. Joe helped arrange music for the Glenn Miller Band. Joan and her very own GI Joe fell in love and married when she was just seventeen. With strict rationing still enforced, Joe's army buddies stole ingredients to make them a wedding cake. Then, after a lengthy wait with thousands of other war brides, Joan and their baby daughter came to the United States on the *Queen Mary* in March of 1946. Just before dawn on the morning they pulled into New York Harbor, she joined the others on deck to see the Statue of Liberty, bathed in brilliant spotlights to welcome them. Almost 70 years later, she still remembered the tremendous wave of emotion of that unforgettable moment.

Joe survived the war, but was killed when a tree fell on him back in the States. She remarried a wonderful man named Howard Shedd, but not long after, she was widowed for the second time. A few years later she was introduced to a recent widower named Bernie Van Spyker. She thought he was "too loud and too coarse!" He thought she was "too old, too tall, and too uppity!" Regardless, they started seeing each other and one day, while on her lunch hour, he took her to the beach and surprised her by serving communion. She still didn't realize he was courting her. They married on "1.1.81" and had 34 wonderful years together.

Last August (2015), Joan enjoyed a fabulous tea party given in honor of her 90th birthday. But her health was declining, and by November, she was more than ready to meet her Lord and Savior face to face. In those last days, our mutual friend Judy Gussler was able to tell her I'm dedicating my book to her. Judy snapped a picture of Joan giving me a "thumbs up" at the news. I only wish I'd finished the book in time for her to read it.

Joan passed quietly into the presence of God on November 23, 2015. And as she did, I have no doubt whatsoever that she heard Him say, "Well done, thou good and faithful servant."

Joan Van Spyker

Discussion Questions

1. What was the main theme of this book?

2. On the day of her wedding, Anya woke from a vivid, recurring nightmare. How is this opening scene indicative of the struggles Anya faces as she begins her post-war life?

3. Why do you suppose English girls were so smitten with American soldiers? What other factors might have influenced the attraction? Would you have had the courage to marry a soldier from another country at such a young age and move to a distant land so different from your own?

4. Once he was back home, Danny had an awkward response from a neighbor who asserted her anti-war position. If you had been in Danny's shoes, would you have said something or walked away? As a Christian, what would be the appropriate response? [*This actually happened to my father when he returned from the war. He was so angry, he walked away rather than say something he'd regret. He took great pleasure in reading Danny's response!]

5. At school, Danny had several encounters with Beverly, his former college sweetheart. How should he have handled those encounters? What lessons did he learn?

6. In my research, I learned how often war-time marriages were destroyed by infidelity. Then, as now, some would say it's just "human nature." As Christians, we know it's much more than that. Is there any way to end the epidemic of infidelity in a world that accepts it as the norm?

7. Unless you're an avid baseball fan, you probably skimmed through those chapters surrounding the 1945 World Series. Still, most Americans know that Chicago Cubs fans are a loyal bunch. What is it about sports that captures the hearts of so many?

8. When Sophie was attacked behind the pub, Anya's training as a Resistance fighter immediately kicked into action as she fought off the brute and almost killed him. But the realization of her ingrained reaction rocked her to the core. How does someone set aside those instincts after years of war?

9. When Danny returned from the war, he had several heart-to-heart talks with his father. For the first time, he began to understand his dad. How has the past shaped Frank's life? How has he changed since the opening chapter in *Of Windmills & War?*

10. Like Frank, Gigi Williams also came from an abusive home. Anya was shocked to learn how much her friend had suffered, but it helped her understand Gigi in a whole new way. Is it possible to help someone overcome the life-wounds like those of Danny's father or Anya's friend Gigi?

11. The war shattered Anya's faith. But gradually, she began to connect the dots between her mother-in-law's prayers and the many obstacles in her path that were inexplicably overcome. Has God used the prayers of a friend or family member to draw you to Him? Have your own prayers made an "inexplicable" difference in someone else's life?

12. We've all known "unique" folks like Cosmos. They can be annoying at times, but harmless. Some are invasive, causing you to duck when you see them coming. Others are more troubling. How do you handle these "irregular" people? [*On a side note, Cosmos's character was based on a peculiar fellow who came to Dad's 390th Bomb Group reunions year after year. The first time I met him, I started taking notes.]

13. What part of the story did you like best?

14. What was the most insightful part of the story?

15. Was there a scene that brought tears to your eyes?

16. What was the funniest scene?

17. What did you learn that you didn't know before?

Resources

Barrett, Duncan and Calvi, Nuala. *GI Brides: The Wartime Girls Who Crossed the Atlantic for Love.* New York: HarperCollins Publishers, 2014.

Billington, Charles N. *Wrigley Field's Last World Series: The Wartime Chicago Cubs and the Pennant of 1945.* Chicago, IL: Lake Claremont Press, 2005.

Childers, Thomas. *Soldier From the War Returning: The Greatest Generation's Troubled Homecoming from World War II.* New York: Houghton Mifflin Harcourt, 2009.

Kaplan, Phillip, and Smith, Rex Alan. *One Last Look: A Sentimental Journey to the Eighth Air Force Heavy Bomber Bases of World War II in England.* New York: Artabras Publishers, 1983.

The Story of the 390th Bombardment Group (H). Paducah, KY: Turner Publishing Company, 1947.

Virden, Jenel. *Goodbye, Piccadilly: British War Brides in America.* Champaign, IL: University of Illinois Press, 1996.

Waller, Maureen. *London 1945: Life in the Debris of War.* New York: St. Martin's Press, 2004.

World War II Stories: 390th Bombardment Group (H) of the Eighth Air Force. Tucson, AZ: 390th Memorial Museum Foundation, Inc., 2008.

WWII: Time-Life Books History of the Second World War. New York: Prentice Hall Press for Time-Life Books, Inc., 1989.

Online Resources

Aldeburgh Museum Online. Retrieved from: http://www.aldeburghmuseumonline.co.uk

American War Bride Experience: Foreign Born GI Brides of World War II. Retrieved from: http://uswarbrides.com

Bert Wilson, Announcer, Chicago Cubs 1944-1945. Retrieved from: http://www.bertwilsonchicagocubs.com

The Billy Goat Curse: The World-Famous Billy Goat Tavern. Retrieved from: http://www.billygoattavern.com/legend/curse

Buckingham Palace: History of London. Retrieved from the History Channel: http://www.history.co.uk/study-topics/history-of-london/buckingham-palace

Information Britain: The History of Aldeburgh. Retrieved from: http://www.information-britain.co.uk/history/town/Aldeburgh6

Kershaw, Sarah. Band of Sisters, New York Times, 6 July, 2008. Retrieved from: http://www.nytimes.com/2008/07/06/nyregion/thecity/06 brid.html?pagewanted=print&_r=0

London Can Take It. Documentary narrated by Quentin Reynolds, October, 1940. [Video file] Retrieved from: https://www.youtube.com/watch?v=bLgfSDtHFt8

London to Tidworth 1946. [Video file] Retrieved from: http://www.britishpathe.com/video/london-to-tidworth

Queen Mary War Brides, as told by June Allen, September 22, 2014. [Video file.] Retrieved from: https://www.youtube.com/watch?v=2m8QtCSlEi8

The Rainbow Corner Red Cross Club in London, 1945. Retrieved from: http://www.303rdbga.com/pp-rainbowcorner.html

Saving an Icon: The St. Paul's Watch and a Flawed Hero. Retrieved from Blitzwalkers: http://blitzwalkers.blogspot.com/2011/03/saving-icon-st-pauls-watch-and-flawed.html

St. Paul's Cathedral History Timeline. Retrieved from: https://www.stpauls.co.uk/history-collections/history/cathedral-history-timeline

The 1945 World Series by Baseball Almanac. Retrieved from: http://www.baseball-almanac.com/ws/yr1945ws.shtml

War and the Abbey, 1939-1945. Westminster Abbey. Retrieved from: http://www.westminster-abbey.org/our-history/war-damage

Women and War: War Brides. Retrieved from PortCities Southampton: http://www.plimsoll.org/SeaPeople/womenandthesea/womenandwar/warbrides.asp

WWII in Colour: The Battle of Britain and the Blitz Over London, April 16, 2010. [Video file]: Retrieved from: https://www.youtube.com/watch?v=euRlmTHpSCI

WW2 People's War: An Archive of World War Two. Stories contributed by the Ipswich Museum. Retrieved from: http://www.bbc.co.uk/history/ww2peopleswar/user/54/u901854.shtml

WW2: The Blitz Hits London. History of London. Retrieved from the History Channel: http://www.history.co.uk/study-topics/history-of-london/ww2-the-blitz-hits-london

Other Books by Diane Moody

Of Windmills & War
Available in paperback and Kindle

The Runaway Pastor's Wife
Available in paperback and Kindle

The Demise – A Mystery
Available on Kindle

The Teacup Novella Series

Book One: *Tea with Emma*
Books Two: *Strike the Match*
Book Three: *Home to Walnut Ridge*
Book Four: *At Legend's End*
Book Five: *A Christmas Peril*
Available on Kindle

The Teacup Novellas – The Collection
(All five novellas in one volume)
Available in paperback and Kindle

Two Blue Novels

Blue Christmas
Blue Like Elvis
Available in paperback and Kindle

Non-Fiction

Confessions of a Prayer Slacker
Available in paperback and Kindle

Also available from OBT Bookz

The Elmo Jenkins Series
by McMillian Moody

Made in the USA
Lexington, KY
29 August 2016